In Kant's Wak

In Kant's Wake

Philosophy in the Twentieth Century

Tom Rockmore

BLACKWELL PUBLISHING
350 Main Street, Malden, MA 02148-5020, USA
9600 Garsington Road, Oxford OX4 2DQ, UK
550 Swanston Street, Carlton, Victoria 3053, Australia

First published 2006 by Blackwell Publishing Ltd

1 2006

Library of Congress Cataloging-in-Publication Data

Rockmore, Tom, 1942–
In Kant's wake : philosophy in the twentieth century / Tom Rockmore.
p. cm.
Includes bibliographical references and index.
ISBN-13: 978-1-4051-2570-3 (hardcover)
ISBN-10: 1-4051-2570-5 (hardcover)
ISBN-13: 978-1-4051-2571-0 (pbk.)
ISBN-10: 1-4051-2571-3 (pbk.)
1. Philosophy, Modern—20th century. 2. Kant, Immanuel, 1724–1804.
I. Title.

B804.R625 2006
190.9′04—dc22

2005024958

A catalogue record for this title is available from the British Library.

Set in 10/13pt Galliard
by Graphicraft Limited, Hong Kong

For further information on
Blackwell Publishing, visit our website:
www.blackwellpublishing.com

Contents

Introduction

> [N]early two hundred years after they were made, [Kant's key insights] have still not been fully absorbed into the philosophical consciousness.[1]
>
> Peter Strawson

> I believe that Kant bequeathes us not one single conception which is both indispensable to philosophy and which philosophy either did not possess before him, or was not destined inevitably to acquire after him through the growth of men's reflection upon the hypotheses by which science interprets nature. The true line of philosophic progress lies, in short, it seems to me, not so much *through* Kant as *round* him to the point where now we stand.[2]
>
> William James

This volume suggests an answer to the obvious, but difficult, question: What happened in twentieth-century philosophy? The present account will be limited to Western philosophy. Though other types of philosophy, for instance Indian or Chinese philosophy, are well worth discussing, I am not competent to do so. The account that follows also makes no claim to exhaustivity. It not intended to compete with histories of philosophy. Unlike historians of philosophy, I have no intention of describing everything, including every main thinker, text, or discussion, even in outline. My aim is rather to depict Western philosophy in general in this period on an introductory level. A reader should come away from this book with an initial sense of the main thinkers, the main problems, and the nature of the debate in the last century. Unlike more specialized accounts, there will be no effort to focus on a single movement, tendency, current, point of view, language, or culture.[3] Since my narrative is selective, it will not be guided by a concern to say everything that should be said on the topic, but rather by the desire to say only a few essential things, but to say them very clearly and simply, at a level within the reach of any educated reader, in contrast to accounts intended for specialists in one or another philosophical domain.

I will be depicting the debate in this period in terms of a series of main movements. This approach is suggested by the self-organization of philosophy itself. Even before Plato founded the Academy in ancient Athens, philosophers organized themselves into schools around those considered to be important thinkers. This practice continues today through the creation of informal or on occasion more formal groups whose members see themselves as working within one or another philosophical paradigm.

It is at least arguable that, as exemplified in Socrates' practice long ago, philosophy worthy of the name depends on dialogue in which different approaches do battle around a series of problems. Descartes's *Meditations* (1641, 1644) were discussed not only by such friendly respondents as Gassendi and Arnauld but also by such less friendly observers as Hobbes and many others. Leibniz, an indefatigable correspondent, was in touch with nearly everyone of importance in his time. When Kant's *Critique of Pure Reason* appeared (1781, 1787), it elicited reactions across the board from thinkers of the most diverse persuasions. Yet at present, the structure of the discussion has narrowed to the point that for the most part pragmatists dialogue with pragmatists, Marxists with Marxists, and analytic thinkers with others of the same persuasion.

In order to keep the discussion within manageable limits, I have chosen to focus on only four main movements: American pragmatism, Marxism, so-called "continental" philosophy, and Anglo-American analytic philosophy. Each of these movements emerged toward the beginning of the twentieth century, which, taken together, they proceeded to dominate. Since no philosophical account is wholly neutral, each reflects a point of view. Marxism seems worthy of inclusion here, even if it was never as popular in the US as in continental Europe, since it was for a long time one of the main philosophical movements in this period.

A further reason for focusing on movements rather than individuals is that we are still too close to the twentieth century to know what is likely to appear important or even to survive as a legitimate concern over time. We simply don't know now at the beginning of the twenty-first century whom our descendants will be reading (or even which problems they will be thinking about) a hundred years from now. One might consider the thought of this period in terms of a very small number of master thinkers who set the terms of debate during an entire period. Though any such enumeration is inevitably controversial, a short list of the most influential figures of the last century might include Husserl, Heidegger, Wittgenstein, and perhaps Quine. Such a list pays more attention to the influence of a given thinker than the staying power or even the importance of a given body of thought. Yet even if we could agree on a list of the most important thinkers, other difficulties arise. Should the importance of a thinker be assessed in terms of that person's own production, the number of people who react to it, or through some combination of both? Since philosophy is not like a presidential poll or a popularity contest, it is still too early to know if these or other thinkers will later be seen as among the most important in this period. Thus Peirce, who was mainly overlooked in his lifetime, and who was notoriously never able to secure a permanent teaching position, is now sometimes regarded as the only American philosophical genius. And Engels, the central figure in Marxist philosophy, is now regarded as at most a gifted amateur.

There are obvious limitations to such an approach, some of which can be indicated immediately. One is that the tendencies in question are not fixed, written in stone as it were, and certainly not hermetic. A number of cross-over figures belong, or can reasonably be thought of as belonging, to more than a single tendency. A paradigm example at present is that most protean thinker, Richard Rorty, who was initially a rising star in the analytic firmament, hence a member of the analytic tendency, which he then ostensibly left for pragmatism, hence a member of the pragmatic tendency, at the same time as he "officially" turned against philosophy of all kinds, to become in effect a member of no tendency at all.

It is also important to avoid the impression that any of the tendencies has a monolithic character. There is a good deal of variety, jousting for advantage, even open opposition, within all the currents featured here, which are mainly depicted in an ideal form that wholly reflects no single position. Thus as will emerge below, the views of Husserl and Heidegger are incompatible on many different levels. Peirce often complains about James's reading of his views. Quine's holism is squarely directed against the mainline analytic effort over many years to solve the problem of reference by understanding how words link up to things. Even Marxism, which exerted tight political control over philosophical issues, was prey to rampant disagreement, for instance in Lukács's critique of Engels, later retracted.

At the time of this writing early in the new century, the fortunes of the four tendencies under discussion here vary considerably. Some of the movements which achieved dominance during the last century are, if not dead, at least apparently moribund. Others are flourishing or even gaining in importance. Marxism once appeared to hold open the political promise of a better life. It has paid the expected price of the break-up of the Soviet Union and, with the important exception of China, as well as Cuba and North Korea, the apparently irreversible decline of "official" Marxism. The political decline of Marxism has led to a widespread philosophical conviction that it has nothing important to contribute to the debate.

The situation is different for continental and analytic philosophy. "Continental" philosophy is a term which can be used in wide as well as in narrow senses. It is employed widely to refer to all forms of modern philosophy written in continental Europe. This includes an enormous gamut of thinkers running, say, from Montaigne and Descartes to the present. They also include the series of thinkers composing German idealism, as well as Kierkegaard, Nietzsche, and various forms of German neo-Kantianism. Or the term is used more narrowly, as is presently the practice in English-language circles, to refer mainly, even exclusively, to Husserlian and post-Husserlian forms of phenomenology, including as well the often lively discussion about them in the extra-European space, including the US and Canada. "Continental" philosophy, which is now mainly used in the latter, more narrow sense, will, following this established practice, be used in this way in this book.

There are still plenty of continental philosophers, that is, thinkers employed in departments of philosophy in universities and colleges in the United States and elsewhere who are committed to one or another version of philosophy as currently or formerly practiced on the continent. Yet it is fair to say that the original inspiration of continental philosophy understood in the more narrow, or Husserlian, sense of the term, as exhibiting some form of the distinctive Husserlian approach to phenomenology, no longer, or only barely still, exists. The impressively large movement which arose in reaction to Husserl's distinctive form of phenomenology quickly and increasingly diverged from his teachings. Not only is Heidegger diametrically opposed to a long series of key Hussserlian ideas, but Heidegger's disciples, including Gadamer and Derrida, long ago stopped using the term "phenomenology" in favor of "hermeneutics."

Analytic philosophy is also now changing or has already changed to a degree where it is questionable whether the same term should still be applied. To be sure, for political reasons relating to power within the academy there is still tight cohesion between those who cast their lot with others considered to be analytic thinkers. Yet it is an open question as to what remains of the original impulse. Anglo-American analytic philosophy as it arose in Britain was always a hybrid movement without anything approaching doctrinal unity. This is probably true to a variable extent of all the movements surveyed here, but it is especially true for analytic philosophy in virtue of the fact that alone of the four movements under consideration it is mainly the product of not one but rather two important thinkers. Russell and Moore, its founding fathers, had very different, often incompatible views. Moore's background lay in classics while Russell came to philosophy from mathematics. Their main area of agreement arguably lay in a shared opposition to British idealism, which was dominant around the turn of the century in Britain, and, by extension, to idealism of all kinds. Beyond the opposition to idealism, there were a number of doctrines characteristic of analytic thought, not all of which were shared. A short list might include traditional British empiricism, the concern with reference or theory of meaning, the analysis of language, the empirical criterion of meaning, and so on. It is remarkable that in different ways and for different reasons, all of these doctrines, which were typical of early analytic philosophy as it emerged in Cambridge in the writings of Russell and Moore, later lost ground or were simply discarded. The commitment to empiricism, which characterized early analytic philosophy and linked it to classical British empiricism, came under sharp attack beginning with the later Wittgenstein. More recently, the analytic movement has begun to or perhaps has already split into a series of fragments. The four main analytic figures in the second half of the last century were Quine, Putnam, Davidson, and Rorty. Putnam has retired, Quine and Davidson have died, and only Rorty, who was always an eccentric presence, never a mainstream figure, is still active. At the time of this writing, no strong figure has emerged to hold together the diverse impulses in the analytic movement.

The analytic movement has further been affected by key "defections" of central analytic thinkers to pragmatism. With the possible exception of Rorty, there are at present no major thinkers sailing under pragmatist colors. Yet in part because of the recent emergence of analytic neo-pragmatism, among the currents discussed here pragmatism seems at present the most lively, and the closest to its original impulse. In discussing pragmatism, it is necessary to distinguish between the original movement, which arose out of and in reaction to the position invented by Peirce, and later developments. Peirce was concerned to work out a post-foundationalist approach to knowledge, with special attention to science. If, for purposes of discussion, we arbitrarily limit the first wave of pragmatism to Peirce, James, and Dewey, we can report that this movement progressively abandoned the original epistemological impulse by turning away from direct involvement with problems of knowledge. James, to be sure, was interested in questions of truth, but that part of his position is perhaps not its most successful aspect. Moreover, though Dewey's later view has many epistemological consequences, he does not directly engage questions of knowledge in the way this is usually undertaken.

Things are, however, a little more complicated in the pragmatist camp because of the regular arrival over many years of important analytic thinkers. It is an open question whether figures like Quine, Putnam, Rorty, and several others could not also be just as well called pragmatists and analysts, or perhaps analytic neo-pragmatists. Since the latter are consistently focused on epistemological themes, it is fair to say that the original post-foundationalist epistemological pragmatic impulse is now still widely considered to be a viable option. It is, then, ironic that as things presently stand this impulse is now only rarely being developed by the conceptual children of the original pragmatists, but more often by the disaffected epigones of the analytic movement.

In a short volume such as the present one, the need to observe strict limits sharply circumscribes the nature, range, and depth of the possible account. The fact that I will be focusing on these tendencies and not others means I will unfortunately have nothing to say about analytic ethics, an area of important work in the twentieth century; I will also leave untouched analytic philosophy of science. This important movement came into its own in the English-speaking world roughly since the Second World War through the emigration of important members of the original Vienna Circle movement, and those associated with it, including Rudolf Carnap, Hans Reichenbach, and others to the US, and Otto Neurath to England.

The limitation of our focus to the four main movements in this period also means that three of its most exciting figures from the present perspective, whose work falls outside these movements, cannot be discussed. One is Thomas Kuhn, a physicist turned historian and philosopher of science. His seminal study, *The Structure of Scientific Revolutions* (1962), is arguably the single most influential philosophical text of the century, even more influential, say, than Heidegger's *Being and Time* (1927) or Wittgenstein's *Tractatus Logico-Philosophicus* (1921), and more popular than Sartre's *Being and Nothingness* (1943). A second figure I will not be discussing is John Rawls, whose *A Theory of Justice* (1971) is widely considered to be the most distinguished work in political philosophy in the last century. A third figure whom I also cannot consider is the linguist Noam Chomsky, who has often interacted with philosophers. Chomsky's revolutionary work in linguistics is often considered to have important philosophical implications. A fourth figure I will not be taking up is the French thinker and novelist Simone de Beauvoir, whose *The Second Sex* (1949) had an enormous effect on the fight for equal rights for women throughout the world.

The present account will be divided into seven chapters. The initial chapter, entitled "Toward Interpreting Twentieth-Century Philosophy," addresses the relation between philosophy and the history of its tradition. There is a widespread conviction in modern philosophy that philosophy can and indeed must be separated from the history of philosophy, which, since it is replete with errors that cannot be corrected, is a record of failure, of no redeeming value. This chapter argues, on the contrary, that philosophy and its history are inseparable. It further argues that later theories are called into being in reaction to earlier ones.

Even a cursory glance at the history of the tradition reveals that only a few main thinkers shape the entire philosophical debate, which unfolds as a series of readings of and reactions to them. The second chapter, "Kant and the Post-Kantian Debate," argues that Kant is a peculiarly influential figure, who provides the problems, the vocabulary, and the main insights that continue to shape the later debate in both the nineteenth and twentieth centuries. Kant's very important but also very rich position is influential in many areas, including ethics, aesthetics, natural science, philosophy of science, but above all as concerns the problem of knowledge. I will be arguing that Kant presents not one but rather two incompatible representationalist and constructivist approaches to knowledge. This chapter suggests that the later discussion of knowledge can be regarded as providing a series of variations on these two main Kantian themes. It finally argues, in setting the stage for the final chapter, that Kant's influence reverberates in the post-Kantian turn, in reaction against Kant's resolutely anti-historical approach, to Hegel's own historical approach to knowledge.

Chapters 3–6 will each describe one of the four main movements that, after their emergence roughly one hundred years ago, formed the main strands of the philosophical debate in the twentieth century. Though in a short book I will need to be selective, I aim to provide enough to whet the appetite of non-specialists in a clear, accessible manner, while offering a thesis which will interest those with specialized concerns. To that end, I will provide a large number of quotations and numerous references to help those who are not very familiar with specific texts as well as to impart something of the flavor of different ways of writing, and even to create the possibility of independent judgment on the part of the reader. My intention is to provide a comprehensive, coherent but relatively simple description of the debate in this period as a whole, emphasizing the dialectical relation between the main elements in opposing tendencies each of which pursues the philosophical discussion from its own perspective. Since I will be concentrating on movements, hence on large alternative ways of proceeding, the focus will mainly be on problems, not people.

For obvious reasons, it will not be possible to begin the discussion precisely at 1900. Philosophy, which has no sharp limits, including temporal constraints, does not obey the dictates of the calendar. I will discuss the movements in the following order: Marxism, pragmatism, continental philosophy, and Anglo-American analytic philosophy. I concede that this order is arbitrary. Pragmatism and Marxism both began about the same time late in the nineteenth century. If Marxism begins in Engels, then it begins as early as the 1840s, for instance in his contribution to the *German Ideology*, which he co-authored with Marx in 1845.[4] But it did not really take off until Engels began to adopt the posture of a philosopher, especially in writings beginning in the 1880s after Marx's death in 1883. It only really emerged in Engels's philosophical reaction to and narration of views he attributed to Marx. Pragmatism sprang into existence very suddenly in a series of articles Peirce published in the 1870s. These two movements precede continental philosophy and Anglo-American analytic philosophy, both of which emerged around the turning of the twentieth century. These two movements commenced at almost the same time, phenomenology in 1900 through Husserl's breakthrough to phenomenology in *Logical Investigations*, and analytic philosophy nearly simultaneously in early articles by Russell and Moore. Hence, from the temporal perspective, the movements to be discussed here will be appearing in roughly chronological order of their emergence.

Alternative ways of ordering these four movements, which ignore the temporal dimension, and concentrate on such other factors as philosophical affinities, are also possible. Thus Marxism and analytic philosophy are united by their common rejection of idealism as well as by a shared investment in science as the conceptual panacea to problems of knowledge and on occasion as a simple substitute for philosophy. Alternatively, Marxism and pragmatism overlap in their adherence to naturalism, roughly the idea that we should disallow anything as an explanatory factor that is not part of nature. Naturalism is contrasted with the naturalizing tendency of analytic philosophy, that is, the view that not only are the results of the natural sciences crucial for epistemology, but epistemology itself belongs to psychology. Continental philosophy and Marxism are continuous with the mainline European tradition, and so on. Indeed, once one abandons the fragile reed of temporal succession as a way of ordering the different movements, a virtually endless series of other possibilities arises.

Though I will be aiming to provide as much information as possible through a simple, accessible, reasonably standard presentation of each of these four movements, each of the chapters will inevitably reflect my own view of what happened in twentieth-century philosophy. Chapter 3, which concerns Marxism in the twentieth century, stresses the enormous philosophical differences between Marx and Marxism. It presents the latter as a conceptual movement following not from Marx, but from Engels, who routinely claims to speak, and is routinely accepted as speaking, in Marx's name. The chapter will cover the relation of Marx and Engels, then Marxism as emerging as the result of Engels's intervention in the debate. It goes on to consider a variety of forms of "Marxism," including Hegelian Marxism, introduced by Lukács and Korsch, and such Frankfurt School thinkers as Horkheimer, Adorno, and, more recently, the early Habermas.

The image of pragmatism is currently obscure, for two reasons. One is a residual uncertainty about its main protagonists, which mainly afflicts analytic refugees in pragmatism's ample bosom. Thus such important recent observers as Rorty and Putnam stress James and, especially in the former's case, Dewey at the expense of Peirce. The other is Dewey's turn away from the problem of knowledge. It seems useful to resist the tendency to deprecate epistemology in calling attention to pragmatism's very useful contribution to that theme. The account of "Pragmatism as Epistemology" in chapter 4 locates the origin of this movement in Peirce's criticism of Cartesian foundationalism, the main modern strategy for knowledge, leading to his own important effort to work out a post-foundationalist approach to knowledge. The chapter considers the decline and even fall of Peirce's concern with theory of knowledge in James's views of truth, Dewey's stance as a public intellectual, ending with Rorty's neo-analytic form of pragmatic skepticism.

The fifth chapter, on "Continental Philosophy as Phenomenology," will situate this current in the larger phenomenological tradition. It is often, but incorrectly, suggested that Husserl invented this approach. Instead it will be argued, through a review of some earlier forms of phenomenology, that he made an extraordinarily influential discovery of a *new type* of phenomenology. Husserl will be depicted as concerned from beginning to end with what he clearly only later identified as the theme of philosophy as rigorous science. His emphasis on phenomenology as a solution to the problem of knowledge disappears in Heidegger's turn to ontology, more precisely in the problem of the meaning of being. Sartre and Merleau-Ponty will be discussed in terms of their dual allegiance to Husserl as well as to Heidegger. In carrying forward the hermeneutical impulse of Heidegger's early position, Gadamer and Derrida, his most prominent disciples, effectively abandon phenomenology in any recognizable sense of the term.

Analytic philosophy has always included very different tendencies, not least because of the very different approaches featured by Russell and Moore, the founders of analytic philosophy in Britain. The account of "Anglo-American Analytic Philosophy" in chapter 6 depicts it as emerging through Russell's own reaction to Frege as well as through Russell's and Moore's shared rejection of idealism. The chapter includes discussion of analysis, analyticity, and analytic philosophy, accounts of Wittgenstein's early and later theories, as well as of his influence on the Vienna Circle thinkers. The chapter ends in a very brief account of analytic philosophy in the US since the Second World War, mainly in reference to Quine, Putnam, Davidson, and Rorty.

The seventh and final chapter takes up the theme of "Kant and Twentieth-Century Philosophy." This chapter makes three connected points. To begin with, it stresses the unsuspected breadth and depth of Kant's impact on the four main currents in twentieth-century philosophy. I will be insisting on the genuine range of possible reactions to Kant, always the case in respect to a great philosopher, in this case even more so because of the genuine obscurity of much of his work and the fact that, as I shall be arguing, he apparently defends identifiably different, obviously incompatible views of knowledge. Then the chapter addresses the question lurking in the background of the discussion throughout this book: What was accomplished in twentieth-century philosophy? Kant's strong, continuous, and deep influence on all the main tendencies in twentieth-century philosophy suggests that its accomplishment can be evaluated against the problems, themes, and concerns of the critical philosophy. I will be arguing that the main accomplishments of twentieth-century philosophy do not lie in advance of Kant with respect to his concerns, but rather in changing the subject, as it were, in order to delineate and respond to a different set of issues and problems. I finally suggest, in a nod in the direction of the earlier reaction to Kant, that the most important innovation after Kant lies in the post-Kantian idealist turn toward history, which is most sharply focused in Hegel, but later quickly forgotten. Though clearly influenced by Kant, twentieth-century philosophy not only does not go further down the Kantian road but, as concerns the turn away from history, largely ignores important later nineteenth-century insights arguably central to working out the epistemological problem.

1

Toward Interpreting Twentieth-Century Philosophy

The following selective account of philosophy in the twentieth century will be limited to Western philosophy only. The reason for this limitation is not because there is no other kind of philosophy, nor because it is the only kind of philosophy of real interest. The Indian and the Chinese philosophical traditions are more than twice as old and arguably just as interesting as philosophy in the West. Nor is it because, as Husserl thinks, that what is called philosophy outside the Western tradition is not worthy of the name. Husserl's view implies a normative conception of the discipline in which other points of view are absent – a conception that one might not care to defend.[1] Although non-Western philosophy could have been considered, there is more than enough to concern us merely in the Western tradition, the only one in which I am competent to provide anything approaching even a selective overall account.

The philosophical debate is highly partisan, often exceedingly sectarian. Philosophy, which is never as wholly disinterested as its participants claim, has a political dimension. Its participants are often more concerned with determining which positions, ideas, or theories are worthy of our attention than in ascertaining through argument which might possibly be true. Though limited to Western philosophy, I will be taking a very wide view about how to understand "philosophy" with the intention if not of wholly eliminating at least of diminishing a clear normative commitment to one or another tendency, movement, or current as the standard of what is correct or even plausible. Since there is no view from nowhere, all accounts of the discussion, including this one, are composed from a point of view. Though I do not pretend to have the only possible approach, I will be deliberately taking as inclusive an approach as possible within the space available to me here.

There is, I believe, no useful way to consider the philosophical texts of the twentieth century without interposing an interpretive framework of some kind. The alternative would be merely to reproduce the texts. As soon as one begins to identify and to describe them, interpretation enters into play. As in every other field, there are different, competing views of philosophy, which affect such factors as the understanding of the nature of the philosophical debate, the relation among different thinkers and positions, the way that philosophy relates to its prior history, and so on. Throughout the modern period and at present there is an important current of opinion holding that philosophy must be isolated from the history of philosophy. This view features an understanding of philosophy as systematic but ahistorical which excludes the history of philosophy from philosophy. Philosophy, according to this model, is not a historical enterprise, and the history of philosophy is neither relevant to it, nor a source of truth. In fact, so as not to be distracted by irrelevant matters, in the process of constructing theories one would be better off leaving earlier philosophical theories wholly out of account, in order to get on with the business of philosophy. As there is nothing worthwhile preserving in the prior tradition, there can be no pretense of simply taking over, selectively appropriating, or building in any way on what comes before. Since there is nothing to save, the proper approach consists in starting over from the very beginning in formulating everything anew. According to this view, we should treat philosophy, like science, as concerned with a series of problems to which it offers definitive answers, solutions which will not and cannot later be brought into question. This normative conception of the discipline, which is widespread in philosophy since Descartes, can be represented by Quine's very Cartesian *boutade* that some are interested in the history of philosophy and others are interested in philosophy.[2]

Aspects of this ahistorical approach to philosophy are pandemic in the modern discussion. They include Descartes's view that people of equal capacity only disagree because they do not use the correct method, for instance through what later was understood, in the rise of scientism, as the scientific method; Kant's idea that all earlier theories are uncritical, or dogmatic, hence fail to demonstrate their claims; the Young Hegelian conviction that philosophy itself has come to an end in Hegel; the Marxist belief that the problems of philosophy can only be solved by leaving philosophy behind in favor of Marxist science; Husserl's contention that there is a single hidden theme in the tradition that is correctly identified, preserved, and developed in his form of phenomenology; and Heidegger's claim that, since the early pre-Socratics, philosophy has diverged from the true path, so its history must be "destroyed" in order that it be correctly recovered.

The alternative view, which I shall be featuring here, holds that philosophy and the history of philosophy are inseparable. On this model, philosophy is like a giant Socratic dialogue in which earlier thinkers advance problems, solutions, and conceptual distinctions which are taken up by later thinkers. Philosophical concerns are debated over time but not necessarily resolved. The debate among philosophers is open-ended, hence interminable, and can be neither ended nor brought to completion through a brilliant insight, or even a series of them, for any position worth examining inevitably leads to further discussion. If this is true, then philosophy is not ahistorical but intrinsically historical, in at least two ways. On the one hand, since philosophical views cannot be demonstrated, say, by being compared to the world, they are, rather, tested through argument among the participants in the discussion. Philosophical theories, which always depend on the ongoing discussion, are constantly in danger of later refutation. Later thinkers continue to grapple with the ideas, problems, distinctions, and solutions proposed by their predecessors. On the other hand, philosophers, like everyone else, are influenced by their time and place, hence by factors which often surpass but also impact on the philosophical debate. One may speculate that the massive changes in Western society which are arguably occurring even now as a result of 9/11, and whose contours no one can foresee or understand, will influence philosophy in years to come in ways we also cannot anticipate.[3]

Aspects of this historical approach to philosophy, which go back to Plato's early dialogues, are represented in the modern debate by many thinkers. Examples include Fichte's view of the subject as finite human being, Hegel's Socratic view of philosophy as an ongoing dialogue between present and past thinkers, Marx's idea that cognitive claims are relative to the social context, Dewey's conviction that philosophical problems arise out of the stresses and strains of existence, the later Wittgenstein's view that constative claims which are true or false depend on conceptual frameworks which are neither true nor false, Fleck's belief that what we call facts are socially constructed, and Kuhn's claim that the practice of scientific inquiry is structured by periodical revolutionary shifts from one scientific paradigm to another.

In constructing an account of the philosophical debate in the twentieth century, I will be taking a dialogical, historical view of philosophy. I will regard the main philosophical tendencies as belonging to a wider debate. Representatives of the different currents work mainly or even wholly within the broadly defined conceptual frameworks of these movements. They compete among themselves to realize the main thrust of such frameworks, for instance by examining proposed ideas or solving problems of interest. Yet even thinkers wholly absorbed in defending a particular point of view are also engaged in dialogue between tendencies competing about which issues are significant and how they should be discussed.

The philosophical debate and calendrical time never wholly coincide. In referring to twentieth-century philosophy, I will understand the term very loosely to include some thinkers, such as Frege, Engels, Husserl, Peirce, and Dewey, who were already active before that century began. I will further be including thinkers important for one or another tendency but whom representatives of other tendencies might find of minor importance or even unworthy of inclusion in a volume of this kind.

Any account of Western philosophy in the twentieth century needs to ask which thinkers and/or tendencies need to be represented even in a general account and how to discuss them. The history of philosophy is replete with thinkers who were important in their own time but were later forgotten or who, though arguably important from different points of view, never succeeded in attracting sustained attention. Since there are so many thinkers who might be discussed, there will need to be some principle of selection, a way of picking out whom to include or to exclude from the story I will be telling.

One might, for instance, consider a series of main figures as absolutely central to any roll call of the most significant thinkers in the period. I have decided against this kind of approach since there is no way to construct a list which would be satisfactory to all observers. Philosophy was already organized into schools even before Plato founded the Academy in ancient Greece around 385 BC. This practice has increased in modern times. Roughly since Kant, philosophers have increasingly been organized within tendencies, currents, or movements following from the intervention of a very few selected thinkers. Another way of putting the same point is to say that a very few "strong," or "master," thinkers tend to act like a magnet in the discussion in attracting other, "weaker" thinkers who think in their wake in adopting their problems, ideas, distinctions, and concerns. Thus the young Fichte attracted the even younger Schelling and Hegel, who, at least early in their careers, depicted themselves as Fichteans before later diverging. This suggests the interest of approaching philosophy in the twentieth century less in terms of specific thinkers than through a few main movements, tendencies, points of view, or ways of doing philosophy.

An approach of this kind is specifically useful in two main ways. On the one hand, in considering major figures within the scope of a few wider tendencies it becomes reasonable to understand the ongoing debate at any given moment as following out the consequences of no more than a small handful of main philosophical options. Though there are, say, about as many approaches to knowledge as there are thinkers who write about it, when the dust settles, and with very few exceptions, most of the positions in play at any time are merely variations on a small number of themes, approaches, vocabularies, and distinctions already available. Though there is no reason why representatives of different tendencies could not debate with those of other tendencies, in practice this is relatively uncommon. At any given moment, there are very few thinkers who are genuinely informed about what is going on in all or even the main areas of philosophy, including the main contemporary currents in the debate. Members of a given current tend to interact with others associated with it while resisting efforts from outside to criticize or diminish its importance.

Different movements are often so different that it is difficult to imagine that a real possibility for productive dialogue between them is possible. In the US at present, two and only two main political parties divide the political landscape in vying for philosophical hegemony. Though there are more than two main philosophical tendencies contending against each other at any given time, the philosophical situation is roughly the same. Just as membership in one political party often means being committed to a series of goals not shared with and antithetical to the other, so identification with one philosophical tendency brings with it the loss of other possibilities, rendering it difficult to enter into anything resembling dialogue with those outside it. The supposed effort of someone like Carnap, an important positivist, to enter into dialogue with Heidegger, an important phenomenologist, is certainly unusual and perhaps incorrectly attributed.[4] Certainly Carnap's sustained polemic against Heidegger as the author of meaningless statements casts extreme doubt upon any claim that he was sincere in his desire to enter into meaningful dialogue with the latter.[5] For these reasons, it seems useful to concentrate on the main philosophical movements in describing the philosophical debate in the twentieth century.

Thomism and neo-Kantianism are candidates for inclusion on the short list of the main philosophical currents in our time. Since late in the nineteenth century, Thomism has been the official position of the Catholic Church. There are important twentieth-century Thomists, such as Étienne Gilson, Jacques Maritain, and Bernard Lonergan. Yet taken as a whole this movement seems less philosophically important, and certainly further removed from the ongoing debate, than other alternatives. German neo-Kantianism, another candidate for inclusion, provides a more difficult choice. Though some of the figures in this tendency, perhaps Hermann Cohen, certainly Ernst Cassirer, are worthy of separate treatment, I have decided not to include it. It is important in the period under study, but it is more significant in the context of the dissolution of the Hegel school after Hegel's death in 1831 and the ensuing anti-Hegelian reaction leading to the return to Kant in the second half of the nineteenth century, a period that falls outside the scope of this book.

Of course, there is more than one way to consider philosophical tendencies in a given period. Different principles of organization might be tried, such as selecting a group of authors in terms of a particular language, a particular national tradition, or again a specific philosophical approach, conception, or problem. Under the heading of *A Hundred Years of Philosophy*, John Passmore usefully profiles British philosophy.[6] Yet there seems no reason to reduce the profusion of philosophical positions in this period either to British philosophers – Passmore includes others, such as Wittgenstein – or merely to what has appeared in English, or even to regard philosophical production in that language as in some way better, more important, or more worthy of attention than in other languages, cultures, or intellectual traditions. Richard Bernstein brings very different philosophical groups together around the concept of action writ large enough to include the Marxist conception of practice (*Praxis*). Yet his effort now appears dated. Action theory, which loomed large when Bernstein's book appeared, no longer functions as a central focus even within analytic philosophy, much less for philosophy in this entire period.[7] Herbert Spiegelberg tells the very rich story of what he calls "the phenomenological movement." Yet this term and his account are misleading since what he has in mind is not phenomenology in general, but rather the phenomenological tendency whose forerunners are Brentano and Stumpf and which is initiated by Husserl.[8] Jürgen Habermas discusses the so-called "unfinished" philosophical discourse of modernity emerging from Kant's form of Enlightenment thinking.[9] Yet we will be concerned with more than the reaction to the Enlightenment project.

The work to follow will be closer in spirit to Bernstein and to Michael Friedman, who take very different approaches than, say, to Passmore, Spiegelberg, or Habermas. Like Bernstein, I will be seeking to provide a broad overview of the philosophical discussion, in this case the discussion in the twentieth century. Like Friedman, I see the main thinkers as engaged in dialogue. Unlike him, however, I will be describing a dialogue which does not follow directly from the effort of a very few important philosophers to engage other positions, but rather from the nature of philosophy, which consciously or unconsciously always takes the form of an ongoing debate over the centuries.

In different ways, each of the movements I will be concerned with here – Marxism, pragmatism, continental philosophy, and Anglo-American analytic philosophy – has so far met the test of time. Each of them originated toward the turn of the twentieth century. Each of them has attracted a number of prominent thinkers throughout the period in question. And from its own distinctive angle of vision, each of them lays claim to be the single most important philosophical tendency, movement, or school in this period.

Approaching the present discussion through these four different angles of vision helps in narrating a wider picture of twentieth-century Western philosophy. Yet this approach is not without its difficulties. One, which is obvious, is that any classification includes some, but also excludes other, possible candidates. In this case, since I will not be including German neo-Kantianism, there is no easy way to say anything about Cassirer, a singularly important, but underappreciated thinker. Someone else who falls outside the grouping proposed here is Whitehead, who, if he belongs to any single tendency, would be a member of the process philosophers – a group that might include James, who also belongs to the pragmatists, as well as Bergson, but which falls outside the scope of this book.

Another difficulty, which arises in any type of classification, including this one, is exactly what is being claimed, for instance with respect to a given tendency. What does it mean to say a given thinker or position belongs to one tendency rather than another? Can one determine with any precision who belongs to which tendency?

These questions, hence their answers, are related. Throughout the Western philosophical tradition, the various currents have routinely been identified with a few individual thinkers. In the case of a small handful of exceptional thinkers, later philosophy is engaged in an ongoing debate that stretches over a period of hundreds or even thousands of years. Whitehead famously claims that all of Western philosophy is a series of footnotes to Plato.[10] If that is true, then in a manner of speaking all Western philosophers should be regarded as Plato's children. In fact, this claim needs to be tempered in a variety of ways. In order to know who is a Platonist, one would need to know what "Platonism" means. Platonism, like other philosophical tendencies, can only be defined normatively, that is, by enumerating different criteria which in the view of the observer belong to what is meant by Platonism. At a minimum, Platonism, which needs to be distinguished from Plato's own position, which is unknown and simply cannot now be determined, includes a series of six related doctrines: first, the ontological claim that the real or reality exists, that is, that there is a mind-independent world, or a way that the world is in itself, as distinguished from its appearance; second, the normative idea that to know is to know reality, or the real as it is; third, the constative claim that we can and, under the proper conditions, in fact do have such knowledge; fourth, the associated descriptive view that such knowledge is absolute, "irrelative," not in any way relative, hence not relative to a particular knower, set of knowers, or again to a given time or place or to a point of view, perspective, conceptual framework, or context; fifth, the claim that knowledge is beyond skepticism, hence beyond doubt of any kind, in a word anhypothetical; and sixth, the idea that, beyond the results of discussion, which is the normal way of dealing with forms or ideas, the real can be directly known, for instance through some kind of cognitive intuition at least by some individuals some of the time.

Someone whose position illustrates these doctrines could fairly be called a Platonist. How would one know? The answer has to be that there simply is no option available beyond subjective judgment in deciding whether, if at all, and if so, to what degree, a particular position deserves to be included within a given tendency. Fortunately, in practice, the problem of who is, say, a Platonist, is not difficult to determine, since Platonists tend to respond to and discuss the views of other Platonists, and so on. Though one cannot determine with precision who is a Platonist, Platonists, like members of other tendencies, are self-selecting, hence self-identifying.

A perhaps more difficult question arises concerning cross-over phenomena, thinkers who are neither fish nor fowl, or rather both fish and fowl, hence neither one nor the other, in a word unclassifiable according to normal criteria. Plato, who is and is not a Platonist, is perhaps one example. Since his position cannot be determined with any degree of accuracy, we cannot say that he is Platonist. Yet since Platonism is inspired by his writings, it is not easy to say he is not a Platonist, or opposed to Platonism. Whitehead, who is a genuine cross-over figure in several senses, provides another example. It is well known that he collaborated over roughly a dozen years with his student, Bertrand Russell, in composing *Principia Mathematica.* Russell, one of the founders of analytic philosophy in Britain, is routinely identified as an analytic philosopher. Does the fact that Whitehead collaborated on a project with an analytic thinker suffice to classify him as one as well? Perhaps in a sense. But in another sense he was close to Bergson and James, both of whom were opposed to analytic philosophy. The moral seems to be that the four main tendencies I will be discussing below, and other philosophical tendencies as well, are merely ideal types, exemplified in varying degrees in different positions, none of which is ever wholly one or the other. Cross-over is common between different positions which in different ways exemplify characteristics of alternative conceptual frameworks, to which they are committed to varying extents, as they "bleed" into each other.

I will be discussing the various positions within the framework of the four main tendencies in the philosophical debate of the twentieth century, and I will be discussing the twentieth-century philosophical debate in respect to Kant. Kant is not only a great philosopher, one of the very small handful of truly great thinkers in the Western tradition; he is also a singularly influential figure, whose position continues to impact on the later debate, often in decisive ways. Like post-Kantian German idealism and German neo-Kantianism, central philosophical tendencies in the nineteenth century, in different ways the main philosophical movements in twentieth-century philosophy are all responding to Kant. The reason for turning to Kant as a standard in terms of which to understand the recent philosophical debate derives from his enormous stature in modern philosophy. The entire modern philosophical discussion is largely determined by a few seminal figures. Whether or not modern philosophy begins in Descartes – this suggestion, which is often advanced, is difficult to sustain since, as has often been noted, his position is continuous with a number of modern and pre-modern positions, particularly Montaigne's and Augustine's,[11] as well as with pre-modern science[12] – it seems clear that Kant is particularly influential in focusing the modern debate on questions of knowledge. I contend that, consciously or more often unconsciously, the main thinkers in the twentieth century are in dialogue with each other on the basis of a shared Kantian tradition, which they understand in different ways, often markedly so. Put differently, to an often underappreciated extent the entire later debate largely consists in alternative, often incompatible, readings of Kant.

The enormous influence of Kant's critical philosophy in the later tradition is felt at four major junctures. Initially, in the debate immediately following the publication of the *Critique of Pure Reason* (1781, 1787), his most important work, Kant's position was quickly recognized as highly important. It was rejected by some contemporaries, including J. G. Hamann, Herder, his former student, and the skeptics Salomon

Maimon and G. E. Schulze. But it was accepted by the majority of other thinkers not only as an instant classic, but, further, as a work of the first rank. The main impression at the time, which Kant did not share, was that his critical philosophy represented an important but unfinished project. Kant was dissatisfied with the reception of the first edition of the book. In the new preface written for the second edition of his treatise, he suggests, in reviving an old religious distinction, the need to distinguish between the letter and the spirit of the critical philosophy.[13] Following Kant's suggestion, an ongoing effort was undertaken by a series of contemporary thinkers, including the post-Kantian German idealists, to reformulate the critical philosophy according to its spirit while, if necessary, disregarding its letter. This effort, which is still under way, is currently most clearly exemplified by Habermas.

K. L. Reinhold, an otherwise unimportant philosopher, was the first to begin this process. He was quickly followed by such major thinkers as Fichte, Schelling, and Hegel, and perhaps even Marx.[14] Their individual and combined efforts to reformulate the critical philosophy gave rise to post-Kantian German idealism. Kant's contemporaries believed his critical philosophy depended on a revolution in philosophy influenced by and roughly equal in importance to Copernicus's famous astronomical revolution. Post-Kantian German idealism, which constitutes the second critical juncture, can usefully be regarded as an effort undertaken by a series of major thinkers to advance and complete Kant's Copernican revolution in working out the critical philosophy.

A third juncture at which Kant was extremely influential was in the anti-Hegelian revolt after Hegel's death. Though Hegel had his enemies, such as Arthur Schopenhauer and J. F. Fries, when he died, at the peak of his influence, he was widely acknowledged as the most important thinker of his time. This was swiftly to change, however, and the anti-Hegel reaction set in immediately after his death in 1831. This was composed of two features. One was the struggle for control of his legacy between the Hegelians, who quickly divided into right-wing and left-wing groups. The right-wing Hegelians, who all had positions in the German university system, proposed a theological version of Hegel's position, which they found admirable. By contrast, the left-wing Hegelians, who included Marx, and who, with the single exception of Eduard Gans, were not employed in the university system – Gans was a professor of law in Berlin – accepted this same theological reading of Hegel, but were opposed to it as a mistaken position.

The second phase of the anti-Hegel reaction occurred in a qualified return to Kant, mentioned above, starting in the mid-1860s. After Hegel's death, Hegelianism declined rapidly, in part because of the increasing development of modern science, which for many seemed to contradict his speculative approach. The return to Kant was prepared by Kuno Fischer and Eduard Zeller, important historians of philosophy. Fischer wrote a ten-volume history of philosophy with two volumes devoted to Kant. Zeller, an important historian of ancient philosophy, apparently coined the term "epistemology" (*Erkenntnistheorie*) while criticizing Hegelianism. Otto Liebmann gave an important impetus to this movement through his slogan "Back to Kant" in his book on Kant and his epigones.[15] Liebmann preached a simplified version of Kant's critical philosophy in maintaining the transcendental dimension, which he regarded as Kant's central discovery, but simply discarding the vexed doctrine of the thing in itself,[16] which, following Hegel, he treated as a mere *caput mortuum*.[17] Liebmann's famous call to return to Kant was a stage on the way to a series of neo-Kantian schools, which flourished in the period 1870–1920. The two main Kantian schools were in Marburg and Heidelberg. The Marburg school included Hermann Cohen, Paul Natorp, and above all the many-sided polymath Ernst Cassirer. The Heidelberg school, also called the Baden or South-west German school – its members also taught at various other places, including Zurich, Freiburg, and Strasburg – included Kuno Fischer, Wilhelm Windelband, and Heinrich Rickert. Others outside these two schools who participated in the revival of Kant studies during this period include Hans Vaihinger, Friedrich Paulsen, Aloys Riehl, Leonard Nelson, and Georg Simmel.

The fourth and most recent phase of Kant's influence on the subsequent debate concerns philosophy in the twentieth century, that is, the quartet of movements under discussion in this book. In different ways, as I will be arguing below, each of these currents can be understood as reacting to and carrying forward Kantian concerns, doctrines, distinctions, and solutions. But before turning to the twentieth-century reaction to Kant to make this case, I will need to describe his position at least in outline, a task which will occupy the next chapter.

2

Kant and the Post-Kantian Debate

Twentieth-century philosophy unfolded against the background of modern philosophy. In the preceding chapter, I suggested that in different ways the discussion in Kant's wake, including twentieth-century philosophy, is decisively influenced by his critical philosophy. This chapter will be devoted to characterizing Kant's philosophy and the initial phase of the post-Kantian debate.

Kant's position unfolds in the many volumes of his collected writings, including three *Critiques* (*Critique of Pure Reason*, *Critique of Practical Reason*, *Critique of Judgment*) and a long series of other texts. His critical philosophy continues to reverberate through, but also to decisively influence, later debate while evoking an enormous and still growing response in the secondary literature. Kant's position is not only extensive, but also very complex. Any account of it within no more than a single chapter is inevitably and severely restricted in what it can say about the position as a whole, its detailed interpretation, and the secondary literature about it.

Kant's often very technical position presents unusual difficulties leading to a very wide range of interpretations. In a famous encounter in Davos, Switzerland (March 17–April 6, 1929), Cassirer defended a traditional epistemological reading of the critical philosophy while Heidegger argued against Cassirer and others that, on the contrary, it provides a foundation for ontology.[1]

Both are correct in that since Aristotle, to whom the term seems to have first been applied by Adronicus of Rhodes, "metaphysics" has taken on two main meanings. In ancient Greek philosophy, it was taken to mean "ontology," or the science of being, which specifically interests Heidegger. Yet since the beginnings of modern philosophy in Descartes and others, it also means "epistemology," or "theory of knowledge." Kant uses the term mainly in the latter sense. In his *Prolegomena to Any Future Metaphysics* (1783), in which he presents a simplified version of his system, Kant studies the outlines of a theory of knowledge which does not yet exist.[2]

Kant's position provides the initial rough sketch of an enormous project, which he bequeathed to later thinkers at his death. He did important work in a huge variety of fields, including at least modern science – he is co-author of the Kant–Laplace hypothesis on the origin of the cosmos – philosophy of nature which later became what is now called philosophy of science, epistemology, ethics, aesthetics, philosophy of religion, politics, and anthropology. It will not be possible to discuss his entire position. In the limited space at our disposal, I will be concentrating on Kant's theory of knowledge, his most influential contribution, which lies at the epicenter of his wider position and which is crucial for his influence on later philosophy. Though Kant made important, often major, contributions to such fields as ethics and aesthetics, his contribution to theory of knowledge, perhaps because the epistemological theme runs throughout the entire Western tradition, is still and has always been the most influential part of his position.

The problem of knowledge, which neither begins nor ends in Kant, is transformed by his intervention in the debate. This problem is as old as Western philosophy, which begins in the cosmological speculations of the pre-Socratics. It is a main theme in Greek philosophy as early as Parmenides, the first thinker to address the question of the conditions of knowledge in anything resembling our current approaches. Plato's *Theaetetus* provides a treatment of epistemology which continues to attract contemporary writers. The problem continues after Kant in new ways in responding to his transformation of the debate. The main post-Kantian philosophical tendencies in the nineteenth (e.g. post-Kantian German idealism and German neo-Kantianism) and twentieth centuries (e.g. Marxism, pragmatism, continental philosophy, and Anglo-American analytic philosophy) all react in different ways to Kant's powerful refocusing of the problem of knowledge.

On the Modern Philosophical Background

The best way into any position, including Kant's, is in terms of the problems leading to its formulation. The epistemological thrust is dominant not only in Kant, who is in that sense typical, but throughout Western philosophy since its origins, particularly in modern philosophy. Through the idea that there is an identifiable foundation to knowledge, Descartes sets modern philosophy on an epistemological path from which it has often strayed but which it has never entirely left behind.[3] The Cartesian impulse culminates in the characteristic twentieth-century idea, the basis of scientism, that science and only science is the real source of knowledge.

The idea of modern philosophy is unclear since, as noted above, despite claims to the contrary, there is no clear break between modern and earlier philosophy. It is often said that modern philosophy starts with Descartes. According to Hegel, he is the first modern philosopher since he is the first to make thinking into a principle.[4] It is unclear if, as often claimed, it begins with Descartes, or earlier, say with Montaigne. Both react to the rediscovery of Pyrrhonian skepticism in the sixteenth century, which Montaigne accepts and Descartes rejects.[5] Montaigne impugns knowledge based on the senses; in reintroducing the concept of epistemological foundationalism, Descartes founds knowledge in independence of the senses. Both base claims to knowledge on the subject in initiating the characteristic modern approach to objectivity through subjectivity. Montaigne famously asks, "What can I know?" (*que sais-je?*) in arriving at the familiar Pyrrhonian conclusion that I can know nothing, nothing at all. Starting from the same perspective as Montaigne, Descartes extends ancient skepticism by questioning the presupposed but undemonstrated existence of the real in arguing for apodictic claims to know that are allegedly sufficient to defeat even the most radical form of skepticism. He responds to Montaigne in claiming there is no end to human knowledge. In linking human being and knowing, subjectivity and objectivity, Montaigne and Descartes commence what might be called a humanist approach to epistemology that is one of the main themes in the later discussion.

When Kant came on the scene, it was dominated by two competing tendencies, rationalism and empiricism, which he later brought together in a powerful synthesis. The relation between these two movements is complex. The two main early figures in rationalism and empiricism, Descartes (1596–1650) and Francis Bacon (1561–1626), are near contemporaries, whose positions develop independently. But already in Locke (1632–1704), empiricism reacts against rationalism.

Rationalism and empiricism present different, diametrically opposing strategies for knowing the world. In both cases, "world" is understood as mind-independent reality, that is, as already constituted apart from and in independence of the knowing subject. The problem of knowledge from this perspective consists in knowing an object which is in no way dependent on, hence is in every way independent of, the knowing subject.

There are different strategies for knowing an independent object. One, which is found in both ancient Greek and modern philosophy, consists of some form of intuitionism, or the claim for a direct, immediate grasp of the mind-independent real as it is. A second strategy has become known as epistemological foundationalism. Epistemological foundationalism is widely identified with Descartes but by no means limited to his position or to those influenced by him. Like realism, foundationalism takes many forms and is deeply rooted in early Greek philosophy. Foundationalism is most easily described in terms of an ideal-typical form. The term "foundationalism" is usually understood to mean an epistemological strategy that relates claims to know to an epistemological foundation, which is asserted to be true, from which the remainder of the theory can be (rigorously) deduced, and which can be correctly applied to yield knowledge of the mind-independent real as it is. The term "real" is routinely used to refer to things in the world and, by extension, the world as well as the nature of the human mind. Forms of foundationalism are widely disseminated throughout the history of Western philosophy, especially in the modern tradition. Foundationalism is arguably the main modern strategy for knowledge. It is sometimes mistakenly thought that foundationalism is no longer a live option. On the contrary, foundationalism, which has remained widely popular throughout the modern period, remains popular, although not always under that name, even today at the beginning of the new century.

Descartes's familiar version of the foundationalist argument runs through a series of stages. They include: first, proof of his own existence; next, proof of God's existence; then, through the inference that since God is no deceiver, the conclusion that clear and distinct ideas are necessarily true; and, finally, the proof of material things. The proof of his own existence consists merely in the observation that one cannot rationally deny one's own existence. Descartes, who desires knowledge of the external world, cannot rest his case with self-knowledge that does not permit him to answer the question of what he knows before knowing that his mind is a reliable source of knowledge. To show the reliability of our intellectual faculties, Descartes proves the existence of God and examines the source of error in the misuse of our rational faculties.

Locke's empiricism is influenced by, but also reacts against, Cartesian rationalism. Like Descartes, Locke builds his theory of knowledge on a conception of ideas, but he disagrees with Descartes about their status. Descartes, who believes that the idea of God is innate, admits innate ideas. In his *Meditations on First Philosophy* (1641, 1644), he uses the term "idea" technically to refer to "images of things"[6] and distinguishes between ideas which are innate, adventitious, or invented by the subject.[7] He further argues we have an innate idea of God and, in reply to an objection by Gassendi, claims that mathematical ideas are not drawn from the senses.[8] Locke, who bases knowledge on empirical experience, insists against Descartes that at birth the mind is a *tabula rasa*, since all ideas are derived from experience, and rejects any claim to innate knowledge.[9] He begins *An Essay Concerning Human Understanding* (1690) in rejecting the very possibility of innate knowledge of any kind. According to Locke, whatever we know comes to us through the use of our faculties in respect to sensory experience.[10]

The empiricist approach to knowledge in all its forms includes two related claims already formulated by Bacon: all knowledge is based on experience; and when we know, the mind in effect acts as a mirror,[11] what Rorty influentially calls the mirror of nature.[12] Locke, who improves on Bacon's view, distinguishes between simple ideas and complex ideas. Our relation to the objects of knowledge is indirect since our only access to the world is through the ideas we have of it.[13] Locke defines "Idea" as "whatsoever is meant by phantasm, notion, species, or whatever it is which the mind be employed about in thinking."[14] Ideas, which have no truth value in themselves, are true or false only when they refer beyond themselves. Locke considers three specific cases: how different people use the same names; the relation between ideas and the independent external world; and whether ideas grasp the essence of whatever it is to which they refer. He locates abstract ideas, which are derived from experience and then accorded a name, between the name of the thing and the thing to which the name refers. Complex ideas in the mind are composed of simple ideas, provided by God, which come into the mind through sensation and reflection, but which the mind cannot create.[15] Error is due to false judgment.[16]

Descartes and Locke differ on the cardinal point of whether ideas are innate or derived only from experience. Both are seminal figures, hugely influential in launching the career of these respective philosophical perspectives, which, however, cannot be attributed to them alone. The relation of rationalism and empiricism is complex. Empiricism both reacts against and continues rationalism. The discontinuity lies in whether the proper road to knowledge leads from the mind to the world, as rationalism asserts, or from the world to the mind, as empiricists affirm. It would be a mistake either to assimilate empiricism and rationalism or to isolate them from each other. Empiricism remains continuous with rationalism in no less than five main ways. It shares the rationalist effort to bring the mind in touch with the world in order to know it as it is. It strives to do so through ideas in the mind. More precisely, rationalism and empiricism belong to the larger framework of the so-called "new way of ideas,"[17] which, before Kant, dominated the discussion of knowledge in modern philosophy. Further, both rely on God to guarantee the veracity of our cognitive ideas. Finally, both take an anthropological approach to knowledge as based on what finite human beings can know. Speaking generally, Kant denies all five points in responding to both rationalism and empiricism in his critical philosophy.

On Kant's Relation to the Contemporary Philosophical Background

Kant's intellectual background includes not only philosophy but also classics, in which he was trained as a young man. In fact, such was his proficiency in Latin (in addition to Greek, Hebrew, and French), which he probably knew well enough to speak it, that there is a recurrent view that the *Critique of Pure Reason*, while written in German, was actually thought out in the former language. Moreover, any account of the genesis of Kant's position needs to consider his deep understanding of science, especially modern science, in which he began his career. His very first article, on Leibniz's concept of force, was followed several years later by others on the earth's rotation, the age of the earth, and so on. His interest in Newtonian mechanics strongly motivated his thought, and he retained a deep interest in natural science throughout his career.

Kant's mature position turns on his seminal distinction between dogmatic philosophy, which is merely asserted but not demonstrated, and critical philosophy, which is both asserted and demonstrated. In the last text he himself published, Kant claims there can only be one true philosophy, and that prior philosophy is not critical, hence is dogmatic.[18] This suggests that philosophy both begins and ends in his critical philosophy. In a word, philosophy worthy of the name, critical philosophy, which alone is true, begins and ends in Kant. It further suggests, since earlier philosophy is dogmatic, that there is nothing to learn from earlier thinkers. In fact, Kant's philosophical position draws on Plato, Aristotle, Christian Wolff, Leibniz, Hume, and many others. He famously suggests he knows Plato better than he knew himself.[19] From Aristotle, he derives the substance-attribute approach which informs his analysis of substance. He thinks enough of Wolff to say that, had the latter been a critical thinker,

Wolff could have anticipated his own effort to transform metaphysics into a science.[20] From Leibniz he borrows the principle of sufficient reason that is the core of his answer to the problem of causality.[21] Kant's well-known remark in the *Prolegomena* that Hume woke him from his dogmatic slumber[22] has suggested to generations of commentators that the most important relation to the philosophical background lies in Kant's effort, as he says, to solve Hume's problem in general form.

Kant's relation to Hume is certainly vitally important, but his relation to Descartes is perhaps even more crucial. In his attack on causality, Hume provides the specific problem which, on Kant's own account, starts him down the road to the critical philosophy. Descartes influences the general approach Kant takes to the theory of knowledge and within which he solves the difficulty posed by Hume. To put the same point in other language: Kant's relation to Hume is negative, but his relation to Descartes is both positive and negative, positive as concerns the outlines of the approach to knowledge, and negative with respect to epistemological representationalism, which, as we shall see in the next section, Kant both accepts and rejects for epistemological constructivism.

The justification for understanding Kant's critical philosophy in response to Hume's attack on causality is clear and persuasive. Hume is important for Kant because of the perceived catastrophic consequences of his destructive attack on causality for modern science, hence for knowledge of all kinds, including what Kant calls the future science of metaphysics. Galileo destroys the old Aristotelian approach to causality without invoking a new conception. Kant's understanding of causality evolves over time. In his early writings, he seems to identify causality with a Wolffian approach to ground.[23] A decade later he suggests we can perceive but cannot demonstrate causality, which must be derived from experience.[24] If true, this latter attitude would have prevented him from ever responding to Hume, who seemingly prevents any possibility of basing causality on experience. In the *Critique of Pure Reason*, Kant understands causality on a broadly Leibnizian model. In the *Monadology* (1714) and in other writings, Leibniz proposes a principle of sufficient reason in arguing that for every fact there is a reason, which he applies, *inter alia*, to prove the existence of God as the ultimate reason in a chain of contingent facts.[25] Kant applies a version of this principle in the form of a universal law of causality in the mature form of this position.[26] The constant element in his changing views of causality is that science depends on it.

Kant's view of Hume arises out of his understanding of modern science as based on a causal analysis of nature. Newton invents a causal analysis of planetary motion, thereby definitively solving a problem for which Copernicus advances a mere hypothesis.[27] Hume undermines this approach, hence modern science, in undermining causality. Thus the defense of knowledge requires a solution which re-establishes causality in the face of Hume's attack on this concept. In the Preface to the *Prolegomena*, Kant outlines Hume's importance for metaphysics in showing that reason cannot think necessary connections a priori. In order to solve the general difficulty, he claims to generalize Hume's problem in noticing that the connection of cause and effect is merely one among a series of a priori connections of which metaphysics consists.[28]

Kant's relation to Descartes, which is not often scrutinized, perhaps because of the many bad things he says about his French predecessor – one of the milder complaints is that Descartes is guilty of doubting the existence of the external world[29] – is deep and important for his own approach to knowledge, hence to solving the enigma posed by Hume. For example, both Kant and Descartes develop approaches to knowledge in which access to the object necessarily runs through the subject. In other words, like Descartes, Kant constructs his theory of knowledge on a conception of the subject as the first, or highest, indubitable and foundational principle of knowledge.[30] Both understand perception as an effect for which the world is the cause. And in both cases the problem of knowledge consists in a causal theory of perception that consists in making out a backward inference from effect to cause, in a word from the representation of the world to the world it represents.

Kant's Letter to Marcus Herz

In replying to Hume, Kant develops a quasi-Cartesian argument. Hume is an empiricist and Descartes is a rationalist: Kant counters Hume's skepticial empiricism by transporting a possible response to the problem of knowledge from the a posteriori to the a priori plane, by insisting on the reality of the external world and through resisting the latent psychologism in Hume's form of representationalism. And in answer to such thinkers as Descartes and Locke who rely on a link between reason and faith, Kant proposes a conception of pure reason, which, since it is self-justifying, is independent of any theological considerations.

In order to outline Kant's theory of knowledge, it will be useful to focus on his famous letter to Herz, and on the *Critique of Pure Reason*, which only emerged nearly a decade later. It is usual to divide Kant's position into pre-critical and critical periods separated by the *Inaugural Dissertation* (1770), the text written when Kant assumed his job as Professor of Philosophy at the University of Königsberg. According to this approach, the text marks the onset of the critical period.[31]

This distinction, which has Kant's support, is questionable. It is not hard to understand why an author, like Kant, who thinks that in his intellectual development after a long series of efforts solid ground has suddenly been reached claims that everything written earlier merely belonged to his juvenilia, hence is not worth taking seriously. It is perhaps more accurate to say that Kant's view of knowledge evolves without breaks or other forms of discontinuity. His theory of knowledge develops over many years from his initial article in the mid-1740s to the first edition of the *Critique of Pure Reason* in the early 1780s, followed by the *Prolegomena* and the second edition of the *Critique.*

The best place to see in abbreviated form how Kant understands the problem of knowledge is in a very important letter (July 21, 1772) he sent early in his critical period to his friend Marcus Herz. In the letter, Kant announces the project which later became the critical philosophy, while pointing obscurely toward the strategy he will later adopt. It is crucial to note the difference between the conception of the problem described in the letter and the solution – in fact, two solutions – Kant later proposes. Kant states the problem of knowledge in terms of three elements: the subject which knows, the object which is known, and the representation through which the subject knows the object. Stated in this way, Kant is denying direct knowledge of the object to which we have access only through its representation. The crux of the problem, which "constitutes the key to the whole secret of metaphysics," consists in grasping "on what grounds rests the reference of what in us is called representation (*Vorstellung*) to the object (*Gegenstand*)?"[32]

In Kant's way of posing the problem of knowledge, it consists in a relation of the representation to the represented, or mind-independent external object. The representation is internal to the mind of the knowing subject. The problem of knowledge calls for a representationalist solution, which explains, to restate Kant's language, the grounds in us of the relation of the representation to the object. We can paraphrase this in the following way: A theory of knowledge requires an explanation of how we know independent objects. If such objects cannot be known directly, then they can only be known indirectly, according to Kant through their representations. This train of reasoning leads immediately to the following crucial question: How can we represent independent objects correctly?

Kant immediately envisages three possibilities in a discussion difficult to paraphrase. One approach, close to current causal theories of perception, is to consider that a passive subject is affected by the object. In this case, the object is the cause and the representation is the effect. On this model, the problem of knowledge consists in explaining how to infer from the representation regarded as an effect to the object regarded as its cause. Yet it seems obvious there is no way to infer from the effect to its cause, say, from the First World War to the assassination of the Archduke Ferdinand. There are many possible causes which could and in fact on occasion do produce the same fact. Since the cause does not uniquely determine this and only this effect, it cannot be shown on the basis of this effect that it is uniquely due to the cause in question.

A second possibility Kant examines is for the representation in some way to produce its object. But, Kant objects, it is only in the moral sphere that the understanding causes the object. An example might be when someone in fact does what one ought to do so that what is corresponds to what ought to be. Yet this condition does not obtain outside morality. If, say, a carpenter constructs a bed according to an idea in the mind, it is not the idea but rather the carpenter who is the cause of which the bed is the effect.

The third possibility, which Kant favors, is to make knowledge depend on concepts in the understanding. In this model, concepts do not depend on the object to be known, which, rather, depends on concepts. This amounts to claiming that the perceptual object does not produce the concepts, which are also not abstracted from experience, but, on the contrary, the concepts produce the perceptual object.[33] The obvious advantage of this approach consists in avoiding difficulties associated with making the representation depend on the object or, on the contrary, the object depend on its representation. Kant's solution, which accounts for the problem of how the representation relates to the object, consists in the idea that there are two objects: one is the mind-independent object, which is already constituted in independence of the knowing subject; and the other is the mind-dependent object, which is constituted, or constructed, by the subject as a condition of knowing it. In this proposal, since the object is constituted by the subject, it corresponds to the structures of the mind, hence is knowable.

Two points need to be noticed to make sense of this solution as concerns representations and concepts. Kant solves the difficulty of the relation of the representation to the object by changing the meaning of "representation." In his solution, he relates ordinary experiential objects to objects standing outside of and unknowable through experience. The objects of experience, which are constructed by, hence dependent on, and for that reason knowable by, the subject are also representations of mind-independent objects, which, since they are not given in experience, are uncognizable. In other words, ordinary objects relate to, thus represent, extraordinary objects, the kind of object which is not given in and cannot be known through experience.

Kant also changes the meaning of the word "concept," which he detaches from experience as an effect in transforming it into a cause. The concepts of the mind are not abstracted from experience, or produced by the objects, which, on the contrary, they construct. Rather, these concepts are, as it were, "hard-wired" into the mind. And the concepts of the understanding do not produce the mind-independent objects, which, since they are independent of us, are already constituted prior to and apart from the knowing process.

This theory, which Kant announces here in barest outline, is new, different, promising, and exciting. It points toward the position he will later work out in detail in the critical philosophy. It in principle provides for the relation of the representation to the object – this is obviously the crux of the problem – at the cost of dropping the idea that the representation is in the mind. Kant rather locates it in the external world, in space and time, where, as a representation, it stands in relation to an object outside experience. This new theory is different from anything Kant has hitherto described in previous writings. In order to indicate what is new, he now characterizes the present version of his theory in comparing it to what he described in *Inaugural Dissertation* only two years earlier.

In the *Dissertation*, he pointed out that cognitive representations cannot be understood as the effects of the object understood as a cause. This means he had moved away from the idea, still frequent in current discussion, that knowledge can be based on a causal theory of perception. But, he says, he did not answer how, in refusing this solution, a representation can refer to an object.[34] From his present standpoint, that means he earlier failed to answer the crucial question of how representations relate to objects. At the time, he merely stated that representations were not produced as the effect of objects acting on the mind. He did not, however, respond to the question he has answered now, that is, how a representation can refer to an object by which it is not affected. Earlier he said that sensuous representations, or what is drawn from experience, provide us with things as they appear, and intellectual representations, which are merely thought without experience, provide us with mind-independent things, that is, things as they really are. His earlier distinction between appearance and reality corresponds to the later distinction between representations and objects. The things met with in ordinary experience are now understood as representations, or appearances, of reality. The difficulty with this line of argument in the *Dissertation*, as Kant now points out, is two-fold. On the one hand, it fails to explain how things, that is, mind-independent objects, are given or made known to us. If it is not by affecting us, that is, through a causal theory of perception, how does it happen? This amounts to saying that we do not understand how our representations relate to what they are supposed to represent, or, to put the point otherwise, how reality manifests itself as appearance. On the other hand, Kant points out that we cannot understand how our concepts – he here uses the term "axioms of pure reason" – agree with, or relate to, these objects unless this relation or agreement is based on experience.

Kant immediately points out that the problem of how representations relate to objects varies in different cognitive domains, which require different solutions. He distinguishes between mathematics, which concerns quantities, and natural science, which deals with qualities. In mathematics, since we produce the objects spontaneously and a priori, it is easy to see that our views of the objects entirely correspond to them.[35] Kant seems to mean that we can represent to ourselves mathematical objects wholly a priori, as when I imagine a triangle, from which I proceed to deduce various properties.

The problem is more difficult in natural science, which consists in making cognitive claims about an independent world. Here the question takes the form of asking how we can know a priori how things must in fact turn out in experience to be in reliably predicting the whole a posteriori world. Science concerns the way the world is, which it attempts to explain by formulating a series of scientific laws. This problem takes two forms, including how we know or can know prior to and apart from experience the way things are in experience, and how we can formulate general scientific laws which must be illustrated in experience. The answer to the question – how can we know how things are or will be given in experience? – lies in the idea that we "construct" them in order to know them. Kant here goes beyond a theory of knowledge based on representing the objects that we know in claiming that we construct them as a condition of knowing them. If we know the way things must be a priori, then we will also be able to know how they must in fact be a posteriori. The answer is more complicated for the specific problem of how we are able successfully to formulate scientific laws. Since Kant thinks that all knowledge worthy of the name, including scientific and metaphysical knowledge, is a priori, this amounts to claiming that the laws of nature do not arise in experience, but are rather prescribed to nature.[36]

I have devoted so much space to this seminal letter since here, early in Kant's critical period, well before he has composed the *Critique*, the main outlines of the theory of knowledge, and its unresolved difficulties, which he will later work out in detail are already apparent. Astonishingly, Kant already has in mind most of the aspects of the solution even as he for the first time clearly poses the problem central to the critical philosophy. Yet despite unremitting labor over many years, one can only agree with him that despite his brilliant effort to solve the problem of knowledge, "such questions always leave behind an obscurity regarding our power of understanding as to how its conformity with things comes about."[37]

Kant's Two Epistemological Solutions in the *Critique of Pure Reason*

Kant strives to elucidate these mysteries in the *Critique of Pure Reason*, his first and certainly greatest book, and one of the very few enduring philosophical monuments. The Herz letter reveals essential aspects about Kant's way of posing the problem of knowledge and the solution he proposes. Since the way the problem is framed influences what can conceivably count as its solution, it is important to see that Kant offers two very different epistemological solutions. The first solution corresponds to the way he originally poses the problem, but fails to resolve it. The second solution, which is very different, is in fact incompatible with the first one, and is also incompatible with the way he poses the problem in the Herz letter. Yet it has the enormous merit of solving the problem of knowledge in another, very different, potentially more promising and exciting way.

In saying that in the letter Kant states the problem of knowledge in representationalist form, I mean no more than that he calls for an analysis of the relation of the representations in us – what earlier thinkers call ideas in the mind – to mind-independent external objects: in short, the world as it is apart from any relation to an observer. This way of putting the problem means that the solution depends on making good on a representationalist approach to knowledge. In taking such an approach to epistemology, Kant renews and carries forward a main epistemological strategy, which is particularly important in modern philosophy. In the modern period, increasing doubt about the idea of a direct grasp of the world as it is has led many thinkers away from direct realism and toward a new solution to the problem of knowledge. The new way of ideas, that is, the approach to knowledge through the relation of ideas in the mind to things, is representationalist. In both rationalism and empiricism, stress is placed on analyzing the relation of ideas to what they represent. For Descartes, ideas are images of things. For a Cartesian, the problem of knowledge comes down to an inference from ideas in the mind to things in the world. For Locke, for whom we cannot create simple ideas, which, on his account, necessarily tell us the way the world is, the problem of knowledge comes down to being sure that we are dealing with simple ideas.

In the *Critique of Pure Reason* Kant utilizes "representation" (*Vorstellung*) where the new way of ideas employs "idea" (a term for which he has another use[38]). As a representationalist, Kant continues and develops the representationalist approach to knowledge which is everywhere in modern philosophy, both before and after him. Since in his capacity as a representationalist, Kant builds on prior thinkers, it is fair to say that in the critical philosophy representationalism reaches a high point which has never since been surpassed. The main difference between Kant and earlier representationalists like Descartes and Locke concerns the resolutely secular character of his approach.

Many philosophical concerns, including Kant's famous questions (What can I know? What should I do? What may I hope?),[39] arose originally in theology. In the West, the link between philosophy and theology has been attenuated but never wholly broken. In famously stating in the *Critique* that he denies knowledge in making room for faith,[40] Kant is not attributing a cognitive role to faith. He is rather pointing to the limits of what can be known through pure reason, which he believes can tell us nothing at all about such items as God, freedom, and immortality. Efforts to extend the reach of reason beyond experience result in dialectical inferences, or contradictions of reason with itself as concerns the topics of the subject (paralogisms of pure reason), the object (antinomies of pure reason), or the relation of subject and object as the world (cosmological ideas).

With the singular exception of Kant, the main representatives of the new way of ideas all depend in different ways on a relation between philosophy and theology, reason and faith. Descartes's knowledge claims explicitly depend on God's existence.[41] He is often said to employ a circular argument, the so-called "Cartesian circle."[42] Claims to know depend on clear and distinct ideas, which he employs to prove the existence of God, who in turn guarantees their veracity. Locke also relies on God in his theory of knowledge. He explains the reliability of simple ideas not through a claim to grasp primary qualities, but rather because they ultimately come from God as the source of our understanding.[43]

For Kant, philosophy worthy of the name must be critical, hence capable of establishing its assertions. Since, according to him, the claims of reason are self-demonstrating, they are independent of faith, and at least in that way divorced from theology. Kant's version of representationalism specifically differs from its predecessors in claiming to provide a rigorously secular demonstration of its assertions.

It differs in another way as well. As the term suggests, representationalists are all committed to representationalism as the proper approach to knowledge. Kant, who is always cautious, and who typically sees different alternatives but is unable to choose among them, is simultaneously committed to representationalism and to what I will be calling constructivism. By representationalism I mean, as should already be clear, that knowledge requires that the representation match up with what it represents, understood as an independent object or objects. Representationalism is a way of making out a claim to know the world as it is through analyzing the relation between the representation and the objects. By "constructivism" I will have in mind the idea that knowledge requires that the subject "construct" the object it knows as a condition of knowing it.

Constructivism, which seems never to have been discussed in detail, is a second-best approach, which bases claims to know on empirical realism. All theories of knowledge of whatever kind claim to provide knowledge of the real, but the real which is known is understood in many different ways. In the West, the main theme in theory of knowledge, which goes all the way back in the tradition at least to Parmenides, is metaphysical realism, that is, the conviction that to know is to know the mind-independent real as it is. Theory of knowledge based on metaphysical realism holds that there is a way the world is and that under the proper conditions the world can be known as it is. There are many different forms of realism. Scientific realism is roughly the view that science and only science determines how the world is. Theories of knowledge are related to conceptions of reality.[44] Empirical realism is the view that claims for knowledge are limited to, hence cannot go further than, whatever is given in experience.

Constructivists typically hold that there may be a way the world is; but we cannot know it, since we cannot know the world as it is in independence of us and knowledge is limited to what is given in experience. Constructivism arises on the ruins of representationalism and all other efforts, including direct realism, to know the world as it is. A constructivist is someone who denies there is any way to know the world as it is but persists in being concerned with knowledge, not about the mind-independent real, but rather as limited to objects we ourselves construct. A representationalist typically claims that our representations point toward something outside experience in inviting an analysis of the relation between the objects of experience, understood as appearances of something else. A constructivist believes there is no way to infer from what is given in experience to something outside it, and limits the problem of knowledge merely to the contents of experience. For a representationalist the epistemological problem consists in knowing how the representation, which is present, relates to the object, which, since it is not given in experience, is absent. A constructivist, who cannot make any sense of the claim about how what is present relates to what is not present, or the relation of representations to independent objects, confines attention to how we can know what is given in experience. The basic claim, which is varied by different authors, consists in affirming that we in some sense construct what we know.

Direct realism is widely thought to be difficult, even not possible, to defend.[45] Representationalism is arguably the main modern approach to knowledge. Constructivism is an important, but minority doctrine, which is specifically modern. It is the kind of doctrine one turns to when approaches to metaphysical realism are seen to fail and skepticism is not an acceptable option. Early modern constructivists include Hobbes and Vico. Kant, who knew Hobbes, seems not to have known Vico, who was, however, known to Kant's student, Herder, but seems only to have become influential later. Kant's constructivism emerges in the famous, often-mentioned, but little understood Copernican revolution in philosophy.

Kant's Copernican Revolution in Philosophy as Constructivism

Kant never uses the term "Copernican revolution in philosophy" to refer to his own position, and there is little attention paid to this concept, especially in the English-language Kant debate. Bertrand Russell, who believed idealism was worthless, thought that Kant's Copernican revolution in philosophy meant "propositions may acquire truth by being believed."[46]

Other, more qualified observers are uneasy about the very idea of linking Kant's position to Copernican astronomy. The most thorough account of the relation of Copernicus and Kant currently available concludes there is no connection.[47] Yet Kant's immediate contemporaries, Reinhold[48] and then Schelling,[49] believed Kant had introduced a Copernican revolution in philosophy based on his reading of Copernican astronomy in relation to the development of modern science.

What is usually called Kant's Copernican revolution in philosophy is in fact a brilliant constructivist approach to theory of knowledge. In regard to representationalism, Kant carries an already existing, important tendency to its high point. Though there are still many representationalists, no one has since taken representationalism beyond the point it reaches in the critical philosophy. In regard to constructivism, Kant breaks new ground in a way which is still underappreciated but which offers an exciting new approach to knowledge.

Kant's constructivism is based on his reading of the history of mathematics and of science. He generalizes the constructivism he finds there to theory of knowledge in general. We can usefully distinguish between Kant's general theory of mathematics and his conception of mathematical constructivism. Kant, who holds a version of the familiar view of mathematics as the queen of sciences, innovates in claiming that all mathematical judgments of any kind whatsoever are synthetic.[50] This view remains controversial. Frege, for instance, influentially argues that geometry is synthetic but arithmetic is analytic.[51] Quine later attacked the very distinction between the analytic and the synthetic.[52] After the rise of relativity theory, physics introduced a distinction between pure geometry, which is exact, but does not describe the world, and applied geometry, which is inexact, but describes the world.[53]

According to Kant, mathematics and physics – for him, physics is the main form of natural science – both determine their objects a priori, that is, prior to and independently of all experience.[54] He explicitly distinguishes between philosophy, which analyzes concepts, and mathematics, which constructs concepts.[55] For Kant, the construction of concepts is the hallmark of the mathematical.[56] Mathematics, he insists, depends on a revolution which, already in ancient Greece, constructed a royal road to scientific knowledge that it has since successfully followed. The revolution consists in discovering that the true method to mathematical knowledge does not lie in simply inspecting figures or their concepts but rather in constructing figures according to a priori concepts. Mathematics only yields apodictic knowledge since it concerns objects we construct a priori in the mind and whose properties we then discover. Mathematical knowledge has a priori certainty since it necessarily follows from what we put into the figure. So, to take Kant's example, we can determine with certainty the properties of an isosceles triangle that we construct in the imagination.[57]

Kant makes a similar but more complex argument with respect to natural science, which he then generalizes from science to metaphysics. The main difference between mathematics and physics is that the former deals only with objects it constructs, but the latter is concerned to know nature as it is. By "nature," Kant understands not things in themselves, which must remain unknown, but rather things as given in experience and determined, as he says, by universal, exceptionless laws.[58] He distinguishes between empirical science, which derives empirical laws from experience, and what he calls pure natural science, his term for theoretical science. The latter is concerned with a so-called "universal natural science" preceding empirical physics, and which formulates apodictic propositions that it prescribes to nature. Kant, who is in this respect his own worst enemy, gives as examples the propositions that substance is permanent and that every event has a single identifiable cause. These claims were widely believed in Kant's time but were later abandoned.[59] Since such laws are formulated a priori, nature as given in experience must necessarily conform to them.[60]

How is it that we can successfully formulate exceptionless laws of nature on an a priori basis? Kant's answer seems to be that we do this through the successful application of mathematics, whose objects are a priori, to nature. His most interesting example is arguably the difference in the contributions of Copernicus and of Newton to modern science. Philosophers of science and historians of science often regard modern science as beginning in Galileo's successful application of mathematics to nature.[61] For Kant, on the contrary, modern science begins with Copernicus's revolutionary change from the Ptolemaic geocentric to a heliocentric conception of the solar system.

As an empirical astronomer, Copernicus introduced his astronomical theory on a posteriori grounds as a mere hypothesis. What for Copernicus was no more than a hypothesis was, Kant suggests, later proven by Newton. This model suggests that the same scientific problems can be approached either empirically, that is, a posteriori, or theoretically, that is, a priori. A problem which yields only a hypothetical solution based on experience can be definitively solved through an a priori approach. For Kant, Newton's discovery of gravitation transformed what for Copernicus is merely a kinetic approach into a dynamic solution. In a famous footnote, Kant writes:

> In the same way, the central laws of the motion of the heavenly bodies established with certainty what Copernicus assumed at the beginning only as a hypothesis, and at the same time they proved the invisible force (of Newtonian attraction) that binds the universe, which would have remained forever undiscovered if Copernicus had not ventured, in a manner contradictory to the senses yet true, to seek for the observed movements not in the objects of the heavens but in the observer.[62]

Kant's answer to how Newton solves the problem lies in reading Newton against himself. In the General Scholium to *Principia Mathematica*, Newton famously claims not to go beyond experience and, hence, not to make hypotheses. He just as famously admits he is not able to explain the origin of gravitation other than by entertaining a hypothesis, which cannot be deduced from the phenomena.[63] This is tantamount to admitting that, and though he eschews hypotheses of any kind, his own proposed solution remains tentative, hence hypothetical, and in any case insufficient to solve the problem. Kant suggests, on the contrary, that Newton is successful in definitively solving the problem since he in effect applies mathematics to nature on an a priori plane in formulating the great inverse square law of gravitation. In an important passage, Kant draws attention to the geometrical properties of a circle in arguing for continuity between mathematics and the laws of physical nature. Since the argument is very technical, we need not follow it in detail. Kant's insight can be informally paraphrased in the following way. If we consider the circle as a conic section, then the rectangles of the segments stand in a constant ratio. In continuing to generalize, we discover that the inverse square, which is the direct physical analogue of the mathematical observation about conic sections, applies to the whole of nature.[64] On this basis, Kant immediately infers that not only does nature rest on laws which can be cognized a priori, but in the law of gravitation Newton has in fact successfully discovered just such a law.

Kant's Copernican Revolution, Science, and Metaphysics

Kant's argument hardly seems conclusive. It scarcely follows that if we successfully apply mathematics to nature, we have discovered a law which is, to use his own words, necessarily inherent in the very nature of things. It remains unclear whether the laws formulated by scientists studying nature are appropriate fictions, inductive generalizations, approximations to what exists, descriptions of reality as it is, and so on. Yet Kant goes further than Newton in making a stronger claim. He feels confident in generalizing the constructive principle underlying his approach both to mathematics and science and to metaphysics, understood as theory of knowledge in general.

His generalization, which is the heart of the so-called Kantian "Copernican revolution" in philosophy, includes two moments. Negatively, there is, as one might expect, an argument against any form of representationalism. For it is only if representationalism fails to know the mind-independent world as it is that it becomes interesting to formulate an alternative approach which precisely argues for knowledge while abandoning this central goal. Positively, it provides a view of a very different strategy for knowledge which makes no pretense to know the world as it is.

Kant's argument, once again, depends on evaluating earlier approaches to knowledge and suggesting an alternative approach. One possibility, which has often been tried, but which for Kant misfires in any possible form, is to make knowledge depend on an appropriate grasp of the independent object. For a representationalist, this means that we grasp mind-independent objects through our representations of them. Yet efforts so far to work out this kind of approach have failed. The solution, Kant suggests, lies in reversing the relation between subject and object, knower and known. Instead of having the subject depend on the object, we must make the object depend on the subject. More precisely, if the knowing subject can determine how the object must be experienced apart from and prior to experience, then a priori knowledge, for Kant the only type of knowledge worthy of the name, will be possible. In a simple, but stunning passage, which encompasses both moments of the argument, and which deserves to be cited at length, Kant writes:

> Up to now it has been assumed that all our cognition must conform to the objects; but all attempts to find out something about the a priori through concepts that would extend our cognition have, on this presupposition, come to nothing. Hence let us once try whether we do not get farther with the problems of metaphysics by assuming that the objects must conform to our cognition, which would agree better with the requested possibility of an a priori cognition of them, which is to establish something about objects before they are given to us.[65]

The argument Kant states here shows he has changed his mind on a basic point: the promise of a representational approach to knowledge.

This argument refutes the representationalism central to his formulation of the problem of knowledge in the Herz letter. Kant here relies on his analysis of epistemological practice as the basis of epistemological theory. He offers two historical examples to support his approach. Both examples focus on a conception of the subject as active in responding to the unstated, but obviously central question of how objects can conform to our cognition. Kant's solution lies in claiming that the subject constructs the object; more precisely, that the knowing subject constructs what it knows according to structures of the human mind. As a direct result, the object we seek to know is "transparent" to, hence knowable by, human subjects. Kant's insight is that we can know only what we "make," "construct," or "produce." One example, which is more recent, concerns the application of mathematics to nature early in the seventeenth century which quickly led on to Newtonian mechanics. The other, which is older, serves to justify the application of the general term "Copernican revolution in philosophy" to Kant's critical philosophy.

The first example concerns recent scientific practice. Kant, who refers to early seventeenth-century scientific figures such as Galileo, Torricelli, and Stahl, observes that, in a famous phrase, "reason has insight only into that which it produces according to its own design."[66] This example illustrates the conclusion that since cognition cannot successfully conform to objects, objects must conform to our cognition in providing a successful instance in modern science.

Kant's second, more interesting example lies in his analysis of the respective contributions of Copernicus and Newton to modern science. Philosophers, philosophers of science, and historians of science usually see modern science as beginning in Galileo's successful application of mathematics to nature.[67] As Kant reads the history of modern science, Copernicus only turned to his heliocentric model when he found the then standard, geocentric model insufficient to explain the movements of the planets. According to Copernicus, who was working with a theory of relative motion, observed movement is due to movement either of the object or of the observer, or both. Since we are located on the surface of the earth, its motion will be reflected in the motions of the planets as they revolve around the sun.[68]

Kant, who did work in planetary astronomy early in his career, would have been familiar with at least the main lines of the Copernican theory, whether or not he was directly familiar with the Copernican texts. Copernicus was faced with a choice of explaining the motions of the planets in one of two ways. The first possibility was based on the assumption that we must fit our theories, or cognition, to the object. This approach commits us to a representational theory of knowledge. The second possibility was to make the solar system revolve around the observer on the very different assumption that the objects, or motions of the planets, must conform to our cognition. Long before Kant, Copernicus chose to make knowledge depend on the observer since he was unsuccessful in explaining the motions of the planets on the assumption that knowledge depends on knowing an independent object. Kant now explicitly links the Copernican innovation in celestial astronomy with his constructivist approach to natural science in writing:

> This would be just like the first thoughts of Copernicus, who, when he did not make good progress in the explanation of the celestial motions if he assumed that the entire celestial host revolves around the observer, tried to see if he might not have greater success if he made the observer revolve and left the stars at rest. Now in metaphysics we can try in a similar way regarding the *intuition* of objects. If intuition has to conform to the constitution of the objects, then I do not see how we can know anything of them a priori; but if the object (as an object of the senses) conforms to the constitution of our faculty of intuition, then I can very well represent this possibility to myself.[69]

Kant's Copernican Revolution in Philosophy and Metaphysics

The moral of this line of reasoning is that we cannot know an independent object since, if it is independent, there is no epistemological link to it; but we can know objects we ourselves construct. Kant now generalizes this claim to metaphysics, or theory of knowledge in general. Its possibility, according to Kant, lies in showing that we know objects we construct, where the idea of construction remains to be specified. More generally, Kant now gives up the approach that to know means to uncover, discover, or reveal what is in favor of the alternative view that to know means to construct, produce, or make what we know. We recall that since the mind-independent world is independent of us, we cannot know it. We know only the world as it is given in experience, or empirical reality, which, Kant argues, is in effect constructed by us as a condition of knowing it.

The idea that we know only what we construct suggests that a conception of metaphysical unity lies at the basis of metaphysics. In the Kantian approach, since the knowing subject knows what it constructs, it knows itself in the form of externality. In other words, there is a unity in difference between subject and object, knower and known, in virtue of which the knower knows the object, which is itself under the form of otherness. Knowledge depends on a deep unity underlying all diversity. This inference, which follows directly from Kant's Copernican turn, is later developed in post-Kantian German idealism, which is often referred to as a philosophy of identity (*Identitätsphilosophie*).

Kant's conception of the subject is central to his critical philosophy. It is obvious that a theory which depends for knowledge on the subject's construction of the object centers on the subject. Kant, who refers to the subject through an infelicitous term as the "synthetic unity of apperception,"[70] clearly says that it is the highest point of the understanding, logic, and transcendental philosophy, in short the *terminus a quo*, the rational origin of his entire position, the logical starting point of the critical philosophy.[71]

Kant's conception of the subject is a large and complicated topic. The easiest generalization is that with respect to the subject he is in part close to Descartes but resolutely opposed to Locke, and, through him, to other British empiricists, particularly Hume. Descartes proposes a two-fold conception of the subject as both the spectator of all that is and an actor in the world. The Cartesian subject is both in the world and, as its condition, transcendent to it. Locke and other British empiricists feature an anthropological view of the subject-related theories of human knowledge. Like such later thinkers as Frege and Husserl, Kant was strongly opposed to what later came to be called psychologism, roughly the reduction of logical processes to psychological processes. Kant strongly favors anti-psychologism. He specifically criticizes Locke for his alleged "*physiology* of the human understanding."[72] Kant also rejects the Humean so-called "bundle" view of the subject – roughly the idea that there is nothing like an unchangeable subject but only a series of fleeting impressions – in claiming that the single subject of all experience is, as he says, "one and the same."[73] In rejecting any form of philosophical anthropology, Kant defends a minimal subject, reduced to its sole epistemological capacity, a subject which, as he says, "must be able to accompany all my representations."[74]

The Kantian subject of knowledge is both active and passive. It is passive with respect to the raw input, which comes from without and which becomes the content of knowledge, and active with respect to working it up into what becomes the output. Kant, who for the first time draws a consistent distinction between sensation and perception, argues that the subject is affected through sensation, or the sensory manifold, whose contents are suitably transformed into objects we perceive, experience, and know. The transformation from mere unprocessed sensory content to perceptual object occurs through the application of the categories, or pure concepts of the understanding, which Kant claims to deduce. The deduction of the categories is a central part of the argument. Kant, who is aware of preceding efforts at a categorial interpretation of experience, criticizes Aristotle's categories as a mere rhapsody – German "*Rhapsodie*," from "*raptein*," meaning "to stitch together."[75] He criticizes Locke for deducing categories from experience but praises Hume, who recognized that they must be a priori.[76]

Kant's deductions in the *Critique of Pure Reason*, which are more elaborate than those in the *Critique of Practical Reason* and the *Critique of Judgment*, are appallingly obscure and very controversial. Descartes, a great mathematician as well as a great philosopher, uses "deduction" in a specifically mathematical sense. Though he is aiming to make a priori and apodictic claims, Kant oddly employs the term not in an empirical (*quid facti*) but rather in a juridical sense to point to what is lawful, in short to what one is entitled to.[77] There are two deductions, a metaphysical deduction which proves the number and type of the categories, and a transcendental deduction which demonstrates the application of the categories, or pure concepts of the understanding, as rules of synthesis serving to pull together the contents of the sensory manifold, in a word the sensory input, in order to construct objects of experience and knowledge. Kant, who was unsatisfied with his initial effort at a transcendental deduction in the first edition of his treatise, provides a revised, even more complicated version in the second edition. The differences between the deductions and the proper way to relate them need not detain us here. Suffice it to say that Kant's consistent aim in all cases lies in rigorously demonstrating that a object given in experience must be a unity, which is constructed by the operation of the understanding, which is itself unified, according to necessary and specifiable rules of synthesis, or categories. To put the point otherwise, Kant insists that we can only experience objects as unified[78] if this unity derives from the application of the categories to content which is given to us in unorganized form.[79]

Since I will be contending that in large part the later discussion consists in a series of responses to Kant's critical philosophy, it will be useful to state as simply as possible the position I am attributing to Kant. His writings swarm with technical difficulties which are grist for the interpretive mill of the specialist. Though the overall theory is less complex than it initially appears, it is not easy but rather unusually difficult to interpret. Kant, who is not always a precise writer, offers two very different theories of knowledge, one representationalist and one constructivist, which both influence the later debate strongly and continuously over more than two centuries. Though the technical details are forbidding, the basic outline, common to both theories, is surprisingly simple. The fundamental structure, which is shared by both, is the scenario of an interaction in which a cognitive subject, which stands outside experience, is affected on the sensory level by an unknown, or transcendental, object, which also stands outside experience. In processing the sensory input, the subject "constructs" objects it experiences and knows. The objects of experience, which are given to us as phenomena, can be understood in two ways. One is that they represent objects, in which case they are appearances of a reality located outside experience, what Kant calls things in themselves. The other is that they are mere phenomena, which can be and are known as they are. From the representationalist side, Kant claims to represent the way things really are in independence of us, in linking knowledge to independent reality. Yet from the constructivist side, he claims no more than to know the empirical world we experience in rejecting any and all cognitive claims to surpass experience. In different ways the later discussion of knowledge continues to dialogue with both aspects of Kant's critical philosophy.

Kant, Hegel, and the Historical Turn

Kant is not only a great thinker; he is also enormously influential, and his influence more than two centuries after his death shows no signs of decreasing. The later discussion, as already noted, can be understood as a series of reactions to Kant. It may be useful to mention here one feature of his position which has attracted particular attention, since I will return to it in the last chapter.

In his very original position Kant simply follows the well-known, traditional ahistorical approach to knowledge. There seem to be at least three reasons for Kant's adoption of an ahistorical conception of claims to know. One is certainly the weight of tradition. A historical conception of knowledge is specifically modern. With the signal exception of Vico, whom, as noted above, Kant seems not to have known, there were no strong figures in the debate prior to Kant who took a historical view of epistemology.

A second reason is the obvious incompatibility between Kant's claim to know with certainty and a conception of knowledge as a mere historical variable. Kant's representationalism provides a form of the familiar metaphysical realist claim to know the world as it really is, which appears to be incompatible with the very idea that the world, hence knowledge, changes over time. Though Kant was by no means ignorant of history, he believes that problems of knowledge can be and in fact are solved in a way that need never later be revised.

The third reason is Kant's commitment to an anti-psychologistic conception of epistemology. His transcendental analysis is clearly intended to discover the conditions of experience and knowledge of objects for all rational beings, including human beings, as distinguished from a description of how human beings in fact come to know. The former study belongs to the logic of knowledge, so to speak, whereas the latter, which Kant rejects as an adequate approach, belongs to psychology.

All of this changes in Kant's wake, in which a series of post-Kantian German idealists transform his position in an effort to carry it forward from where its author left it in the critical philosophy. Two centrally important changes in post-Kantian German idealism are the formulation of a drastically revised view of the subject as early as Fichte, and, as a direct result, a turn to history in both Fichte and Schelling, which is enormously deepened in Hegel, the most historical of all the German idealists.

The theme of the subject is in fact a series of complex, difficult, and interrelated questions. To understand Fichte's transformation of the Kantian view of the subject, we can look at the typical modern insistence on subjectivity as the necessary passage to objectivity. Descartes proposes a dual theory of the subject both as a mere passive epistemological spectator of all that is, who is outside the world but seeks to know it, and, on the contrary, as an actor, in the world. Kant develops a version of the former view. In rejecting the Kantian reduction of the subject of knowledge to its mere epistemological capacities, Fichte rethinks the subject as finite human being within the social context. The result is to revive a version of the underdeveloped Cartesian actor theory.

Fichte's revision of the Kantian subject is closely linked to a turn to history. Though Kant follows historical events, throughout his writings even in the texts left unpublished at his death he maintains a rigorous separation between history and philosophy, between fact and knowledge.[80] He consciously insists on knowledge, hence philosophy, as surpratemporal, hence as ahistorical. This conception of knowledge as ahistorical immediately breaks down in the reformulated view of the subject as a finite human being within context.

Kant is an anti-contextualist who holds that knowledge is independent of context; Fichte is a contextualist who insists that all cognitive claims finally depend on context. Since contexts change, there is no way to separate finally between context and history, between knowledge which is socially determined and knowledge which is historically conditioned.

Fichte never gives a coherent form to his view of history, which receives its first systematic treatment in German idealism in Schelling's *System of Transcendental Idealism* (1800). In this influential work, among other themes Schelling works out a theory of the relation of art and history. The historical turning quickly becomes central for Hegel, who is, even in his earliest writings, concerned "to think life,"[81] which is inseparable from history. In his mature writings, Hegel works out a theory of knowledge as intrinsically historical. He understands philosophy not as transcendent to but rather as fully integrated within its historical moment. For Hegel, philosophy is nothing other than its historical moment captured in thought.[82] His resolutely historical view of philosophy is tightly linked to a historical conception of knowledge that is taken up by such figures as Marx, Dilthey, Cassirer, and Croce before largely disappearing from the debate. We will return to this point below.

3

On Marxism in the Twentieth Century

In sketching the philosophical movements of the twentieth century, we will begin with Marxism, which, more than any other main philosophical tendency in the last century, needs to make a case for its importance, for its worth, other than on political grounds, as a philosophical approach which should still be taken seriously. Its perceived significance has greatly altered as a result of the political changes of the twentieth century. There was a time when it seemed to be central in the political arena and in the philosophical arena as well. During several decades after the Russian Revolution, Marxism enjoyed about the same status as an official philosophy in communist countries as Thomism has continued to enjoy within the Catholic Church since the late nineteenth century. After the Second World War, the Frankfurt School and Heidegger were widely regarded as of roughly equal importance in the German-language debate. Yet Marxism's fortunes changed rapidly as a result of the dramatic transformation of the political situation late in the last century. The rapid, unforeseen, and irreversible disintegration of the Soviet Union cast its main philosophical tendency into disrepute from which it has not recovered, nor is it likely ever to do so. It is, then, not surprising that T. I. Oizerman, the very capable main spokesman for Soviet Marxism over several decades as an approach able to meet any and all philosophical challenges, the author of many important books in this domain,[1] has recently adopted a softer, more conciliatory line in admitting that, perhaps, after all, the separation between Marxism and utopia is not complete.[2]

The problem of demonstrating that, despite its relation to politics, Marxism is philosophically important is not unique to this tendency. But at least for Marxism, it is posed in unusually focused fashion. One of the main philosophical fictions is that somehow philosophy could really be above the hurly-burly, hence independent of its surroundings. At least since Plato, philosophy has always pretended to be unaffected by the surrounding world, but indispensable for the good life. This founding myth of the Western philosophical community has never seemed more doubtful than at present. Few observers now think of philosophy either as a unique source of knowledge or even as very useful outside the academy. When we are called upon to act in the great struggles of our time, philosophers seem to have little relevant to say and often not to be very interested in historical events. It further seems doubtful that philosophers or indeed philosophy is independent of the historical context.

All segments of philosophy are inevitably responsive to social, political, economic, and other changes, such as war, revolution, and scientific discoveries. The emergence, rise, and fall of different theories, even their ability to attract scholarly attention, is probably never wholly independent of what else is happening. The reciprocal relation between philosophy and its surroundings is manifest in the attraction of philosophers toward the political realm as well as its influence on the philosophical debate. Socrates' conviction that the unexamined life is not worth living suggests that the philosopher must leave the library or at least pay attention to the surrounding world. More more than two thousand years later it still motivates philosophers like the Nazi Heidegger, the Bolshevik Lukács, and the democratic liberal Dewey to participate in the life of the city. It is not an accident that immediately after the Vietnamese War, in an uncertain time, when the myth of an omnipotent but supremely good United States was called into doubt, Rorty's message that there is nothing philosophically important to say would garner attention. Yet Marxism, which differs from many, perhaps all, other major philosophical movements in insisting that philosophy is political, hence never simply neutral, is arguably that movement most affected by the sweeping changes of the twentieth century.

Marxism's philosophical fate has always been tied to the prevailing political forces. In Hegel's wake, it seemed to many that philosophy, which supposedly peaked and ended in his thought, changed nothing in leaving everything as it was. Hegel's left-wing students believed that the main contemporary task was to link philosophy to practice, or praxis – this is the proximate source, in the German idealist tradition, not of the problem of theory and praxis, but of the well-known Marxist concern with it[3] – in making theory actually serve human needs. Everyone knows Marx's famous "Eleventh Thesis on Feuerbach": "The philosophers have only *interpreted* the world, in various ways; the point is to *change* it."[4] Marx formulates this view with the specific political intent of surpassing mere interpretation through action. He seems to suppose, in drawing attention to this distinction, that interpretation can be brought to an end through action. Attention to the relation of theory to practice is a central theme for Marx and, building on his position, in Marxism.

Marxism includes a changing series of political and philosophical doctrines which are difficult, perhaps not fully possible, to separate. The interest of Marxism as a way in principle to transform philosophy into an effective social force attracted many followers in the last half of the nineteenth century. This continued in the twentieth century until it was called into question by the end of the cold war. Most of the twentieth century was taken up by a stern confrontation between the Soviet Union, the eastern bloc countries, as well as China, on one side, and Western countries led by the United States, on the other. This political confrontation was reflected through Marxism, which, as a direct consequence of the Bolshevik Revolution, came to power in Russia and then throughout Eastern Europe and China. During the 1960s, the tardy publication and intensive discussion of some of Marx's unpublished early writings, especially the *Economic and Philosophic Manuscripts*, also known as the *Paris Manuscripts of 1844*, sparked an important debate on Marxist humanism.[5] It seemed then that Marxism, or at least a certain form of Marxism, offered a viable alternative to other, more traditional types of philosophy. Yet the political demise of the Soviet Union produced a conceptual turn away from Marxism as if it had nothing to say, and as if it had only been a kind of political fantasy that no one ever should have accepted. Thus the same Leszek Kolakowski who earlier called attention to the epistemological promise of Marxism[6] later attempted, in his self-appointed role as Marxism's historian and gravedigger, to unmask it as nothing more than a giant mistake, a mere tragic error.[7]

If, as I believe, no single approach has a philosophical monopoly, then a reliable estimate of Marxism's importance, or at least of its philosophical importance, seems to lie somewhere between the two extremes. Marxism was never, as Lukács famously claimed, the single royal road leading to all the problems and solutions confronting capitalism[8] – according to Lukács all the problems of capitalism point to the structure of commodities, hence to Marx's theory of modern industrial society – and it is not, as Kolakowski later came to believe, a merely political movement devoid of philosophical interest. In taking a more moderate approach, this chapter will depict Marxism as a specific philosophic approach which has a legitimate claim to figure in the main quartet of leading tendencies of the period.

Marx, Marxism, and Feuerbach

I will be focusing here on Marxist philosophy, which is a subset of Marxism, which has always claimed to speak in Marx's name. Marx is not only one of the most important philosophers[9] but also a seminal intellectual whose precise field is as difficult to delimit as his immense influence, which stretches from philosophy through economics in passing by literary studies, anthropology, psychology, sociology to philosophy of science, psychoanalysis and countless other fields. Marxism is, or at least once was before its sudden collapse, a vast, sprawling conceptual continent, including at the very least all of the above.

Marxism is a diverse movement composed of intellectuals and others, including political figures, who claim conceptual allegiance to the thought of Karl Marx. During the period of Marxist political hegemony, the uncomfortably close relation between Marxist philosophy and politics made it possible for political figures like Lenin or even Stalin to pretend to be philosophers of the highest rank. It also sometimes exposed Marxist philosophers to political repercussions if they deviated from whatever shifting political line was at a given moment regarded as politically orthodox. Thus Lukács, who published *History and Class Consciousness* in 1923, was obliged, when Lenin's *Materialism and Empiriocriticism* (1908) became known in the West in the very next year, to perform public criticism of his own work.

Twentieth-century Marxism is a variation on a theme which originates in the second half of the nineteenth century. Marxism, which authorizes itself to speak for Marx – Lenin defines "Marxism" as "the system of the views and teachings of Karl Marx"[10] – was invented by Friedrich Engels, Marx's close friend, staunch political colleague, longtime financial supporter, and tendentious editor of his unpublished writings. There is a widespread, deep-seated tendency in Marxism to blur any differences between Marx and Marxism, which naturally creates the erroneous impression that they are one and the same. Yet, philosophically speaking, they are not only different but often utterly opposed. There is no alternative to distinguishing between Marx and Marxism in order to understand philosophical Marxism. A brief way to describe the difference is to say that though the political views of Marx and Engels coincide, their philosophical views, which interest us here, are very different, arguably obviously antithetical.[11] Marx belongs by inclination and training to the great German idealist tradition from which he can only be distinguished on political grounds. Engels today would be understood to belong to the positivist camp.

Marx, like Kierkegaard and Nietzsche, was one of the three most important figures in the reaction against Hegel after his passing. Like Kierkegaard and Nietzsche, Marx disdained the appellation "philosophy" for his own writings. He was trained as a philosopher – he held a Ph.D. awarded in 1841 for a dissertation "On the Difference in the Epicurean and Democritean Philosophy of Nature" – at a time when Hegel still largely dominated the debate. Marx was thoroughly steeped in Hegel. He claimed to have read all Hegel's writings as a teenager.[12] Though he criticizes Hegel, he continues to think within a Hegelian framework, against which he rebels but which he very usefully appropriates for his own purposes. As noted in chapter 1, after Hegel's passing, his school split into different fragments, including the Hegelian right, which defended a theological reading of his writings, and the Hegelian left, also called the Young Hegelians, who, from a vantage point opposed to religion, accepted the right-wing reading of Hegel as correct and rejected it.[13] Marx belonged to the Hegelian left. Hegelian logical categories are everywhere present in his masterpiece, the first volume of *Capital* (1867), the only one Marx was able to finish before he died in 1883.[14] Engels, who did not have formal philosophical training, was at best a gifted amateur, with a weak understanding of the key concepts of German idealism, a tradition he pretended to know and clearly rejected. Marx's main ideas are continuous with classical German philosophy, to which at least philosophically he clearly belongs. Engels, who is much closer to what is now called scientism, is concerned, as Popper later was,[15] with drawing a line between philosophy and science while aligning Marxism with the latter. He also has a gift for a simple, even a simplistic, statement of both the problem and its solution. Since Marx wrote the turgid prose of the German professor he never became, Engels continues to attract readers who desire an easy way into hard topics.

The Marxist tradition considers Marx to be a political economist and Engels to be a philosopher. In a speech at Marx's grave, Engels credited Marx with discovering the law of motion of modern society.[16] Engels, who only studied philosophy for a short time – in 1841 he attended some of Schelling's lectures at the same time as Kierkegaard – wrote a number of semi-popular philosophical texts. They include *Herr Eugen Dühring's Revolution in Science* (1878), often and not inaccurately known as *Anti-Dühring*,[17] a polemical work directed against a contemporary German professor; the unfinished *Philosophy of Nature*, in which Engels, like Hegel, but unlike Marx, extends dialectic to nature; *Ludwig Feuerbach and the Outcome of Classical German Philosophy*, a slim brochure in which he broke with German idealism; and a small contribution to *The German Ideology*, a work which contains the best exposition of the canonical Marxist view of ideology,

Ludwig Feuerbach, who was a contemporary left Hegelian figure, is important in the post-Hegelian transition. He was initially a follower and then later a strong critic of Hegel, whose philosophical and theological views influenced Marx. In his effort to come to grips with Hegel, Marx was attracted by such Feuerbachian writings as *Preliminary Theses for the Reform of Philosophy* (1842)[18] and *Foundations of the Philosophy of the Future* (1843),[19] which are explicitly empiricist-materialist in character. Today Feuerbach is known less for his interesting philosophical contributions than for his influential contribution to theology, especially *The Essence of Christianity*.[20] The right Hegelians view Hegel as a basically religious thinker. Yet in the *Phenomenology of Spirit* he develops an anthropological perspective to religion in suggesting the thesis, more familiar in Freud's view of religion as an illusion,[21] that religion is a human conception, created by human beings, in which we know only ourselves.[22] Though Feuerbach studied Hegel carefully, he failed to detect Hegel's deep critique of orthodox Christianity in favor of an anthropological approach to religion. As a theologian, Feuerbach builds on the work of D. F. Strauss. The latter, who began as a Hegelian, quickly turned to study of the records of Jesus' life. Strauss's famous two-volume work, *The Life of Jesus Critically Examined* (1835–6),[23] resulted in public criticism leading to the loss of his job at the University of Tübingen. Strauss argues the Gospels are not direct evidence of historical events, but rather the record of human efforts to understand something transcending our finite historical condition. They are not evidence of the divine but rather evidence of the history of what is sometimes called human expression not very different from myths, legends, epics, in short merely another form of literature. In his famous study of *The Essence of Christianity* (1841),[24] following the lead of Hegel and Strauss, Feuerbach employs transformational criticism – he exchanges subject and predicate – in contending that God does not create human beings, they create Him.

In an early article, "Contribution to the Critique of Hegel's Philosophy of Right: Introduction" (1843), Marx follows Hegel, Feuerbach, and others in claiming that human being is the "root" of God. Yet he goes even further in claiming that man is the root of man.[25] Marx here adopts an anthropological perspective that he will conserve throughout all his later writings. In the *Paris Manuscripts of 1844*, he credits Feuerbach with being the first thinker to show that philosophy is only a form of religion,[26] and he adopts Feuerbach's conception of the species-essence in his brilliant account of alienation.[27] This is not to say, however, that Marx is wholly uncritical, and in the "Theses on Feuerbach" he criticizes the form of materialism he attributes to Feuerbach as static and inadequate to grasp human practice.[28]

Marxism and Engels's *Feuerbach*

Marxism was largely shaped by Engels's very different, negative reaction to German idealism and his positive reaction to Feuerbach, understood as a critic of Hegel and, by extension, of German idealism. Feuerbach, who began as a Hegelian, was knowledgeable about Hegel's position. Engels was less knowledgeable but more critical. In simple terms, Engels follows but alters Feuerbach's own informed critique of Hegel in rejecting German idealism and philosophy while claiming to solve the very real problems of philosophy through Marxism.

The very slim volume on Feuerbach – it runs to only about fifty pages – was composed by Engels after Marx's death as a series of articles in *Die Zeit* (1886) and quickly republished in book form (1888). This text was influential in stating Engels's view of his friend's legacy in easy, bite-size form with a touching simplicity utterly devoid of philosophical nuance, but hugely influential on generations of Marxists unable or unwilling to read Marx's own often difficult but infinitely more rewarding texts. Marx famously said that religion is the opium of the masses. Engels, pretending to expound Marx's position, presents in fact a mere travesty which substitutes a series of banalities creating for the unwary the conceptual equivalent of a drug-induced stupor in place of genuine philosophical insight.

In the very short foreword, Engel cites Marx's Preface in *A Contribution to the Critique of Political Economy* (1859), where the latter talks about "our view," that is, "Marx's materialist conception of history," in opposition to "the ideological view of German philosophy." Despite their common desire to settle accounts with post-Hegelian philosophy, including "Hegel," they never were able to do so in the form of "a comprehensive, connected account."[29]

Engels's suggestion that Marx and he share a single non-ideological view of philosophy as ideology implies that there is in fact a shared view, that it is not ideological, and that there is in fact a break with Hegel and philosophy. Suffice it to say that Marx, who, despite what Engels says, never breaks either with Hegel or with philosophy, does not share Engels's philosophical position. Marxism is and always has been highly ideological, which says nothing about Marx's position. There is further no demonstrable break between Marx and Hegel. It is more accurate to say that Marx, like every major thinker, criticizes important predecessors in working out his own position, but that, despite claims to the contrary, his position remains within the framework of the debate leading from Kant through Hegel to Marx. It follows that Marx's position is not extra-philosophical, but, rather, belongs to German idealism.

Engels provides his account of German philosophy in the body of his book on Feuerbach. In referring to the famous, enigmatic statement in the *Philosophy of Right* – "All that is real is rational; and all that is rational is real"[30] – Engels begins by depicting Hegel, without argument, as an unabashed supporter of the contemporary political repression.[31] The main thrust of his effort consists in turning Hegel against Hegel. Though the Hegelian School has disintegrated, Hegel has still not been refuted. Hegel, who suggests that all stages of development are merely transitory, also suggests that in his system all contradictions have been resolved and history has come to an end.[32] "But if all contradictions are once for all disposed of, we shall have arrived at so-called absolute truth – world history will be at an end."[33] This is a claim Hegel never makes and is based on a misunderstanding of his position. Nonetheless, it has acquired a life of its own in the literature. It is later echoed in Kojève's Marxist reading of Hegel (who first located the end of history in Napoleon, and later in post-war Japan), and then it arises in more simplistic form in Fukuyama's conviction that Ronald Reagan defeated communism and brought history to an end.[34]

In correctly observing that Hegel's position has important political implications that have not so far been realized, Engels implies that in refuting Hegel it will be possible to turn the latter's system against him. In Hegel, Engels contends, philosophy itself terminates, for two reasons. Hegel sums up the prior development and shows us how to go beyond philosophical systems, which are merely transitory, to "real positive knowledge," Engels's term for scientific cognition.[35] The difference between Hegel and philosophy, on the one hand, and science, on the other, can be seen with respect to nature. For Hegel, nature is merely the other of the Idea. In contending, on the contrary, that for materialism only nature is real, Engels anticipates later Anglo-American physicalist and extentionalist efforts to restrict meaningful statements to those relating only to the spatio-temporal world. Feuerbach's revolutionary importance lies in the transition from idealism to materialism, which refutes philosophy in re-establishing nature as independent and simply destroying the (Hegelian) "system."[36] Engels's point is that if philosophy culminates in Hegel, and if Hegel is refuted by Feuerbach, then philosophy is over. Yet to sustain this argument, it would need to be shown that Feuerbach has successfully criticized Hegel.

Engels, who makes this assumption, argues, in terms of the distinction between idealism and materialism, that there is a watershed question opposing philosophy and science. All philosophy turns on the relation of "thinking and being."[37] It would obviously be considerably easier to come to grips with philosophy as a whole if the amazing profusion of different theories could be reduced to no more than a single theme with only two possible attitudes, yes and no, true and false, spirit or nature, materialism or idealism. In that case, it would suffice to ask someone a simple question ("which side are you on?") to close the debate. Engels, who is interested in cognition, is concerned with whether thought can know being. He sees philosophers as divided on the question of knowledge – for Hegel we know the world but for Hume and Kant, whom he lumps together as skeptics, we cannot know it. Engels takes the view that knowledge is the result of the proper attitude toward nature. In a very crude passage, which reveals his misunderstanding of Kant, he writes that "practice, namely experiment and industry," suffices to show us what is correct, which brings him close to pragmatism, and puts "an end to the Kantian ungraspable 'thing-in-itself'."[38] Conversely, there are definitive answers to scientific questions. For instance, in observing that Leverrier's calculation of the orbit of Pluto, later discovered by Galle, proves the Copernican system,[39] Engels echoes Kant's view of Newton.

Engels reads Feuerbach as reformulating Hegelian idealism in a materialist manner. In observing that the Hegelian idealistic system is an inverted materialism, he echoes Marx's famous observation that, to find the rational core of dialectic, it must be inverted.

> The mystification which dialectic suffers in Hegel's hands by no means prevents him from being the first to present the general form of its working in a comprehensive and conscious manner. With him it is standing on its head. It must be turned right side up again, if you would discover the rational kernel within the mystical shell.[40]

Engels attributes to Feuerbach a supposed transition from idealism to materialism in which philosophy is left behind while the resources of Hegel's system are effectively marshalled. But Feuerbach, who never wholly overcame his earlier commitment to idealism,[41] stopped short of an adequate materialism. Since he conflates natural processes and history, he is lacking a historical view of nature.[42]

As proof of his belief that Feuerbach never left idealism wholly behind, Engels criticizes the latter's stance on religion – he wants to perfect, but not to abolish, it – and ethics. Up to now he has argued that Feuerbach goes beyond Hegel. Now he maintains that, as concerns ethics, Feuerbach fails to attain Hegel's level. Feuerbach's new religion leads to a cult of abstract man that "must be replaced by the science of real men and of their historical development,"[43] which is only a stepping stone on the path to an adequate materialism. Though the only important philosopher among the left Hegelians, since he remained half-idealist and half-materialist, Feuerbach is unable to overcome Hegel. In suggesting that Marx alone was able to criticize and overcome Hegel by making the transition to the materialist standpoint,[44] Engels, faithful to his view of the watershed separating idealism and materialism, locates Marx, as a non-idealist, firmly in the materialist camp.

Marx overcomes Hegel by overcoming Hegel's view of dialectic, which is an "ideological perversion,"[45] in favor of concepts as "images of real things."[46] In putting forward the idea that knowledge mirrors an independent reality, Engels clearly parts company with Hegel, and with anything Marx ever says, in restating a reflection theory of knowledge familiar in forms of empiricism. This theory was later adopted and made canonical for Marxism. Engels suggests that knowledge must be knowledge of independent objects, or at least of processes concerning them. Dialectic, for Engels, is "the science of the general laws of motion, both of the external world and of human thought," and "the dialectic of concepts becomes the conscious reflex of the dialectical movement of the real world," resulting from the fact the "the dialectic of Hegel was placed upon its head; or rather, turned off its head, on which it was standing, and placed upon its feet."[47] The result is to free Hegel's method from its idealist moorings in transforming it into an instrument of revolution based on an interpretation of Marx's suggestion that his own position inverts Hegel's. Engels ends with a sketch of the Marxist conception of history which, he claims, puts an end "to philosophy in the realm of history"[48] in revealing the general laws governing historical processes, which in the last instance reflect economic interests.[49]

Lukács, Korsch, Kojève, and Hegelian Marxism

Marxism in the twentieth century includes political revolutionaries, academic figures, and those, like Lukács, who at different times and places play both roles. Among political figures with often interesting philosophical views, the most important are V. I. Lenin and Rosa Luxemburg. Beginning with G. V. Plekhanov, Lenin's teacher, there have been numerous Marxist thinkers. A short list might include Karl Korsch, Georg Lukács, Ernst Bloch, Lucien Goldmann, Leszek Kolakowski (who, as noted above, later turned violently against Marxism), Antonio Gramsci, Alexandre Kojève, Max Horkheimer, Theodor Adorno, Herbert Marcuse, for a time Jürgen Habermas, Karel Kosik, and the later Jean-Paul Sartre. Twentieth-century Marxism tends to contradict Engels's version of the Young Hegelian view that philosophy has come an end in Hegel in building on the very fertile philosophical consequences of the Marxist conflation of Marx and Marxism.

Certainly, Marx and Marxism take different stances on Hegel. Marx criticizes, but also appropriates, transforms, and develops Hegelian themes. Engels rejects Hegel as incompatible with Marx's position. One of the most interesting developments of twentieth-century Marxism is the rise of Hegelian Marxism, which uncovers Marx's considerable Hegelian roots, hidden in the facile Marxist claim that Hegelianism, as ideological, must simply be cast aside. Hegel, and the Hegel–Marx relation, have been interpreted by a long list of important Marxists and non-Marxists,[50] of which the most important Western Marxists are Lukács, Korsch, and Kojève.[51] Twentieth-century Marxism reflects a struggle for Marx's legacy between Hegelian Marxists, who stress the continuing importance of the philosophical dimension, and anti-Hegelian Marxists, such as Louis Althusser, who argue for an anti-philosophical conception of Marx's mature position, hence Marxism, as simply beyond philosophy in any form.[52]

Hegelian Marxism began in 1923 with the independent, nearly simultaneous publication of books by Lukács and Korsch. Karl Korsch was a German who studied law and philosophy. He took a doctorate in law in Jena in 1910, and, after studies in London and membership in the Fabian Society, became a member of the German Communist Party, from which he was expelled in 1926. Korsch, who remains closest among the Hegelian Marxists to Engels, contends in *Marxism and Philosophy* that Marxism aims to abolish bourgeois social reality, and, in the process, its ideal component, philosophy.[53] Noticing the term "critique" in the title of many of Marx's works, Korsch understands Marxism as carrying out trenchant criticism of the economic bases of capitalism. This approach takes seriously the idea that the basis of modern industrial society is economic. It understands concrete materialistic dialectic as an integral part of revolutionary practice.[54] In Korsch's version, Marxism takes the form of a specific form of critique aimed at tearing down the walls of bourgeois society as the precondition to building socialism.

Korsch is a gifted but otherwise typical Marxist intellectual. Lukács and Kojève are more gifted but very atypical Marxist intellectuals. Lukács, a Hungarian who wrote in German, was trained in Germany, where he had ties to Max Weber's circle in Heidelberg. A polymath, he wrote an impressive number of works in philosophy, aesthetics, literature, and literary theory. His initial attraction to Kantianism resulted in two books on aesthetics before he became interested in Marxism. After his conversion to Marxism in 1918, he turned his fertile pen to Marxist themes. His famous collection of essays, *History and Class Consciousness*, mentioned above, which appeared in 1923, identified him as the most important Marxist philosopher of the Stalinist period.

Like all of Lukács's Marxist writings, this work is a mixture of political orthodoxy and philosophical non-orthodoxy. This book centers on a famous essay, "Reification and Consciousness of the Proletariat." In a previously mentioned early text, "Contribution to the Critique of Hegel's Philosophy of Right: Introduction" (1843), Marx suggests that the importance of philosophy lies in creating class consciousness leading to revolutionary action. Lukács now develops this idea in applying Marxism to the solution of the main philosophical problems. He emphasizes Marx's use of the category of totality, inherited from Hegel, and reification, Lukács's term for alienation. At a time when Marx's *Paris Manuscripts* had not yet been published, Lukács brilliantly infers this latter concept from Marx's later writings. The brilliance of his inference is not diminished by his unfortunate conflation, which he later conceded,[55] under the heading of reification, of objectification, as when one "concretizes" oneself in what one does, a concept already clear in Hegel,[56] and alienation, or the various kinds of separation of self from self that Marx famously analyzes in the *Paris Manuscripts*.[57]

Lukács's main argument concerns his very ingenious effort to justify the Marxist view of Marx as solving the problems of philosophy. Lukács's Kantian reading of German idealism turns on the claim that philosophy is inadequate to solve its problems, which are solved on an extra-philosophical plane by Marxism. In Lukács's narrative, all of German idealism turns on the unsolved problem of the thing in itself. In passing, he rejects the reflection theory of knowledge introduced into Marxism by Engels and exposes the latter's misunderstanding of Kant's thing in itself.[58] The limit of German philosophy lies, according to Lukács, in Hegel's mythological theory of history.[59] This problem, which is insoluble on a philosophical basis, is solved through Marx's discovery of the proletariat "as the identical subject-object of the social and historical processes of evolution."[60] In leaving the terrain of bourgeois thought behind, on which the greatest bourgeois thinkers struggled in vain, the problems of capitalism are solved by proletarian thought.

Lukács went on to write numerous other important works, which, while often important, never quite reached the level of his early breakthrough to Marxism. Notable is a work on *The Young Hegel*[61] in which he unmasked the Marxist claim that Hegel did not understand economics by highlighting the important role of political economy in Hegel's early thought. His late, unfinished *Ontology of Social Being* is an important effort to create a Marxist social ontology. He also made major Marxist contributions to literary theory[62] and aesthetics.[63]

Lukács was ambivalent about the choice between the academy and political action. In his long career, he was not only active in the Rákosi government in 1919, but also over decades a leading academic presence. Later Marxists progressively abandon revolutionary action and even a revolutionary attitude in adopting more ordinary academic or other pursuits. In Kojève, for instance, Hegelian Marxism entirely loses its revolutionary ardor in becoming a respectable philosophical approach. Though he presented a Marxist (and Heideggerian) interpretation of Hegel, Kojève was not interested in revolutionary activity. He later became a civil servant of the French government – he died in 1968 during the French student revolution while participating in a meeting of the Common Market in Brussels. He was also uninterested in demonstrating the correctness of various Marxist dogmas about Hegel. This is perhaps the reason why Kolakowski, who ranges widely over Marxism in all its forms, has no more than a sentence about Kojève in his important three-volume history of the Marxist movement.[64]

Alexandre Kojève (pseud. for Alexandr Kojevnikov) was a naturalized Frenchman who left Russia after the Russian Revolution. On the way, he spent some eight years in Heidelberg, where he studied with Jaspers and acquired a doctorate in philosophy before coming to France. The story is well known how when in 1932 Alexandre Koyré, another Russian emigrant to France, was obliged to give up teaching his course on Hegel, Kojève, with only a summer to prepare, stepped into the breach with an unprecedented course on Hegel's *Phenomenology of Spirit*, which had not yet been translated into French. The impact of those extemporaneous lectures on the select group of gifted students, many of whom went on to become leading French intellectuals, was simply enormous. It raised Hegel's profile in France to the point where it has been seriously argued that he is the master thinker around whom everything in philosophy has turned since that time.[65]

Kojève's famous course lasted until 1938, when, just as the Second World War was about to break out, it ended with the claim, mentioned above, that with Napoleon history had come to an end. The manuscript was later edited and published by the French poet Raymond Queneau. Kojève's approach is by turns arbitrary, but often brilliant. An example of his arbitrariness is the unsupported, simply mistaken claim that Hegel, Husserl, and even Heidegger employ the same phenomenological method.[66] This claim, which is later repeated by Jean Hyppolite, a famous French Hegel scholar, and Jacques Derrida, could not be correct since Hegel has no method in, say, Husserl's sense. In his interpretation, Kojève, who is strongly influenced by Feuerbach, stresses philosophical anthropology to the point of reading Hegel's entire treatise through the lens of the master–slave relation.[67] His analysis contains a number of anachronistic elements, such as the interpretation of Hegel's concept of death in terms of Heidegger's view.

Horkheimer, Critical Theory, and the Frankfurt School

Engels's canonical Marxist view that after Hegel philosophy has no specifically philosophical role to play is contradicted in Hegelian Marxism. It is further contradicted in the Frankfurt School view of social theory. The main thinkers grouped under this framework developed a critical social theory influenced by Marx and selected Marxists. They were independent of political parties and never doctrinaire or mere followers of any thinker, trend, or doctrine.

Much could be said about the relation of the Frankfurt School to the period in which it flourished. This School emerged between two World Wars, in the aftermath of the Great War, after the collapse of the working-class movement, the transformation of the hopes of the Russian Revolution into Stalinism and the emergence of Nazism in Germany.[68] The School, which was socially critical, coincides almost exactly, as Kolakowski notes, with the rise and fall of National Socialism,[69] which was also socially critical, though in a very different sense. Formally known as the Institute for Social Research (Institut für Sozialforschung), the Frankfurt School was founded within the University of Frankfurt in 1923. It functioned from that time (it was directed by Max Horkheimer, starting in 1930) until it was closed and its members emigrated – most of them were German Jews – in 1933. After the Second World War, Horkheimer and Adorno returned to Germany and resumed their teaching activities, but Marcuse remained in the US.

This School grouped together a remarkable collection of academic thinkers, critical of both Stalinism and Nazism, as well as the various institutional forms of Marxism, ranging widely from philosophy over various forms of social theory through the social sciences. Though the School was influenced by Lukács and Korsch, who were politically active, its members were mainly uninterested in Marxist revolutionary activity, institutionalized Marxism, or communist politics.

The influence of and critical relation to Marx and Marxism is a central but unclear theme in the Frankfurt School. Unlike Marx, Engels, or Lukács, as a whole the Frankfurt School turned away from the idea of the proletariat as the motor of revolutionary change. The result from a Marxist point of view, or even from a Marxian perspective, is an effort to define a particular kind of theory that, since it is deprived of social force, is incapable of transforming society. Philosophy was neither intended to guide the proletariat, as in Marx and Lukács, nor subservient to political criteria, as in Lenin's conception of partyness (*partiinost'*). The concern with alienation, which Lukács earlier addressed as reification, was met through the proper sort of theory. An acceptable theory cannot be pure in a Kantian sense, but must be social, and a social theory must be dialectical. The aim is not truth in a classical sense but rather the general advancement of social interests in a way common not only to Hegel, but also to Marx, and all the Marxists, and many others as well.

The work of the Frankfurt School can be divided into two generations. The initial generation included the philosophers Horkheimer, Theodor Adorno and Herbert Marcuse, the literary critic Walter Benjamin, the sociologist Raymond Aron, the political economist Karl Wittfogel, the psychoanalyst Erich Fromm, the economist Friedrich Pollock, and others. The most prominent member of the second generation is the social theorist Jürgen Habermas, who has since moved in a different direction.[70]

The most significant philosophers associated with the Frankfurt School are Horkheimer, Adorno, Marcuse, and, if he is a philosopher, Habermas.

One way, certainly not the only way, to describe the development of critical theory is in terms of the perceived relation to Kant and the philosophical tradition he represents. In simple terms, critical theory, which correctly sees itself as working out a flexible, non-doctrinaire approach influenced by Marx and Marxism, can be described as drawing out many of the implications of Hegel's critique of Kant. In reaction to Kant's concern with pure, non-situated reason, grounded in nothing more than itself, Hegel contends that reason is always situated, hence always "impure," never fully grounded, but always dependent on a shifting categorial framework, thus never independent of the historical moment.

The traditional Western philosophical view of philosophy, which comes to us from Plato, is that it is independent of its surroundings, but indispensable for the good life. Like Hegel, the Frankfurt School thinkers were concerned to work out a rival view of philosophy as never wholly independent of its surroundings, and not indispensable but, under certain conditions, socially useful. The philosophical agenda of the Frankfurt School can be described in terms of Horkheimer's seminal, programmatic article on "Traditional and Critical Theory" (1937).[71] This text proposes a key distinction presupposed in the writings of many of the members of the Frankfurt School between traditional theory, represented by Descartes, and critical theory, whose standard-bearer is Marx.

Horkheimer's essay identifies a canonical absolutized model of theory for which he offers an alternative. Traditional theory aims at a universal systematic science encompassing all possible objects in natural science, social science, and philosophy. Descartes gives philosophical voice to the ideal of a chain of deductions that in Husserl take the form of a single propositional system "as though it were grounded in the inner nature of knowledge as such or justified in some other ahistorical way."[72] In occulting the relation of theory to its context, traditional theory takes the form of a purely formal sequence without a conscious social function. The result is the false consciousness of the savant who illegitimately generalizes personal categories as universal.

This one-sided understanding of the knowing process reaches a peak in Kant. Horkheimer follows Lukács's view that for Kant reality is finally irrational. Kant presents a false view of the objects of experience as the inexplicable, purely intellectual result of so-called "supra-individual activity," hence not "as a product of a society's work."[73] Kant, who believes that the real source of the objects of experience is uncognizable, famously describes it in an appallingly obscure passage on the schematism in the *Critique of Pure Reason* as "an art concealed in the depths of the human soul."[74] Horkheimer, for whom this view merely reflects a failure to understand social reality, unfavorably contrasts Kant's concept of the schematism with Hegel's concept of the cunning of reason.[75]

Unlike traditional theory, critical theory turns on a concern with reasonable conditions for life. Critical theory takes society as its object. Its aim lies in relativizing the separation between individual and society in reconceiving the knowing process on a social basis. The subject is no longer the autonomous subject of bourgeois thought, but a definite individual or set of individuals in a definite context. The knowing process is redescribed as not only logical but also historical. The aim of knowledge is to produce social change. Theory is not disinterested, as Kant holds, but rather, as Hegel and Marx think, directed toward a new and better social world. "It is the task of the critical theoretician," Horkheimer writes, "to reduce the tension between his own insight and oppressed humanity in whose service he thinks."[76] Critical theory concerns the possibility of social change in order to bring about a rational organization of society,[77] whose future literally depends on adopting a "critical attitude."[78]

On Marcuse and Adorno

In casting critical theory as indispensable for human beings, Horkheimer contrasts it with traditional theory, which, hewing to an absolutistic model, can no longer claim more than accidental social relevance. Marx's point that theory must not be self-encapsulated but change the world in which we live reappears in the basic distinction of critical theory. In different ways, all of the thinkers associated with the Frankfurt School follow some version of Horkheimer's distinction between traditional theory, which is rigorous but socially useless, and critical theory, which is in principle socially useful.

In discussing the thinkers associated with the Frankfurt School, it is important to avoid imposing an artificial unity. Their writings had significantly different foci. Horkheimer wrote many articles but only a few books. His invitation to criticize contemporary rigorous, detached but socially uncritical conceptions of reason is particularly interesting. His suggestion that the mindless development of technology only strengthens social oppression, so that progress leads to barbarism,[79] was later developed by Marcuse.[80] It contrasts strongly with Heidegger's nearly contemporary argument that the failure of modern technology lies in being unfaithful to the Greek notion of *techne*.[81]

Adorno, who was Horkheimer's closest colleague, was trained equally in philosophy – he took a Ph.D. with a doctorate on Husserl – and music – he studied composition and piano with Alban Berg and Eduard Steuermann. His enormous knowledge of music is the basis of Thomas Mann's creation of the character Adrian Leverkuhn in his novel *Doctor Faustus* (1947).

Adorno's philosophical work reveals a kind of pessimism foreign to both Marx and the early Horkheimer, but which later became a prominent feature of Horkheimer's writing. In *Dialectic of Enlightenment* (1947), Horkheimer and Adorno analyze not the eighteenth-century Enlightenment, but enlightenment (with a small "e"), understood as "the most general sense of progressive thought . . . aimed at liberating from fear and establishing their sovereignty."[82] Following Max Weber, Lukács objects to the well-known mathematical approach which objectifies everything. In echoing Lukács, Horkheimer and Adorno claim, in objecting to system of any kind, that "enlightenment is as totalitarian as any system."[83] This anticipates André Glucksmann's facile suggestion that German idealism is tyranny.[84] Progressive thought, which seeks to liberate human beings, has turned into its opposite. Instead of seeking to enfranchise human beings, a totalitarian mathematical approach to the world can only grasp what recurs, which objectifies itself in mathematical form in enabling some to have power over others.[85]

Adorno's own contributions range unusually widely over cultural criticism, music theory, detailed criticism of contemporary German phenomenology, and sociological studies of the authoritarian personality.[86] His style, which is aphoristic in such texts as *Minima Moralia* (1951),[87] is forbiddingly intellectual, nearly or even totally impenetrable in *Negative Dialectics* (1966).[88] In the latter, Adorno develops what can be described as a mere negation of metaphysics and epistemology as obscure as anything in Heidegger, an onslaught similar, say, to Derrida's attack on Hegel and system in *Glas* (1974).[89] Adorno is less obscure and more perspicuous in his critique of contemporary German phenomenology. In his study of Husserl, which originated as a dissertation, he considers Husserlian phenomenology as epistemology. He raises two points which he later raises in different form against Heidegger: a theory of knowledge dealing with ultimate foundations (*Ursprungsphilosophie*), what was earlier called first philosophy, must settle for a kind of pseudo-givenness. Despite phenomenological claims, it cannot reach pure givenness, hence cannot legitimate itself. And the movement introduced by Husserl leads to a mere jargon of authenticity.[90] The difficulty of taking the abstract as the concrete recurs in Adorno's unsystematic but wide-ranging study of Heidegger, whom he regards as a philosopher of language centering on fundamental ontology.[91] Heidegger distinguishes between authentic speech (*Sprache*) and mere idle talk (*Gerede*).[92] For Adorno, Heidegger's position is formulated in supposedly concrete, technical language which, since it has lost any direct relation to what it describes, is no more than philosophical chatter, a form of idle talk merely pretending but failing to grasp the essence of what it describes. In abstracting from the exchange relationships which lie at the basis of social reality, Heidegger advances an abstract jargon which merely pretends, but is simply inadequate, to grasp concrete social life.[93]

Marcuse, the younger colleague of Horkheimer and Adorno, studied briefly with both Husserl and Heidegger, and wrote a *Habilitationsschrift*, or second dissertation, on Hegel directed by the latter.[94] His early articles illustrate a kind of Heideggerian Marxism later developed by Yugoslav thinkers like Gajo Petrović. Marcuse, who, as noted, stayed in the US when Horkheimer and Adorno returned to Germany, wrote in an agreeable way, leading to his acquiring a semi-pop star status as a popular philosopher in the American New Left at the time of the Vietnamese War. His work covers a vast range. It includes classical Marxism, which he discussed in detail in a book on Soviet Marxism;[95] self-emancipation through polymorphous sexuality in a book combining Freud and Marx called *Eros and Civilization* (1955);[96] but also popular culture[97] and aesthetics.[98]

Marcuse, who was closer to German phenomenology than were Horkheimer and Adorno, was also closer to the Hegel–Marx tradition, which he studied in detail. His work on the relation of Hegel's ontology and historicity is an early effort to apply Heideggerian insights to the German idealist tradition.[99] Its value is undiminished by Marcuse's later effort to distance himself from Heidegger. When Marx's *Paris Manuscripts* were finally published in 1932, Marcuse was one of the first scholars to recognize their importance in themselves and for understanding Marx. His *Reason and Revolution* (1941),[100] which appeared early in the Second World War, criticized positivism from a dialectical perspective and depicted Hegel's right- and left-wing students as arrayed on the field of battle against each other. In his work on Soviet Marxism, he provided an early, informed critique by someone steeped in the Hegel–Marx tradition. In *One Dimensional Man* (1964),[101] he proposed a general critique of technological civilization with many similar insights, but expressed in a more accessible way than in Horkheimer and Adorno's *Dialectic of Enlightenment*.

Excursus on Habermas and Marxism

The second-generation Frankfurt School thinkers include Alfred Schmidt, author of an interesting book on Marx's concept of nature;[102] Iring Fetscher, a historian of Marxism and author of an important work on the concept of the individual in Hegel;[103] and Jürgen Habermas, the leading contemporary German social theorist, who in the meantime has left the Frankfurt School behind.

Habermas, who has been unusually productive in philosophy and several related fields, is difficult to characterize. His interests lie both within and beyond philosophy, which he studied in addition to politics and sociology. His dissertation was on Schelling, and he later produced an important study of the public space.[104] He then wrote a series of books on an almost bewildering variety of topics, ranging from Marxism,[105] the theory of communication,[106] later developments in the Enlightenment concern with reason,[107] ethics,[108] legal theory,[109] and so on. At the present time, after Gadamer's passing (2002), he is widely recognized as the most important living German thinker, though it is unclear whether he is best described as a philosopher. In keeping with the theme of this chapter, our comments on Habermas will be limited to his relation to the Frankfurt School and to Marxism writ large.

Habermas, who was for a time Adorno's assistant, later left any form of neo-Marxism behind while returning to orthodox philosophy, particularly neo-Kantianism, but still in the guise of social theory. In Habermas, Horkheimer's distinction between traditional theory and critical theory disappears. Even in his early writings, when Habermas was closest to the first-generation thinkers of the Frankfurt School, his aim was never to formulate a conception of theory intended to realize itself in practice; he was concerned with theory itself, often theory as a conception of practice. At the time he was close to Kant's idea of philosophy as incorporating the self-realizing ends of human reason.[110] For Habermas, as for Kant, the problem is not, as it is for Marx and Marxism, how to formulate a theory that will change the world, since theory is itself self-realizing; it is rather, as for German idealism, but in a different way, to work out an adequate conception of human reason that will finally make good on the intention animating Kant's critical philosophy.

In the present context, it will not be possible to follow Habermas's often very interesting writings after he left the Frankfurt School and hence Marxism. It will be sufficient to discuss his early writings as they bear on this theme. Marxism often uses the terms "historical materialism" and "dialectical materialism." Engels applies the former term to designate the discovery he attributes to Marx of the law of history.[111] "Dialectical materialism," which does not occur in Marx, was probably first used by Plekhanov in 1891 after Marx's death to designate the philosophy of Marxism. Under the general heading of historical materialism, many of Habermas's early writings were concerned with various facets of Marx and Marxism. Unlike Marcuse, Habermas is not concerned with realizing a social utopia. Unlike Horkheimer and Adorno, he is also not interested in preserving a distinction between critical theory and traditional theory. The thrust of Habermas's account of historical materialism lies in rejecting the notion of a non-traditional theory that is both socially responsive, hence emancipatory, and defensible as theory according to prevailing intellectual norms. In making a qualified return to what Horkheimer calls traditional theory, Habermas leaves any form of Marxism behind. In its place, he confides the responsibility for social change to theory as it has developed in the Western tradition without attempting to sketch out an alternative to that tradition.

Habermas's effort can be reconstructed in four stages, beginning with interpretation of Marx and Marxism, which, following Marxist practice, he did not distinguish. This was followed by critique and then by reconstruction, culminating in a post-Marxist phase when, having concluded that this line of argument could not be saved, he retreated to what is best characterized as a neo-Kantianism of his own devising. Though Marx and Marxism themes were present in his writings for a time, they later faded as Habermas worked out his views on such themes as communicative action, discourse ethics, and the law. More recently, he has moved closer to analytic philosophy through studies of epistemological justification, realism, and philosophy of mind, all central themes in analytic philosophy.[112]

Even when he was interested in the traditional themes of the Frankfurt School, Habermas was also concerned with many other things. He began to publish in 1953 with two articles calling attention to the relation between Heidegger and Nazism. There is no single synthetic statement of his views of Marx and Marxism, which emerged in piecemeal fashion. Habermas follows Marxism in insisting on the continuity of Marx and Marxism. His reading of historical materialism, which began in a lengthy survey article (*Literaturbericht*), originally published in 1957, continued in a series of articles and books until he lost interest in the topic in the late 1970s. In his output over the last thirty years we can differentiate texts directly or indirectly devoted to the interpretation of Marx and Marxism from those in which they are at most of peripheral interest. As concerns this theme, the main texts, many of which are available in English, include: the articles "Report on the Philosophical Discussion on Marx and Marxism" (1957), "Between Philosophy and Science: Marxism as Critique," the so-called inaugural lecture "Knowledge and Human Interests," as well as the book bearing the same title (both 1971), an article entitled "Towards a Reconstruction of Historical Materialism" (1979), and the massive treatise called *Theory of Communicative Action* (1984, 1987).[113]

The early report on Marx and Marxism interprets historical materialism as a philosophy in terms of the canonical Marxist distinction between idealism and materialism. Even at this early stage, Habermas displays a good grasp of Marx's position, especially the early writings, and a wide acquaintance with various parts of the immense secondary literature. Habermas insists on the concept of the subject, or philosophical anthropology, which is strongly present in the early Marxian writings, particularly the *Paris Manuscripts.* He further insists that Marx proposes a theory of history with revolutionary intent, which Habermas, at the time influenced by Heideggerian phenomenology, discusses under the heading of "Typical Answers to the Question Concerning the Meaning of History and the Answer of Historical Materialism" (1957).[114]

In the initial, or interpretive, phase of his discussion, Habermas is focused on historical materialism, as distinguished from traditional philosophy, and philosophical interpreters of Marx. He is not, however, critical of historical materialism as such. He immediately widens his critical attitude to englobe the views of Marx and Marxism as well in the next, or critical, stage of the discussion. Here he elaborates an epistemological critique of Marx that he extends in subsequent writings, and which becomes the basis of his theory of communicative action. The critical phase of the discussion begins in an attempt to locate historical materialism between science and philosophy. Here Habermas, tacitly following Korsch, maintains that, as critique, historical materialism is a falsifiable theory of history with practical intent. He also raises the initial form of his epistemological criticism of the theory.[115] Second, in the so-called "inaugural lecture" he examines the relation of knowledge and interest through study of the opposition of traditional and critical theory, exemplified in the views of Husserl and Horkheimer. Habermas's point is that the traditional assumption of the relevance of reason cannot be sustained, although it can be sustained from the perspective of critical theory. Here he also introduces his important triple distinction in order to correlate forms of knowledge and forms of interest.[116] In the third stage, in an essay on Hegel, he maintains that Hegel in fact separates work and interaction, or communication, which Marx conflates.[117] The final stage occurs in *Knowledge and Human Interests*, which may eventually be perceived as his most important contribution. Here he restates his epistemological critique. He situates Hegel and Marx in the alleged turn away from epistemology leading to the rise of positivism due to the decline of reflection; and he locates appropriate analyses of knowledge and interest in the views of Fichte and Freud.[118]

In simplest terms, there are two main changes in Habermas's reading of historical materialism at this point. On the one hand, he further develops his earlier analysis of the theory in several ways. These include a shift in the focus of attention to the period of the *German Ideology*, which only accentuates the supposed separation of idealism and materialism, and an increasing, but paradoxical, emphasis on the theory as empirically falsifiable. On the other hand, he introduces an epistemological criticism of the theory which he continually modifies and restates in later writings. According to Habermas, who tacitly accepts a Kantian angle of vision, Marx fails to raise the question of the possibility of the conditions of his philosophy of history with practical intent. Historical materialism simply lacks a self-reflective dimension. In a later formulation of this point, Habermas suggests that Marx, who relies on a conception of goal-oriented work, or labor, as his basic concept, is unable to separate or otherwise to distinguish work and interaction. In other words, Marx's very approach obliges him to assimilate the reflective dimension to physical labor, that is, to reduce the entire cultural sphere to the underlying economic dimension.

Habermas's critique at this stage can be summarized as a two-step argument: Marx's position lacks a reflective dimension since it assimilates interaction, or communication, to work; and Marx's position cannot have a reflective dimension since the conceptual net is cast too narrowly and does not permit the necessary distinction in kind of work and interaction. In effect, this is a negative argument concerning the impossibility of a satisfactory epistemological analysis from the Marxian angle of vision. In terms more closely related to the critical philosophy, we can describe this as a transcendental analysis of the unavoidable epistemological deficit of historical materialism. The problem lies in how to correct this epistemological deficiency.

Habermas turns to this problem in the third, or reconstructive, phase of his reading of historical materialism. This brief, but important, moment comprises two parts: a metatheoretical reflection on the idea of theory reconstruction in general, and an effort to carry out this task with respect to historical materialism. The metatheoretical reflection, which covers no more than a single paragraph in the introduction to a volume of essays entitled *On the Reconstruction of Historical Materialism* (1976),[119] is intended to ground the possibility in question. Habermas differentiates among the concepts of renaissance, restoration, and reconstruction. He understands the latter term to mean that one takes a theory apart and puts it back together in order better to reach its intrinsic goal. He maintains this is the normal procedure to follow for a theory which requires revision, but whose potential is not exhausted.

This statement is more an indication of intent than a justification of the procedure employed. Nonetheless, it clearly underlies the effort to reconstruct historical materialism. Habermas undertakes to do so in the long paper, cited above, appropriately called "Towards a Reconstruction of Historical Materialism."[120] His view has slightly shifted now from the *German Ideology* to include as well the later, more economic writings, especially the famous Preface to the *Critique of Political Economy.* At this point he regards historical materialism as a theory of the evolution of society whose limitation lies in an over-investment in the economic perspective. Not surprisingly, since he objects to Marx's alleged reduction of communication to work, Habermas is primarily concerned to reconstruct what he will later describe as a trivial superstructure/base distinction.

We do not need to pursue the theme of theory reconstruction further, since in the fourth and final stage of his reading of historical materialism Habermas quickly abandons this effort. He has since maintained, in what is obviously a tacit criticism of his earlier effort to achieve a viable form of the theory, that historical materialism is itself flawed, but incapable of further development to overcome its deficiencies. This phase represents the outer reaches of his effort to come to grips with Marxism. It is mainly devoted to showing that historical materialism must now be abandoned in favor of his own position. The latter, which he expounds in the abovementioned treatise of more than 1,100 pages entitled *Theory of Communicative Action*,[121] is meant to succeed in the socially relevant task of human emancipation where Marx and Marxism have putatively failed.

At this point, Habermas regards historical materialism as an economic theory. His attack centers on the Marxian theory of surplus value. He offers three criticisms of the Marxian value theory, which are surprisingly formulated in quasi-phenomenological language. First, Marx, in virtue of his indebtedness to Hegel's *Logic*, fails to presuppose the separation of system and life-world. Second, Marx is lacking criteria required to differentiate the destruction of traditional forms of life from the objectification (*Verdinglichung*) of post-traditional forms of life. The third criticism lies in Marx's alleged overgeneralization of a special case of the subsumption of the life-world under so-called "system imperatives."

In his claim that the latter criticism is decisive, Habermas implicitly concedes that his objections are of unequal value. Only the first among them even directly concerns the theory of surplus value. Now this Marxian view is obviously controversial. At this late date it is perhaps not plausible to envisage a calculation of exchange-value as a function of work-time. But it does not follow that the value theory is less useful as an indication of the effect of the normal working of a market economy on the individual worker. The more general problem is why Habermas thinks that the fate of historical materialism turns on the validity of the labor theory of value. He implicitly holds that a position which he has earlier regarded from different perspectives, and in terms of which he reads different parts of the Marxian corpus, is in fact mainly or even exclusively a theory of political economy; but he needs to show that this is the case for it even to be possible to refute historical materialism in this manner.

4

Pragmatism as Epistemology

Pragmatism was founded in the 1870s, around the same time as Marxism, but became important as a philosophical tendency in the twentieth century. Also like Marxism, pragmatism's place in the debate changed rapidly during the last century. After a period of great promise – mainly through the efforts of William James, a popular thinker in every sense of the word, it dominated the American debate during the first quarter of the century – it later fell into eclipse. But unlike Marxism, which has continued to decline, pragmatism is currently in the ascendant. Largely through Richard Rorty's intervention, and the widespread conviction that analytic Anglo-American philosophy was increasingly losing its way, the last two decades of the century witnessed a strong return of pragmatism. As the century came to a close, it seemed the most popular of the four major twentieth-century philosophical currents. Wih the exception of continental thinkers, virtually everyone claimed to be a pragmatist, but it was increasingly unclear what, if anything, self-professed pragmatists shared in common.

Kant's position encompasses a great many themes, but above all epistemology. His main influence was felt in his time and in the later debate in a series of reactions to the central epistemological thread of the critical philosophy. A reading of the twentieth-century discussion in whole or in part that suppresses or even minimizes the continuing philosophical concern with knowledge in many forms and as many theories runs the risk of distorting our understanding of its relation to Kant's critical philosophy. While it would be a mistake to accept the idea, surely incorrect, that there is one and only one way to approach the theory of knowledge, a single royal road as it were, an approach which Kant claims to illustrate, it would be an equally important error to reject any further concern with knowledge, however formulated. The twentieth-century debate amply demonstrates that Kant's critical philosophy did not close the discussion but, rather, stimulated a very wide series of later approaches to knowledge, including pragmatism.

This point is worth emphasizing with respect to pragmatism, whose very interesting, rich contribution to theory of knowledge is often passed over in silence. The fault is due equally to its followers, who are not well versed in the problem of knowledge, to its critics, who are often not sufficiently knowledgeable about pragmatism to recognize its achievement, and again to the deeply rooted, but unfounded suspicion that claims to know are somehow not central to pragmatic concerns. Yet the genuine originality of pragmatism is obscured in merely identifying it with a series of prior movements, or in turning away from, or failing to perceive, its interesting contributions to the problem of knowledge.

We will be concerned with American pragmatism, which is often regarded as the most important specifically American contribution to philosophy. In turn, C. S. Peirce, its proximate source and central early figure, is often regarded as the most important and original American philosopher. As for the other main philosophical tendencies in this period, it is difficult, perhaps not possible, to provide a definition, much less a description, of pragmatism acceptable to all observers. This seems particularly difficult for pragmatism. Depending on how it is understood, pragmatism overlaps with aspects of the critical philosophy, with Marxism – the pragmatist John Dewey was interested in Marxism and Sidney Hook, who studied with Dewey, later turned from Marxism to pragmatism – with some main forms of continental philosophy, and even with most austere strains of Anglo-American analytic philosophy. Josiah Royce, a Harvard colleague of James, knew German idealism extremely well. Royce believed that the idealists were in fact whom people early in the twentieth century were calling pragmatists.[1] Royce, who perhaps mistakenly equates "idealism" and "pragmatism," uses the latter term in a broad, but still restricted sense. Others, who are not similarly restrained, go much further. According to Richard Rorty, who employs "pragmatism" is an unusually wide manner, not only Donald Davidson but even Nietzsche are pragmatists.[2] Robert Brandom, Rorty's former student, employs the same term even more loosely so as to exclude virtually no one. He applies it not only to W. V. O. Quine, but also to Michael Dummett, Ludwig Wittgenstein, and even Gottlob Frege.[3] Other observers attribute "pragmatism" even to main figures in continental philosophy. Mark Okrent's view that Heidegger's thought features transcendental pragmatism[4] has been furiously refuted by Hubert Dreyfus.[5]

Another major difficulty in describing pragmatism is its great diversity. A. O. Lovejoy, a qualified observer, famously distinguished no less than thirteen varieties.[6] "Pragmatism" is characterized in different ways and from different points of view, as a general position that, in its pure form, has probably never been held by any single thinker. It is approximated in numerous thinkers belonging more or less closely to the pragmatic fold, in terms of its proximate origins in Peirce and William James, and in other ways. Pragmatism is understood very differently by practicing pragmatists as well as critics and scholars of the doctrine. Peirce felt that James, a notoriously enthusiastic admirer, misinterpreted his main ideas, and this led him to attempt to free himself from his unwelcome embrace. Analytic thinkers have often been put off by the apparently subjectivist aspect of pragmatism. For Bertrand Russell, for whom the question of truth is paramount, Protagoras' idea that man is the measure leads to the view that some propositions are more useful than others, pointing toward pragmatism.[7] According to A. J. Ayer, who distantly follows Russell, pragmatism reaches back in the tradition to Protagoras' view that man is the measure.[8] These and other critics of pragmatism object to a supposedly subjective side to the pragmatic approach to truth. Nicholas Rescher, who sympathetically stresses the pragmatic contribution to cognition, refutes any description of pragmatism as freewheeling relativism.[9] John E. Smith, who takes pragmatism as coinciding more or less completely with American philosophy, emphasizes the themes of purpose, experience, community, and religion,[10] and again that "All thought is for the purpose of action."[11]

On the Origins of Pragmatism and the Theory of Practical Action

There is no doubt that pragmatism is older than the American pragmatist movement. The unfortunate tendency to divide the discussion into exclusive tendencies that coexist but supposedly do not interact works to conceal the continuity between pragmatism and the prior discussion. Anticipations of pragmatism, though not under that name, are scattered virtually throughout the entire Western tradition. It is important to distinguish the origins of American pragmatism, an important philosophical movement that arose on American soil within the context of the philosophical tradition in America, from the origins of pragmatism in general. Pragmatism is not necessarily American or situated in the US. In the absence of anything like agreement, much less unanimity, about "pragmatism," we can do no better than to look to Kant. The author of the critical philosophy, who distinguishes opinion, belief, and knowing, refers to pragmatic, or contingent, beliefs guiding someone, such as a doctor, who needs to act in a specific practical context.[12] Such a person relies on a claim that, since it is based on mere belief, is theoretically insufficient for a truth claim, hence not yet knowledge, but adequate for action.

In identifying pragmatic belief, Kant is assuming that the distinction can be made between an objective truth claim, the prerequisite for knowledge, and a mere belief. For Kant, belief is what one resorts to when there is no knowledge, as when a doctor is obliged to make a diagnosis, which is no more than a bet, or educated guess, based on the symptoms. Kant is not recommending that action in general be based on belief since he thinks that, as concerns practice, there is always knowledge, more precisely rules, that can serve as a universal and necessary guide to action in any and all cases.

The general distinction between knowledge and belief, on which Kant relies, goes all the way back in the tradition. The Academic skeptics recommended the probable (*to pithanon*) as the alternative to truth (*episteme*) in abandoning any effort to know in a strong sense in favor of coping through belief. Aristotle's canonical distinction between the theoretical and the practical domains points to the difference between supralunar exact and sublunar inexact sciences. Sublunar sciences like ethics, economics, and politics aim at approximate knowledge. The relation of pure theory and practical theory in Aristotle is unclear. If practical theory depends on pure theory, then Aristotle privileges theory over practice. If the practical sciences are autonomous, hence independent of the theoretical sciences, then already in Aristotle we encounter a recognizable form of practical theory as self-sufficient that is an important ancestor of what later came to be called pragmatism.

Aristotle restricts pure theory and practical theory to different domains. When this relation is revisited much later in German idealism, stress is placed on subordinating theory to practice in what, following Marx, has come to be called the relation of theory and practice (*Praxis*).[13] Marx, who famously insists on the need to change the world, is opposed to mere theory but also to action based on a false grasp of the social surroundings. His position presupposes a form of theory that cannot be disjoined from, hence is based upon, and correctly grasps practice as an alternative to other, more standard forms of theory.

In privileging practice, Marx is extending a concern running throughout German idealism. Kant's position on this question is complex and self-contradictory. He tries to absorb theory into practice, notably in the realm of the moral law that applies to everyone in all times and places without exception in a universal and necessary manner that simply overlooks local differences. Yet in the *Critique of Judgment*, he twice argues in the opposite way in suggesting the subordination of theory to practice.[14] Fichte, who is at least more consistent, maintains that theory arises only within and in order to solve the problems raised by life. His view of philosophy as dependent on human existence influences Marx and largely anticipates Dewey's later conception of philosophy as called forth by the stresses and strains of existence.

Peirce on Cartesian Foundationalism and Knowledge

Any account of pragmatism needs to begin with that long-neglected, distinctively American genius, C. S. Peirce. There would be no need to make such an obvious statement if Peirce's role in the pragmatic movement were as well known as his contribution to it. Yet for various reasons his role in the invention of what became American pragmatism is often depicted in a way that tends to hide and even distort the relation of the three main figures of pragmatism's golden age: Peirce, William James, and John Dewey. A not untypical example is the treatment accorded to these figures by Bertrand Russell. In *A History of Western Philosophy* (1945), he accords a chapter to James, another to Dewey, but no more than two references to Peirce, one each to his influence on James and on Dewey.[15]

Pragmatism as it is known today is mainly but not exclusively a home-grown American position that arose on American soil before increasingly gaining an audience in the far reaches of the globe. Since there is no agreement about "pragmatism," it is hardly surprising that there is also no agreement about when it began in the New World or even who counts as a pragmatist. While some observers start with Peirce and James, others see pragmatism as starting to emerge in Ralph Waldo Emerson[16] or even earlier. Still others include among the pragmatists such figures as Rudolf Carnap and Nelson Goodman.[17]

Whatever else it is – and there are many different views – pragmatism as we know it is a post-foundationalist approach to knowledge. Peirce is arguably not only the first but also the single most important pragmatic thinker, whose contributions continue to overshadow those of later philosophers attracted to the movement he created. A systematic thinker with unusual breadth, he wrote on a huge number of themes. They include formal logic – independently of Frege and with the help of his students Peirce worked out a logic of quantifiers and relations after

1880; epistemology; scientific method; semiotics; metaphysics; cosmology; mathematics; as well as ethics, aesthetics, history, phenomenology, and religion.

Yet, despite his undoubted achievements, for a variety of reasons Peirce was for many years a comparatively neglected figure. One reason is that he was never able to pull together his various insights in a single accessible exposition of his position. Another is that since he never had a permanent teaching position, he was unable to exert the usual kind of academic influence on other contemporaries and on a series of students. A third, once again leading to his relative eclipse, is the current tendency to concentrate on James, who, according to Peirce, misunderstood his position, as noted above, as well as on Dewey. Though clearly an important pragmatist, Dewey never knew much about Peirce. In part for that reason, Peirce criticizes Dewey,[18] who was himself more generous in commending Peirce.[19] Yet the simple truth is that, though certainly important, James and Dewey were less important than Peirce, to whose doctrines they were mainly reacting directly, or, in the case of Dewey – he knew Peirce even less well than did James – indirectly. Without Peirce there would not be anything approaching pragmatism as it has come to be known.

The original formulation of Peirce's distinctive approach to pragmatism arose in a very short period in a series of six articles that appeared in the late 1870s (1877–8) in the *Popular Science Monthly*[20] and, suitably developed, led to Peirce's new position. Here in less than a hundred pages of text Peirce founded an entire philosophical movement, which has continued to prosper and develop as one of the major philosophical tendencies of the twentieth century.

Peirce's enormous contribution to American pragmatism as it took shape in his and other positions is two-fold. On the one hand, he decisively refutes Cartesian foundationalism, the main and still the most influential modern approach to knowledge. On the other, he sketches the outlines of a non-Cartesian, post-foundationalist view of knowledge based squarely on practice.

The son of a prominent mathematician, Peirce studied chemistry, and worked as an astronomer and as a physicist while privately pursuing studies in philosophy and logic. He later taught for a while in various universities, but was unsuccessful in gaining tenure, before retreating into the difficult life of a private scholar. Peirce's failure to land a permanent academic job is no doubt reflected in the sprawling character of his vast philosophical production. His position, in fact a series of related positions, was worked out in an enormous series of articles – when published, they are expected to fill some 130 volumes – which turn on various problems of logic and science. Today he would be classified as a non-standard philosopher of science with strong historical interests. He was extremely knowledgeable in the history of philosophy. His review of a new edition of Berkeley's collected writings typically shows a deep grasp of the Irish philosopher.[21] His main philosophical background lay in Kant – he claimed to know the *Critique of Pure Reason* almost by heart – but the origins of his own distinctive position lie in his incisive critique of Descartes.

The sprawling nature of Peirce's work leads to controversy about where its center lies. Knowledgeable experts disagree. For C. J. Hookway, he is most important for his contribution to formal logic.[22] H. S. Thayer insists on the importance of Peirce's theory of signs and its use to clarify communication.[23] Murray Murphey distinguishes no less than four different systems that emerged as Peirce struggled over many years to solve a related set of problems in terms of successive conceptions of logic.[24]

In criticizing Descartes, Peirce examines and rejects an earlier form of the Kantian architectonic model of knowledge as a series of apodictic assertions about the possibility of experience and knowledge not later revisable in the light of further developments. Descartes and Kant share the commitment to a single univocal, but different, conception of method, in effect a pre-established, fixed, invariant royal road to science and knowledge of all kinds. In reaction to Descartes and Kant, Peirce, like Hegel, favors a version of the developmental model of science and knowledge. As he grew older, Peirce increasingly stressed his growing agreement with Hegel. Yet unlike Hegel, who emphasizes the historical character of knowledge, Peirce, who also stresses that knowing is a process, stops short of characterizing it in historical terms.

Peirce's critique of Descartes shows that the general foundationalist epistemological model – one or more propositions known to be true and from which the remainder of the theory can be rigorously deduced to make the transition from an idea in the mind to the mind-independent external world in acquiring apodictic knowledge – is simply a false description of how we go about the knowing process. For this reason, he rejects foundationalism as a proper approach to knowledge, apodicticity as the epistemological standard, as well as any effort to identify knowledge with metaphysical realism. In place of the familiar foundationalist model, he proposes a more flexible approach in which advances in science depend on advances in reasoning. Peirce, who did not acknowledge a specifiably final conception of science, believes that each step in the history of science exhibits the defects of the art of reasoning on which it is based.[25]

In his seminal series of articles, Peirce was concerned with inquiry, understood as the struggle to overcome doubt through belief.[26] He begins in contrasting the methods of authority, tenacity, and apriority with the scientific method, the only one able to produce belief by confronting it with reality as given in experience.[27] The first duty of logic, Peirce thinks, is to clarify our ideas.[28] In clarifying his notion of belief, Peirce suggests that belief leads to a habit, that is, a habit of action,[29] or a way of going about things. Extending this idea, Peirce writes in a singularly important passage, which is repeatedly cited and often seen as expressing a central insight of pragmatism: "Consider what effects, which might conceivably have practical bearings, we conceive the object of our conception to have. Then, our conception of these effects is the whole of our conception of the object."[30]

Peirce here provides a general conception of meaning in linking practical bearing, or effects in practice, to what we mean by an object. He immediately connects this view of an object understood in terms of its practical effects to the idea of reality. Reality can be understood in two ways: as what is independent of you or me – he says what you or I think about it[31] – and what, on the assumption that the correct application of scientific method will produce no more than a single result, will eventually be accepted by all concerned at the end of the inquiry – in a word, in the long run. According to Peirce, "the opinion which is fated to be ultimately agreed to by all who investigate is what we mean by truth, and the object represented in this opinion is the real."[32] Peirce, who rejects the more frequent appeal to a mind-independent real as the object of knowledge, here provides his own rival operational view of the real, understood as whatever will ultimately emerge from the process of inquiry.

The first two papers in the series – "The Fixation of Belief" and "How To Make Our Ideas Clear" – address basic questions of knowledge in the context of a redescription of epistemology using as the model scientific method. Like many observers, Peirce thinks of modern science as arising from the elaboration of a mathematical approach to nature. The last four papers in the series, which are less well known – "The Doctrine of Chances," "The Probability of Induction," "The Order of Nature," and "Deduction, Induction and Hypothesis" – consider mathematics as the appropriate tool for knowing nature before returning to scientific method. In "The Doctrine of Chances," Peirce shows that the assumption of continuity so important for science allows the development of a quantitative theory of probability, before continuing in "The Probability of Induction" to discuss the addition of probabilities.

The latter article ends with a very important extension of the quantitative approach to probability to Kant. In his remark, Peirce simply assimilates inductive and synthetic reasoning that is the source of all knowledge. According to Peirce – who here anticipates Quine's later attack on the analytic–synthetic distinction – Kant, who asks how synthetic a priori judgments are possible, should have asked the prior question about how any synthetic judgments at all are possible. Implicitly relying on the continuity of nature, Peirce contends that we can be certain about results since the same processes have in the past proved reliable. Though synthetic inferences are not deductive, in the long run induction is reliable.[33] Yet it is doubtful that a line of reasoning relying on the working assumption of the continuity of nature would satisfy either Hume, who denies there is any reason to hold that the future is like the past, or Kant, who counters him through an appeal to a priori arguments.

The account of "The Order of Nature" argues there is no reason to invoke religion in the domain of science, but that the Christian religion, whose basic principles are widely accepted, is not otherwise affected. Peirce is here separating religion from science as it unfolds in practice. Finally, in the last paper in the series, "Deduction, Induction and Hypothesis," Peirce distinguishes three main tools in the scientific arsenal (deduction, induction, and hypothesis) while seizing the occasion to bring together other distinctions. Though sometimes conflated, for Peirce induction and hypothesis differ in that the former relies on what we have directly observed and the latter on what we have not directly observed.[34] Induction, which is stronger than hypothesis, is, Peirce says, "the logical formula which expresses the physiological process of formation of a habit."[35] He goes on to maintain that the various natural sciences can be classified through the difference between induction, hypothesis, and theory that rests on laws of nature.

Peirce, who set out the main lines of his emerging theory of pragmatism in this series of seminal articles, continued to toil in obscurity until attention was called to his position by his friend James, who, he believed, also distorted it, as we have seen. With characteristic generosity, James, who took to calling himself a pragmatist, describes Peirce as the inventor of pragmatism.[36] Peirce was displeased by what his friend James and the English philosopher F. C. S. Schiller made of his ideas. Instead of accepting credit for himself, he surprisingly credited the invention of pragmatism to Berkeley.[37] Later Peirce tried to describe his position in a way that would distinguish it from what his uncomprehending disciples said about it in a series of seven lectures at Harvard in 1903 and again in a series of three articles on pragmatism in *The Monist* in 1905–6.

In the Harvard lectures, Peirce begins in characterizing pragmatism as a "certain maxim of Logic," by which he means it is concrete, hence not speculative. He then attempts, but without notable success, to bring out the force of his basic claim that, as he earlier famously said in his account of "How To Make Our Ideas Clear," in referring to "an object of conception," "our conception of those effects is the whole of our conception of the object."[38] In the first lecture, Peirce is critical of Hegel while affirming that his own theory is a variant form of Hegelianism,[39] but in the last lecture he identifies pragmatism with Kantianism (Kantism), curiously defined as also including Aristotle and Thomas Reid.[40]

In the first article in *The Monist*, Peirce repeats again his pragmatic maxim in pointing now to the link between rational action and rational purpose as central to pragmatism.[41] In Kantian terms – Peirce here affirms that he learned philosophy in reading Kant – he is favoring the pragmatic (*pragmatisch*), as concerns action, but not the practical (*praktisch*), which, for Kant, relates to practical reason, or morality. Though Kant links practical reason and moral action, Peirce here disjoins them in making practical reason the instrument of scientific inquiry. In a word, "pragmatism," for its inventor, signifies drawing attention to the future consequences of cognitive affirmations without any further claims about action. Notable here as well is Peirce's important contention, a conclusion from his pragmatic maxim, that claims about metaphysical realism – he uses the term "ontological" realism – that is, assertions about knowing the mind-independent world as it is in itself – are just so much rubbish. Peirce, who rejects Cartesian foundationalism, clearly intends to break with any view that knowledge depends on knowing the mind-independent world as it is. In response to the question of the meaning of his pragmatic maxim, Peirce writes: "It will serve to show that almost every proposition of ontological metaphysics is either meaningless gibberish . . . or else is downright absurd. . . ."[42] This statement definitively aligns Peirce's view of pragmatism with a view of the real as the final result of the scientific process of inquiry, in drawing the consequences of his initial idea that the real is independent of whatever anyone thinks about it.[43] Instead of claiming, or at least striving, to get closer to the mind-independent real, Peirce lowers his sights to aim at no more than agreement in practice among qualified observers.

James and Pragmatism after Peirce

In retrospect, it is hardly surprising that such confusion reigns in the literature about pragmatism. Though Peirce, in the course of rejecting the Cartesian idea of clarity, arrived at the pragmatic maxim that the meaning of anything lies in its future effects, he was unable ever satisfactorily to clarify his understanding of pragmatism. Even his celebrated pragmatic maxim was misunderstood by his followers, or at least they understood it differently from him, beginning with James. A further factor is his change of mind with respect to the real from a traditional approach centering on the proposed grasp of what is as it is, on knowledge of the mind-independent real, to a more modest, but infinitely more interesting effort to arrive at an agreement based solely on experience. With respect to the real, Peirce is only navigating between two different views, one he accepted earlier and later abandoned in favor of another view. By the time we get to James, the idea of the real has apparently dissolved in a series of hazy pronouncements about radical empiricism.

The three main thinkers in the golden age of American pragmatism are about as different as three thinkers can be and still share a tendency in common. James, unfailingly generous, is the brilliant jack of all trades endowed with a vivid imagination and even more vivid sense of language who was always in the process of producing yet another popular version of his view. Though Peirce, when he wanted to, could write splendidly well, James certainly wrote on the whole rather wonderfully. But unfortunately he seems never, except perhaps in his discussion of psychology, to exhibit real intellectual discipline in his writings. In truth, James was a public philosopher, who worked out his ideas in front of the public. Dewey, a very good philosopher but a deadly dull writer, is the public intellectual in a sense akin to the European intellectual in our time, always taking stands on the problems of the day from A to Z.

The relation of the main pragmatists within pragmatism is not well understood. Any number of accounts exist in which the three most prominent members of the golden age of American pragmatism are discussed one after another as if they were seamlessly linked. In fact, in the same way as important members of other important philosophical movements, they worked within a shifting body of theory in which their own views were never quite the same and just as often at odds. If the truth be told, though their views are related, there is no single common garment that clothes them all.

Peirce is the great central pillar on which pragmatism is constructed. Yet one must concede that not only did his position change as he dealt again and again with old questions and took up new ones, but from his own angle of vision no one claiming to be influenced by him ever understands his position in quite the same way as he did. The divergence between the views of pragmatism in the eyes of Peirce who invented it and others reacting to him began very early. James, who claimed to be the first one to notice Peirce's discovery of pragmatism,[44] was also, from Peirce's viewpoint, the very first one to get it wrong. The matter is important since James, by far the more popular thinker, now serves with (or without) Dewey as the main source for classical pragmatism, even pragmatism *tout court*. Though Peirce is the deeper thinker, for various reasons those writing on or interested in pragmatism are now far more likely to turn to James than to him.

James's distance from Peirce becomes apparent about as soon as he became interested in his friend's views. One reason is certainly James's unusually accessible philosophical style of composition in contrast to what, in reference to the style of the inventor of pragmatism, in a typically wonderful turn of phrase, he calls "flashes of brilliant light relieved against Cimmerian darkness!"[45] Toward the end of his life, James was regarded as perhaps the most important living American philosopher. It is, then, not by accident that a number of his books have been reprinted literally dozen of times while we are still waiting for anything approaching a complete edition of Peirce's writings in any form.

We perceive something of the nature of the difference between James's and Peirce's conceptions of pragmatism in James's reference to his friend's invention. In a passage cited above, Peirce awkwardly wrote: "Consider what effects, which might conceivably have practical bearings, we conceive the object of our conception to have. Then, our conception of these effects is the whole of our conception of the object."[46] In his article about "What Pragmatism Means" (1904), James characterizes pragmatism as a method and refers to the passage just cited as Peirce's principle and again as the principle of pragmatism.[47] These varied references to the same idea suffice to fix Peirce's claim to invent the doctrine, and to identify it with a view Peirce continually interprets and defends. In the article in which this passage appears, and in the passage itself, Peirce is concerned with gaining clarity about cognitive affirmations, above all in respect to the process of scientific inquiry. Like Peirce, James also had a strong scientific background. He studied chemistry, comparative anatomy, and physiology, later acquired a medical degree, and made unusually important contributions to the fledgling science of psychology. Though very well grounded in science, he was interested in pragmatism less as a clue to appropriate scientific method, which interested Peirce, than as a guide to action. This difference in emphasis becomes decisive in James's reading of Peirce, hence in his conception of pragmatism. James, in interpreting what he correctly identifies as a basic tenet in Peirce's view, gives it an altogether different twist in writing that for Peirce "our beliefs are really rules for action," and "that to develop a thought's meaning, we need only determine what conduct it is fitted to produce."[48] The difference is one between action and science. James, who here conflates habits with meanings, is mainly concerned with action, but Peirce is mainly concerned with meaning within the context of scientific inquiry.

James, who had many concerns, made important contributions, often simultaneously, not only in philosophy, but also, as just noted, in psychology – he was Professor of Psychology and Philosophy at Harvard – as well as in religion. His interest in religion came to him from his father, Henry James, a religious thinker interested in Swedenborg – to be distinguished from his brother Henry, the famous novelist. His work in philosophy naturally grew out of his study of psychology.

All of James's work has a strongly phenomenological cast. It is, then, not by accident that James later exerted an important influence on the phenomenologist Edmund Husserl. Yet unlike Husserl, James resisted the very idea of pure unadulterated description. Much of what he did had a lighter character, engaging, probing, unsystematic, always interesting, but rarely worked out in detail. In part because he was a convinced pluralist, there are many tensions, paradoxes, even outright contradictions in his writings.

James's contributions to psychology are singularly important. He is sometimes described as the most important American psychologist. His approach was neither Freudian nor behaviorist, nor cognitivist, views that only developed later. His *Principles of Psychology*, his first book, appeared in two volumes in 1890;[49] a less voluminous version appeared as *Psychology: The Briefer Course* two years later.[50] In psychology, his most important theme is the stream of consciousness. He rejects the synthetic approach, starting with simple ideas of sensation, which simply assumes that higher states of consciousness are composed of lower units. In a famous chapter on "The Stream of Consciousness,"[51] James provides a rich introspective description of consciousness as states of mind succeeding each other within the subject. James here develops the view that every thought or idea belongs to a constantly changing personal consciousness that never recurs in precisely the same way. Consciousness, he says, is akin to a river or a stream,[52] without sharp breaks, and the present is no more than a specious present, without duration,[53] never again to recur.

James's interest in religion is odd since, although plagued with doubt, he was not a believer in any ordinary sense, and perhaps not a believer at all. In *The Varieties of Religious Experience* (1902), he studies the phenomena of mysticism and religious experience with a view to an eventual empirical assessment of their validity. This work in turn led to interest in psychical research. As in his studies of psychology and philosophy, James's work on religion is highly descriptive, but empirical, concerned not to go beyond ordinary scientific principles and laws – the initial chapter is entitled "Religion and Neurology" – in classifying and explaining religious phenomena. In emphasizing individual, subjective phenomena, James is consistent with his introspective approach to psychology. In the chapter on "Philosophy" he examines whether anything about religion is objectively true.[54] A correct view of experience, including religious experience, contains both subjective and objective parts, neither of which can be omitted.[55] Ever the psychologist, James stresses an enlarged view of the self as the key to a general theory of religion.[56]

For James, philosophy often took the form of actively engaging with other views, many of which he rejected. Whereas Peirce, who originally despised Hegelianism, grew steadily closer to Hegel, James, who knew next to nothing about Hegelianism, was content to ridicule it. In "On Some Hegelisms" (1882), an article that is appropriately accompanied by apologies for its superficiality,[57] James begins by writing that "Hegel's philosophy mingles mountain-loads of corruption with its scanty merits. . . ."[58] He goes on to say that Hegel's system "resembles a mouse-trap, in which if you once pass the door you may be lost forever."[59]

Two themes on which James made substantial, if controversial, philosophical contributions are empiricism and truth. As an empiricist, James favors radical empiricism, or the view that the ultimate stuff of reality (or at least knowable reality) is pure experience.[60] Pure experience means either lived experience in which we focus on an object or do something, or a limit concept reminding us that we contribute to what we experience. Radical empiricism means that reflection must be limited to experience. It is radical since it favors a non-reductive pluralism, and empirical since claims about experience are mere empirical hypotheses later modifiable. But perhaps because he favors pluralism, James does not propose any single radical empiricist account of the physical world. Within the same collection of essays, he typically embraces no less than three disparate perspectives. They include a phenomenalist view for which the physical consists in possible experience, a "new realist" view for which it consists in sensory vistas, only some of them minds, and a panpsychist view that the physical consists in its own inner experience.

James, who was not skilled in technical argument, sometimes ventured opinions he was hard put or simply unable to defend. In discussing truth, after raising the question directly and indirectly in a number of contexts, he seems rather to circle around the problem than to advance a single central idea. In the essay "The Will To Believe" (1896), he argues there is no agreement about what is meant by "true," no single test acceptable to all parties, even, as he incautiously ventures, no objective evidence. According to James, ideas of the true include: perception, revelation, *consensus gentium*, the instincts of the heart, and the systematic experience of the race – hence no objective evidence.[61] In "What Pragmatism Means," he casts pragmatism as a theory of truth, where truth is a form of the good.[62] In "Pragmatism's Conception of Truth" (1907), he contrasts the pragmatic view to the familiar correspondence theory in incautiously proclaiming the identity between truth and usefulness.[63]

James's suggestion that truth is less than objective was attacked unmercifully, particularly by Russell, who made fun of what he called the transatlantic view of truth. Russell, who examines the view of truth developed in the book *The Will To Believe*, suggests that James desires to place his positive beliefs on a skeptical foundation, which consists in ignoring objective facts. Though James scorned idealism, Russell, who incorrectly links idealism with subjectivism, obscurely sees a hint of Berkeley lurking in James's background. He describes James's effort to identify the true and the useful – which goes all the way back in Greek philosophy to Plato's identification of the true, the good, and the beautiful – as "a form of the subjectivistic madness which is characteristic of most modern philosophy."[64]

Dewey, or the Pragmatist as Public Intellectual

It has already been noted that the classification of James as a pragmatist is not entirely obvious. He is sometimes also put in the camp of such process philosophers as Henri Bergson and Alfred North Whitehead. Dewey came from a background in St Louis Hegelianism. But no one has ever doubted that the mature Dewey, who is now widely considered, since Peirce is once again in eclipse, as the quintessential American pragmatist, perhaps as the most important American philosopher,[65] belongs to pragmatism.

Dewey, who was born in 1859, the year Darwin published *Origin of Species*, was twenty years younger than Peirce and seventeen years younger than James. He belongs just barely to the first generation of American pragmatists. Dewey briefly studied logic with Peirce as a graduate student at Johns Hopkins University, where he took a Ph.D. in philosophy in 1884. Before going to graduate school, while still a school teacher, three of his early essays were published by W. T. Harris in the *Journal of Speculative Philosophy*. As a graduate student, Dewey came under the influence of George S. Morris. Dewey then spent ten years at the University of Michigan, where he collaborated with G. H. Mead, followed by ten years at the University of Chicago, where he shifted from idealism to pragmatism under the influence of James's views on psychology. Though he studied with Peirce, and though he later reviewed the edition of Peirce's collected works that appeared in the 1930s,[66] Peirce, whose work, as noted, he did not know well, never exerted a strong influence on Dewey.[67] Other than differences of emphasis, the reason is that for a long time Peirce, who never succeeded in acquiring a stable academic address, was simply unknown. By the time his friend James succeeded in calling attention to Peirce's work, Dewey was already well launched on his own career. Dewey's entry into pragmatism, hence his early conception of it, was derived from James. But the influence of James on Dewey is mainly through James's work in psychology, much less so through his philosophy. Yet Dewey shares James's concern with the focus on practice instead of knowledge. Unlike Peirce, but like James, Dewey was more interested in action than in theory. He goes so far as to claim later on in an article on "The Development of American Pragmatism" (1925) that pragmatism can be reduced to the view that concepts are meaningful in respect to possible applications. "It is therefore not the origin of a concept, it is its application which becomes the criterion of its value; and here we have the whole of pragmatism in embryo."[68]

Dewey was not only an important philosopher but also, as mentioned earlier, a genuinely public intellectual, who participated in various ways in the affairs of his time. In this regard, he was something of a rarity in the US, where, unlike in Europe, philosophers and other cultural figures are seldom called on to comment on the events of the day. While in Chicago, Dewey founded an elementary school supervised by the Department of Philosophy and worked with Jane Addams at Hull House. He then moved to Columbia University. He taught there and at its Teachers

College from 1904 to 1930. During this period, he also collaborated with Teachers College in sponsoring progressive education, founded the American Association of University Professors, and was involved in founding the teachers' union movement in New York City. He also found time in 1937 to chair the commission of inquiry into the charges brought against Leon Trotsky in the Moscow show trials orchestrated by Stalin. When Russell was denied the right to teach at the City College of New York, Dewey defended him on grounds of academic freedom. And all the time he wrote voluminously on more technical philosophical issues as well as numerous small monographs on various social topics, such as liberalism,[69] and a huge number of articles on current affairs for journals like *The New Republic.*

Like Peirce, then, Dewey was extremely prolific. His voluminous writings – his enormous bibliography runs to more than 150 pages[70] – span an impressive list of themes, many of them theoretical, but at least as many of them practical, running from psychology[71] and education[72] to the reconstruction of philosophy,[73] experience,[74] individualism,[75] and aesthetics.[76] In one way or another, all of those who sail under the pragmatist label write about epistemology, but they do it in very different ways. It was stressed above that pragmatism taken as a whole offers a very fertile anti-Cartesian, post-foundationalist approach to epistemology.

Though Dewey wrote little directly about the classical conception of epistemology, it would be an error to say that he was not interested in theory of knowledge. His Gifford Lectures, which became *The Quest for Certainty*, are, distantly following Peirce, a thoroughgoing critique of the very idea of basing knowledge on the Cartesian criterion of certainty.[77]

Though Dewey was uninterested in traditional epistemological theory for the sake of theory, he was intensely interested in working out specific approaches to concrete problems. In this sense, pragmatism for Dewey is different than it was for Peirce and James. Peirce's focus on philosophy of science and related problems is transformed in James through his emphasis on radical empiricism and truth. These themes, which are still recognizably related to traditional epistemology, give way in Dewey to a revolt against the traditional conception of epistemology as wide-ranging, general, non-specific theory of knowledge. Though he still addresses epistemological themes, he does so rather differently than Peirce, or James, who are still concerned with finding a practical, instrumentally oriented approach to knowledge. Dewey, who turns away from such issues, at least as they are usually debated, is, rather, concerned with less general, more concrete themes, centering on what is sometimes described as a series of reflections on democracy in America. In an article from his middle period, he links the rise of American philosophy to the experience of democracy.

> American philosophy must be born out of and must respond to the demands of democracy, as democracy strives to voice and to achieve itself on a vaster scale, and in a more thorough and final way than history has previously witnessed. And democracy is something at once too subtle and too complex and too aspiring to be caught in the midst of a single philosophical school or sect. It is, then, to the needs of democracy in America that we turn to find the fundamental problems of philosophy; and to its tendencies, its working forces, that we look for the points of view and the terms in which philosophy will envisage these problems.[78]

Dewey's admonition that philosophy should concern itself with problems drawn from the American experience was certainly an important motivation in his position. Yet this suggests a local approach that does not do justice to the breadth of his thinking about traditional figures and problems that he transformed from his own perspective. Though not as deeply grounded in the history of philosophy as Peirce, he certainly addressed traditional figures more often than did James. Unlike James, who wanted to break with the German tradition, which he did not know well, throughout his career, even after his interests changed from idealism to Darwinism, Dewey retained the influence of his early grounding in German philosophy. This background is apparent in his critical comments on Kant, his general description of his own position as objective idealism, and his general stress on practice in distinction to theory.

Dewey's relation to Kant was important for his effort to define his relation to Hegel and then later, as he left idealism and Hegel behind, to Darwinism. In an early article on "Kant and Philosophic Method" (1884), Dewey refutes Kantian dualism in favor of Hegel's organic model.[79] A quarter of a century later in the process of turning from Hegel to Darwin as a basic model, in a study of "Intelligence and Morals" (1910), Dewey again defends Hegel against Kant in suggesting that Hegel's contribution consists in giving concrete historical content to Kant's empty concept of reason.[80] Yet Dewey, who never engages in close textual analysis, even in his early writings, later reduces his direct references to specific thinkers. It is, then, not surprising that in *Experience and Nature* (1927) there is only a single reference to Kant in passing.

Dewey's interest in, and contribution to, epistemology has been passed over for two reasons. On the one hand, it is sometimes but incorrectly thought that he was uninterested in the problem of knowledge. While it is correct that he was mainly concerned with particular problems of knowledge, he devoted a series of important works, including the *Quest for Certainty*, *Reconstruction in Philosophy*, and *Experience and Nature*, to describing and criticizing the mainline philosophical conception of knowledge as well as to working out his own version of the pragmatic alternative in the form of empirical naturalism (or naturalistic empiricism). His general attraction to the Darwinian biological model – he is the only major pragmatist to have this interest – should not distract attention from his interest in epistemological issues.

For Dewey, Darwinism is useful in helping us to abandon the idea of species as tending toward the realization of a fixed *telos*, or *eidos*, an idea that goes back in the tradition to Aristotle. The Darwinian insight that life depends on transition eliminates the idea of a designer, hence intelligent design, while suggesting the need for a new logic. "The influence of Darwin upon philosophy," Dewey writes, "resides in his having conquered the phenomena of life for the principle of transition, and thereby freed the new logic for application to mind and morals and life."[81]

Dewey, who was not a logician, here uses "logic" in a non-standard sense. By "logic" he does not mean methods of formal reasoning but rather the logic of inquiry. In this respect, it is clear that Dewey overlaps with Peirce. Peirce, of course, was a formidable logician, whose insights, had Dewey known them better, would have enabled him to sharpen his own account. There is a further a difference in the scope of their respective approaches to logic. The logic of scientific inquiry, Peirce's field of predilection, is only a subset within Dewey's much wider concern with inquiry in general.

Dewey studies what he calls the pattern of inquiry in *Logic: The Theory of Inquiry* (1938). Inquiry is a process in which what initially appears unformed and inchoate is transformed into a determinate situation. "Inquiry," he writes, "is the directed or controlled transformation of an indeterminate situation into a determinately unified one."[82] This may include introducing hypotheses that are tested in determining claims that provide what Dewey, in a rare arresting turn of phrase, calls warranted assertibility. He has in mind conclusions roughly defensible in terms of a particular pattern of inquiry, as ascertained through testing different possible solutions, as distinguished from traditional claims for certain knowledge.

Dewey's view of logic as experimental inquiry turns him against the traditional philosophical approach to knowledge and in the direction of philosophical reconstruction. His most extended discussion of the traditional philosophical approach to knowledge occurs in *The Quest for*

Certainty (1929). Typically for Dewey, his approach lies in confronting the question of knowledge not in isolation, but rather in relation to its social function. Dewey's thesis is that insecurity generates the quest for certainty in both philosophy and religion. "The quest for certainty is a quest for a peace which is assured. . . ."[83] The interest in certainty leads to an emphasis on stability, in which science in the true sense meant grasping the real that, as Dewey says, traditionally "glorified the invariant at the expense of change."[84] The success in providing certainty was earlier guaranteed by religion through a synthesis between belief and authority that came undone through the rise of modern science. This synthesis can be restored not by holding to religion or returning to ancient philosophical views, but only by abandoning certainty and adopting an experimental or operational view in practice.

Already in the discussion of Darwin, Dewey calls for philosophy to turn away from eternal concerns in dealing with pressing temporal issues. He urges that "philosophy must in time become a method of locating and interpreting the more serious of the conflicts that occur in life, and a method of projecting ways for dealing with them."[85] Taking his cue from experimental science, he proposes an experimental view of philosophy that yields no more than experimental results. Dewey develops his new vision of the discipline in *Reconstruction in Philosophy* (1920, 1948), his most popular work. Here he argues in a way reminiscent of such thinkers as Aristotle in some of his moods, as well as Fichte and Marx, that the "problems and subject matter of philosophy grow out of stresses and strains in the community life in which a given form of philosophy arises."[86] In this passage, Dewey is positioning himself against the search for a final, unalterable philosophy as it comes into the modern debate through Descartes and Kant. According to Dewey, there is not and cannot be a single philosophy true in all times and places since philosophy is merely a secondary enterprise arising within and limited to different situations in different historical moments. As in his study of certainty, so here he sketches a view of philosophy as intrinsically experimental.

Dewey's most important concept is his concept of experience, whose most important statement is *Experience and Nature* (1925). In this book, he favors empirical naturalism or, as he also says, naturalistic empiricism and again naturalistic humanism. By "naturalism" he has in mind an account based on and limited to the natural world or nature, an approach very different from naturalizing epistemology in analytic thinkers. By "empiricism" he means that whatever claims philosophy raises about the world must be traced back to experience, and that general conclusions must be brought into line with experience. In accordance with Dewey's experimental approach to philosophy, naturalism is intended to reveal the inconsistency of old accounts with the nature of things. Dewey's whole effort is intended to overcome the supposed separation of human beings and nature in formulating a philosophic method that reveals human beings within nature and nature as cognitively accessible to us.[87] His account denies the transcendent status accorded to reflection by Kant and many of his followers. As a natural event, reflection occurs within nature.[88] "These commonplaces," Dewey writes, "prove that experience is of as well as *in* nature."[89] For him, when used intelligently, an experiential approach to nature progressively reveals it. Unlike many scientists and too many philosophers, he is not claiming to know nature in itself, or to grasp metaphysical reality. In taking an instrumental approach, he claims no more than that physical science discovers how to appropriate nature for human purposes, that is, as he says in the preface added in the second edition, "those properties and relations of things in virtue of which they are capable of being used as instrumentalities."[90]

Rorty and Neo-Analytic Pragmatism

When Dewey died in 1952, pragmatism entered into a form of conceptual hibernation from which it was only reawakened about a quarter of a century later by Rorty. Rorty, a cross-over figure, belongs to analytic philosophy, in which he has long played an important role. Yet at least since his public renunciation of many of the ideals and ideas of analytic philosophy in *Philosophy and the Mirror of Nature* (1979), he claims to be tilling the pragmatist garden as well. Rorty's turn to pragmatism and his turn away from analytic philosophy are interrelated. Since Rorty is also discussed in the chapter on analytic philosophy, the remarks here will be limited to his role in American pragmatism. With respect to pragmatism he contributes in three ways: in calling attention, through his unusual notoriety – Rorty is at the present time one of the most visible philosophers in the world – to the considerable resources of pragmatism as a prominent option in the contemporary debate; in focusing attention specifically on Dewey, who, for Rorty and increasingly through him, has become the master figure of American pragmatism; and through his own distinctive form of neo-analytic pragmatism – despite the change in allegiance, Rorty continues to conserve in his post-analytic writings the writing style and vocabulary of his earlier analytic beliefs.

Neo-analytic pragmatism begins earlier, perhaps much earlier, than Rorty, who is only the most prominent later thinker to have taken up the cause. Pragmatism has long served as a point of refuge for disaffected members of the analytic fold. In general, neo-analytic pragmatists are united by the conviction that the traditional analytic concern with the specific problem of reference, or more broadly semantics, cannot be solved on formal grounds. Such thinkers tend to see pragmatism, suitably reinterpreted and understood in different ways, as offering an acceptable alternative to more traditional analytic approaches to knowledge.

Depending on the observer, the growing roster of neo-analytic pragmatists, thinkers who also count as among the most prominent analytic thinkers, include such names as Otto Neurath, Rudolf Carnap, C. I. Lewis, W. V. O. Quine, Hilary Putnam, and, most recently, Robert Brandom. Like Peirce, who criticized Cartesian foundationalism, Neurath's contribution to pragmatism lies in his sweeping refutation of Carnap's early foundationalist effort to ground science in experience through what he called protocol sentences. These are roughly basic statements similar to the atomic propositions featured in Russell and the early Wittgenstein. In a famous paper, Neurath decisively criticizes the very idea of protocol sentences.[91] Carnap immediately gave up his foundationalist program in favor of indexing claims to know to alternative categorial frameworks.[92] C. I. Lewis, who influenced Carnap, is important for his pragmatic relativization of the Kantian a priori.[93] Distantly following Neurath, in an unusually important paper, Quine employs a holist approach in denying that ideas match up one to one with the world, in what he simply characterizes, without any effort to clarify the claim, as a shift to pragmatism.[94] Putnam has long been interested in pragmatism, which he reductively tends to identify with the thought of James.[95] Brandom identifies his own view of inferentialism as pragmatism.[96] Other analytic figures sometimes classed as pragmatists include Gottlob Frege, Donald Davidson, and Nelson Goodman.[97]

Since pragmatism was comparatively neglected after Dewey's death, Rorty contributes usefully in calling attention to it. But the way in which he does this is questionable, beginning with his identification of pragmatism and the pragmatists. Rorty is not looking for another, better approach to knowledge. He is skeptical about the very idea of discussing knowledge. He consistently says that if someone brings up this problem, then the best thing to do is to change the subject. Unlike Peirce, who describes pragmatism as a new, post-foundationalist epistemological approach, Rorty consistently depicts it as an alternative to epistemology.

There is an analogy between Rorty's aversion to the problem of knowledge and the Young Hegelian view that philosophy terminates in Hegel. In both cases, emphasis falls not on going further in a different way but rather on simply breaking off the conversation. Pragmatism in Rorty's hands no longer appears as a way of picking up the pieces to continue the debate after the failure of the main epistemological strategy of modern times. It rather appears as what one does, or at least should be doing, after one gives up the whole enterprise as a bad bet, no longer worth the effort to take seriously. In *Philosophy and the Mirror of Nature*, Rorty reacts against analytic philosophy understood as the high point of Western philosophy. Here he depicts traditional philosophy as concerned with "rationality," "objectivity" as the result of some form of accurate representation, and pragmatism as giving up the "Greek contrast" between, as he says, "representing the world and coping with it."[98] From Rorty's perspective, accepting something like Dewey's warranted assertibility means being able to cope, in short, to get through the day, as distinguished from being able to claim to know or to have knowledge.

Rorty, who only turns to pragmatism as a substitute for epistemology, is opposed to any form of the traditional effort to work out the problem of knowledge. In writing about pragmatism he plays up those who strike his skeptical fancy while impugning the credentials of those hardy souls still committed to anything resembling knowledge. In an article on "Pragmatism, Relativism, and Irrationalism" from Rorty's middle period, shortly after the *Mirror* book, when he is still in the process of establishing his pragmatic bona fides, he sketches a description of pragmatism he has continued to defend in other writings. Rorty here calls attention to James and Dewey while casting aspersions on Peirce. Pragmatism, he suggests, is not merely a variant of logical empiricism, itself a variant of Kantianism, but, rather, simply breaks with the Kantian epistemological tradition. James and Dewey are misunderstood as having theories of truth, knowledge, or morality. They should, rather, be understood as turning away from any effort to make philosophy into a foundational discipline. This part seems correct since in different ways all the early pragmatists share Peirce's reaction against Cartesianism. Yet Rorty, who talks about the various pragmatist figures in contrast to interpreting their texts, sees the situation differently. Though he concedes Peirce's technical competence, according to Rorty, Peirce did not himself contribute to pragmatism. "His contribution to pragmatism," Rorty writes, "was merely to have given it a name, and to have stimulated James."[99] Even worse, in Rorty's eyes, Peirce remained a Kantian, hence, by extension, committed to a Kantian approach to epistemology. Yet it would be more accurate to say that he was thoroughly knowledgeable about but deeply critical of the author of the critical philosophy.

Rorty's skeptical approach, opposed to any effort to take the problem of knowledge seriously, leads to an influential, but foreshortened view of pragmatism. One difficulty is the basic distortion in the account of pragmatism as a movement introduced by the virtual elimination of Peirce, the founding father, as well as all concern with the specifically pragmatist approach to knowledge. A second is the proliferation of "pragmatists," who, in Rorty's fertile imagination, tend to spring up like mushrooms. For pragmatism as for any other tendency there is considerable difficulty in identifying the main doctrines as well as their representatives. Rorty, who opposes the very idea of coming up with an acceptable theory of knowledge, which he identifies with Kantianism, charitably extends the term "pragmatist" to virtually anyone who appears non-Kantian, including Nietzsche, Davidson, and Rorty's personal *bête noire* Putnam. In introducing a volume of his collected papers, Rorty suggests that Nietzsche did for European philosophy what James and Dewey did for American philosophy in criticizing Cartesianism, essentialism, and representationalism in favor of perspectivalism.[100] Yet this way of reading Nietzsche seems too rapid, since the familiar claim in favor of the unavoidability of endless interpretation[101] only counts as going beyond epistemology if claims to know must lie beyond it.

Rorty compares Davidson very favorably to James. In an important essay, "On the Very Idea of a Conceptual Scheme" (1974), Davidson extends Quine's attack on the analytic–synthetic distinction to what he calls the "scheme–content distinction."[102] Though he abandons the idea that sentences correspond to anything, Davidson denies that his view commits him to pragmatism.[103] In reading Davidson against himself, Rorty compares him to James in supposedly simply dissolving the problem of truth through dropping epistemology and empiricism.[104] In an "Afterword" to his paper, Davidson later replied in distancing himself from his own effort to work out a coherence theory of truth. His reason is that coherence implies correspondence as well as, from Rorty's "pragmatic" angle of vision, the effort to dismiss the epistemological tradition as a hopeless muddle.[105]

Davidson is respectful of Putnam's efforts on behalf of pragmatism. Rorty, on the contrary, regards his Harvard colleague both as the main contemporary pragmatist[106] and as an important foe to be vanquished. The feeling is apparently mutual. Putnam has classed Rorty with various

French thinkers as a cultural relativist. Rorty, who is not to be outdone, and who apparently thought he had been mistreated by Putnam, quickly rose to the bait. In "Hilary Putnam and the Relativist Menace" (1993), he gets even in exposing supposed distortions of his view.[107] In a complicated discussion, whose point seems to be to dissociate himself from any accusation of relativism, perhaps because that would mean he is still attached to a form of the theory of knowledge, Rorty describes Putnam as still unfortunately committed to saving from the realist position some version of the universal validity claim.[108] For Rorty, who eschews claims to truth and knowledge on the basis of skepticism, this description of Putnam, who sees himself as a pragmatist, as still holding on to universal truth claims, amounts to unveiling him as finally not a pragmatist at all.

5

Continental Philosophy as Phenomenology

Unlike Marxism and pragmatism, which began in the 1870s and 1880s before coming into their own in the twentieth century, so-called "continental philosophy" and Anglo-American analytic philosophy both emerged around 1900. The term "continental philosophy," which has no non-normative meaning, can be understood in different ways. One might be as including all philosophy of whatever kind in the geographical space of continental Europe, as distinguished from Great Britain. Understood in this way, the continental philosophers would be those who write in any one of the European languages except English, though mainly in French and German. Continental philosophy would include among its representatives not only the continental rationalists (Descartes, Spinoza, Leibniz) but also the German idealists, such later nineteenth-century figures as Kierkegaard, Marx, and Nietzsche, the German neo-Kantians, and many others. In practice, especially in the US, the term has come to be used more narrowly to refer to no more than a subset of philosophy originating in the continental European space beginning with Edmund Husserl, hence as simply omitting European thinkers either earlier than or unrelated to Husserlian phenomenology. In this chapter, I will be using "continental philosophy" to refer to what is sometimes called the phenomenological movement,[1] meaning forms of phenomenology understood in a broad sense to include hermeneutics, structuralism, postmodernism, and allied movements, that is, the various forms of philosophy, beginning with Husserlian phenomenology, invented by Husserl and his many successors.

If we follow entrenched custom in taking "continental" philosophy to refer to Husserlian and post-Husserlian phenomenology and allied movements, we run into two obvious problems. One is the risk of conflating Husserl with phenomenology and Husserlian phenomenology. The other is the risk of conflating Husserlian and post-Husserlian phenomenology with philosophy in continental Europe. Both of these problems create distortions. Despite what some of his followers may think, Husserl did not create phenomenology, though he did invent a form of it that proved extremely influential on a series of very talented thinkers over many years. What has come to be called the phenomenological movement is in fact the large-scale debate set in motion not by phenomenology, but rather by Edmund Husserl. Husserl's students sometimes exaggerate his importance through simply denying that phenomenology existed before he came on the scene. Yet this is simply false. Before Husserl, Hegel and many others, including A. G. Baumgarten and even Kant, were either phenomenologists or exhibited phenomenological tendencies. Husserlian and post-Husserlian forms of phenomenology represent at most variations on a pre-existing theme. They are clearly new kinds of phenomenology, but represent neither the initial appearance of phenomenology in the debate nor perhaps even a wholly new type of philosophy.

Further, continental philosophy neither begins nor ends with Husserl, who begins to participate in the debate nearly three centuries after such earlier continental thinkers as Montaigne and Descartes. One can further point out that there were many philosophers who were working in the European space from the beginning of the twentieth century who were never part of the Husserlian phenomenological movement. A short list might include not only European Marxists, but also Wittgenstein, an Austrian who wrote in German but worked mainly in England, Bergson, Jean Wahl, Thomists such as Étienne Gilson and Jacques Maritain, the German philosopher of science and culture Ernst Cassirer, a whole raft of German neo-Kantians besides Cassirer, including Hermann Cohen, and so on.

Phenomenon, Phenomenalism, and Early Forms of Phenomenology

The question of the meaning of "phenomenology" is difficult to answer since the main phenomenologists are very far from agreement. The term "phenomenology" can be distinguished from such other near synonyms as "phenomenalism" and "phenomenon." In the famous passage on the divided line in the *Republic*, Plato distinguishes between what for Kant would be phenomenal and noumenal objects, that is, those which lie below the line and are given through the senses, hence can be seen, and those that lie above the line, cannot be seen, hence are invisible, and are given only through the mind.[2] Kant later controversially distinguished between noumena, which can be thought but not known, and phenomena, which can be experienced and known.[3] "Phenomenalism" can be generally described as the doctrine that objects can be reduced to (and reconstructed out of) sensory experiences, which is associated in the twentieth century with such thinkers as A. J. Ayer and C. I. Lewis. Etymologically, phenomenology (Gr. *phaenomenon* + *logos*) is literally the science of phenomena.

Since observers differ widely in what they understand as "phenomenology," it is difficult to generalize. Yet all known forms of phenomenology appear to adopt an anti-Platonic approach to appearance. In the *Republic*, his most influential dialogue, Plato features an intuitive grasp of the true, or mind-independent real, access to which is limited on grounds of nature and nurture to a select group of philosophers in drawing a strict epistemological distinction between phenomena, appearances, and reality. According to Plato, no road leads through phenomena to reality. In his criticism of art and literature, he notoriously denies that mere appearance leads to access to the true, or the real. Phenomenologists of all stripes typically take an anti-Platonic stance in seeing phenomena, properly understood, as providing access to the real, which, hence, appears. To put the same point in other language, phenomenologists deny at least three central Platonic beliefs: (1) there is a transcendent real; (2) the transcendent real cannot be known through mere appearance, or phenomena; (3) the transcendent real can be directly grasped by at least some individuals some of the time. For phenomenologists, on the contrary, study of phenomena, of what appears, provides access to what is, hence to the real and the true.

The term "phenomenology" (Ger. *Phänomenologie*) seems first to have been used by J. H. Lambert, a contemporary of Kant, in his *Neues Organon*, published in Leipzig in 1764.[4] Kant employs "phenomenology" only twice. In a letter to Lambert written in 1770 as he was beginning to formulate what later became the critical philosophy, he mentions he is working on a theory of metaphysics that presupposes a negative science he calls "general phenomenology" (*phaenomenologia generalis*). This science is concerned with determining the limits of the principles of sensibility.[5] About a year and a half later, Kant comes back to the topic in the famous letter to his friend Marcus Herz. In describing the plan of the book that later became the *Critique of Pure Reason*, Kant indicates it will contain a theoretical and a practical part, and that the former will be divided into two sections: (1) general phenomenology and (2) metaphysics.[6]

Lambert and Kant, while understanding "phenomenology" differently, do, however, both understand it in anti-Platonic fashion as marking out the legitimate limits of what can be known with reference to experience. Plato rejects the very idea of restricting analysis to the world of appearance instead of the world of reality. In the *Phaedo*, he attacks the Sophists for refusing to go beyond mere appearance, hence as refusing genuine philosophical explanation.[7]

In reaction to Kant's critical philosophy, Hegel rethinks phenomenology, which he grasps, in a reference to the human community, as the phenomenology of spirit. He understands the latter as the science of the experience of consciousness. Spirit is a general term referring to the conscious life of human beings. Hegel revises Kant's understanding of experience and knowledge in putting the accent on consciousness and, unlike Kant, on self-consciousness. The science of the experience of consciousness refers to a process of knowledge with no preconditions that studies not the abstract conditions but rather the real practical conditions of knowing understood as unfolding in a social and historical context. The *Phenomenology of Spirit* traces the historical process of working out the real conditions of and in fact acquiring knowledge. The process begins in immediate consciousness, or knowledge of what is immediately given. In subsequent stages it continues and rises through a dialectical discussion centering on understanding the nature of knowledge through such stages as natural science, morality, art, and religion. The process culminates in the highest or properly philosophical standpoint that Hegel characterizes as absolute knowing (*das absolute Wissen*), which is often misdescribed in the literature as absolute knowledge.

In the Introduction to the book, Hegel depicts knowledge as a process in which various theories of the object are formulated, tried out in experience, and reformulated. Truth appears as the limit in which, since the theory of the object is adequate to the object of the theory, further experience no longer reveals a distinction between them. Hegel later describes the *Phenomenology of Spirit* as the first part of the system of science, whose content is then worked out in detail in the *Logic*.[8]

Phenomenology is not eccentric within but rather central to Hegel's mature position. Hegel is a major philosophical figure, one of the very few whose enormous influence, like Kant's, continues to echo through the later debate. Hegel is in many ways a deep Kantian, often opposed to specific Kantian ideas but basically committed to working out the critical philosophy, which continues in Hegelian phenomenology. In virtue of Hegel's impact, phenomenology is mentioned by others prior to and around the same time as the early Husserl, including Hermann Lotze, Gustav Class, Henri-Frédéric Amiel, Eduard von Hartmann, William Hamilton, and C. S. Peirce.[9] Yet Hegel is by far the strongest thinker prior to Husserl for whom phenomenology plays a central role.

Husserl, whose background in the history of philosophy was relatively weak, seems to have inherited the prejudices of his teacher, Franz Brentano, concerning his phenomenological predecessor.[10] Husserl, who never studied Hegel with care, perhaps not at all, remarks that the impulse toward philosophy as rigorous science is hindered in Hegel's Romantic philosophy, which lacks a critique of reason.[11] This reference is doubly inaccurate since Hegel was opposed to Romanticism, which he criticized. Further, the central thrust of Hegel's position consists in criticizing Kant's theory of pure reason (*Vernunft*), for which he substitutes a theory of spirit (*Geist*). More neutral references in Husserl's later writings never reveal specific knowledge of any Hegelian texts.

Husserl's unhistorical attitude toward prior phenomenology, particularly Hegel, leads to two very different, but equally inaccurate reactions among his followers. One, already noted, is to deny that there is any significant phenomenological precedent in the prior debate. Works on Husserl and Husserlian phenomenology often maintain that phenomenology was discovered or invented by Husserl, or at least that it can be discussed without any account of historical precedents.[12] A second approach consists in suggesting that Husserlian and other forms of phenomenology are indistinguishably similar. Following Husserl's emphasis on method, French observers often make versions of the mistaken claim that Hegel, Husserl, and Heidegger employ the same method.[13] Yet Hegel has no discernible single method, and, in virtue of his critique of Kant, it seems that his position excludes the very idea of one, while the differences between Husserl and Heidegger are so profound as to call into question the idea that they share a common approach.

Husserl and the Origins of the Phenomenological Movement

Edmund Husserl (1859–1938), the German phenomenologist, was one of the most inventive and most influential thinkers of modern times. He was a very prolific writer, who published several books during his lifetime but at his death left some 45,000 pages composed in shorthand that have still not been fully transcribed.

Husserl, who was born in Bohemia, studied in Leipzig, Berlin, and Vienna, and taught at Halle, Göttingen, and, from 1916 to 1928, at Freiburg im Breisgau. He came to philosophy from mathematics. He studied with Karl Weierstrass and Leopold Kronecker, and took a Ph.D. on the calculus of variations. He then attended lectures by Franz Brentano and Carl Stumpf, eventually writing a second dissertation (*Habilitationsschrift*) about the psychological analysis of the concept of number. At the time, he was close to J. S. Mill, who took a psychologistic approach in reducing epistemology to psychology. He studied Mill's *System of Logic* (1843) with care. In his never completed *Philosophy of Arithmetic*, Husserl tried to derive the fundamental concept of number, hence mathematics, from psychology. The first volume, which was published in 1891, criticized the views of the German logician Gottlob Frege's *Foundations of Arithmetic* (1884) from a psychologistic standpoint. Frege famously replied to Husserl. In his extremely critical review of Husserl's book, Frege objected to its psychologistic effort to base logic, in this case mathematics, on psychology.[14] After this point, Husserl turned radically against psychologism – the precise reason is controversial – either in reaction to or independently of Frege's criticism.[15]

The first fruit of Husserl's rejection of psychologism appeared in *Logical Investigations*, which was published in two volumes in 1900 and 1901, his breakthrough to phenomenology. This enormous work – more than 800 pages – was the foundational text of the nascent phenomenological movement, widely influential on those attracted to Husserlian phenomenology. Yet Michael Dummett could write as late as 2000, that is, a century after its initial publication, that it was still largely unknown to English-speaking students of philosophy.[16] In the first volume, which bears the Kantian title *Prolegomena To Pure Logic*, Husserl, who has by now turned against his own earlier approach, provides a very strong, highly detailed refutation of psychologism.[17] Husserl oddly regarded the critique of psychologism not as a special subject but as integral to phenomenology.[18] In passing, he also acknowledged the correctness of Frege's anti-psychologism.[19] In the tradition of Leibniz's universal mathematics (*mathesis universalis*), Husserl here develops a conception of logic as a pure, a priori science of ideal meanings, and as a pure theory of science, or science of science.

In the second volume, entitled *Phenomenology and Theory of Knowledge*, Husserl draws attention to a link between logic, epistemology, and phenomenology in characterizing pure phenomenology as ancillary to empirical psychology. Empirical psychology studies forms of experience treated as real events. On the contrary, "phenomenology," Husserl writes, "lays bare the 'sources' from which the basic concepts and ideal laws of *pure* logic 'flow', and back to which they must once more be traced, so as to give them all the 'clearness and distinctness' needed for an understanding and for an epistemological critique, or pure logic."[20] Husserl is clear that phenomenology has a foundational role. But he is not yet clear about how to understand its precise relation to empirical psychology.

The discussion of logic displays a unity lacking in the sprawling nature of the six "systematically bound chain of investigations," or "series of analytical investigations" that together make up the second volume.[21] The six Investigations study such epistemological themes as meaning, concept, proposition, and truth. Husserl here takes the view that logic studies ideal objects that are independent of, but accessible to, and graspable by the human mind.[22] At the time he wrote the *Logical Investigations*, on his own account, Husserl had not yet become aware of the explicit difference to which he later drew attention between pure, or transcendental, phenomenology and descriptive psychology.[23]

It goes beyond the limits of this chapter to follow the six Investigations in any detail. Suffice it to say here that the Fifth Investigation explores intentionality. Brentano, with whom Husserl studied, revived the medieval concept of intentionality – from *intentio*, a Scholastic term for ideas or representations formed by the mind – to mean "reference to a content, direction toward an object . . . or immanent objectivity."[24] Husserl here reworks Brentano's distinction in distinguishing between the content and the quality of mental acts.[25] He further suggests that an observer only sees a mind-transcendent object from a particular angle, profile, or aspect. The Sixth Investigation, in which Husserl explores the connections between meaning and truth as they figure in various conscious acts, attracted the attention of Heidegger.[26] Husserl here discusses what he calls categorial intuition as a kind of perception through widening the conception of perception and intuition.

After publishing the *Logical Investigations*, Husserl published almost nothing in the next decade prior to the important programmatic article, "Philosophy as Rigorous Science" (1911).[27] This text provides an occasion for Husserl to respond to Wilhelm Dilthey, a contemporary German philosopher known for his contribution to Hegel studies as well as for his own theory of vitalism. In an important paper which appeared in 1910, Dilthey argued in a vaguely Hegelian manner inimical to traditional philosophical claims of unrevisable knowledge that philosophical positions manifest a bewildering series of worldviews while denying that they lead to epistemological skepticism.[28] Though personally friendly with Dilthey, Husserl read Dilthey's claims in an altogether different way than their author. He understood Dilthey's position as leading to relativism and skepticism. In response, Husserl proposes a traditional view of philosophy as the source of apodictic knowledge in promoting phenomenology as the only acceptable version of philosophy in the rigorous, or scientific, sense.

As in the *Logical Investigations*, so here Husserl defends a broadly Kantian view of rigorous philosophy. In the *Prolegomena*, Kant aims toward the future, as yet unrealized, metaphysics. This normative Kantian view now recurs in Husserl's clarion call for a philosophy that is nothing less than science and indispensable "to teach us how to carry on the eternal work of humanity."[29] Philosophy claims to be rigorous science, however, in a way that can only be fulfilled in the future. "I do not say that philosophy is an imperfect science; I say simply that it is not yet a science at all, that as science it has not yet begun."[30]

Husserl, who takes over a normative conception of philosophy that he attributes to Kant, finds, other than the impulse to science, nothing positive in the preceding debate, not even in Kant,[31] nor in Descartes before him and Fichte after him. According to Husserl, these thinkers, who fully share Kant's concern with rigorous philosophy, also fail to make even the least progress toward reaching this goal.[32] Husserl is optimistic about the promise of his own approach. But he is pessimistic about other thinkers and, again like Kant, about all prior philosophy. Writing early in the twentieth century, Husserl thinks the goal of philosophy as rigorous science is not drawing closer but only receding. The emergence of three rival views – naturalistic philosophy,[33] historicism, and *Weltanschauung* philosophy (*Weltanschauungsphilosophie*)[34] – prevents the attainment of apodictic claims to know. Hence, they lead and can lead only to skepticism. Husserl, who composed this article before the analytic interest in naturalized epistemology associated with Quine and other later analytic figures, is not thinking of an aspect of analytic philosophy that, had he known about it, he would surely have rejected. He is rather thinking of the reduction of everything, specifically including ideas, ideals, and norms of all kinds, to physical nature.[35] This tendency is associated, as he points out, with the rise and spread of modern science throughout modern life, which always takes nature as a given.

In discussing naturalism, Husserl contrasts empirical psychology with the wholly different science of phenomenology. Psychology is concerned with empirical consciousness, but phenomenology is concerned with what he calls pure consciousness. Psychology sets aside pure consciousness, which is the subject matter of phenomenology, which, as a kind of non-empirical psychology, "brings social phenomena to direct givenness and investigates them according to their essence."[36] Phenomenology studies phenomena in which no difference can be drawn between appearance and being.[37] It is not concerned with phenomena as appearances of something else, say metaphysical reality, but only with what is immediately given, which it undertakes to study as it is given. The immediately given psychical content is not nature in itself. Phenomena, which have no nature, instead have an essence that can be directly grasped. Husserl insists that phenomena are directly given, that they are directly given through intuition, and that the relevant concepts correctly describe essential intuition. "All the statements that describe the phenomena in direct concepts do so, to the degree that they are valid, by means of concepts of essence, that is, by conceptual signification of words that must permit of being redeemed in an essential intuition.[38] Husserl believes that essences grasped in intuition can be described in conceptual statements which are objectively valid, hence are not in any way subjective. He goes on to distinguish the intuitive grasp of essences from such obvious rivals as "experience," including perception or recollection, empirical generalization, matters of fact.

Husserl, whose grasp of the history of philosophy was never good, had odd views of his relation to it. He goes so far as to claim that his phenomenological critique of other sciences corresponds to the secret longing of modern philosophy.[39] Like Kant, who famously claims that Hume awoke him from his dogmatic slumber, Husserl also relates his position to Hume's. Husserl claims to understand as essence what Hume was grasping for in his positivist conflation of essence and idea, as distinguished from impression. Hume's problems need not have driven him to skepticism, since they belong to and can be solved through phenomenology.[40] Hume needed to turn away from existential claims about nature to the science of pure phenomenology, for psychology, hence psychological knowledge, can only be based on what Husserl clearly labels as "essential knowledge of the psychical."[41] To put the same point in other words, it is only possible to go beyond the confusions of modern psychology, illustrated by Hume, if psychology, as well as all the other sciences, is based on phenomenology, for, as Husserl unblinkingly reports, "every real theory of knowledge must necessarily be based on phenomenology."[42]

Husserl also rejects historicism and what, following Dilthey, he calls *Weltanschauungsphilosophie*, or philosophy based on a worldview. Husserl understands Dilthey's position as an attack on the very idea of philosophy as science. For Husserl, these two kinds of philosophy are related. Historicism, which reduces everything to history, is the opposite of naturalism, which reduces everything to nature, and, like it, leads to relativism, hence to skepticism. Following Dilthey, Husserl understands the philosophy of the worldview as the result of according objective validity to one or another worldview, whose simple proliferation, as Dilthey points out, destroys any belief in the universal validity of any philosophical system. Husserl sees a philosophy based on worldviews as weakening a traditional view of philosophy as yielding apodictic knowledge. The result of adopting historicism is that the "ideas of truth, theory, and science would then, like all ideas, lose their absolute validity."[43] Like Kant, Husserl rejects any form of the view that science can emerge from reasoning based on history. While Husserl is willing to grant that a worldview reaches the highest level of wisdom, he is unwilling to grant that it in any sense reaches truth. A worldview is different in different periods, but the idea of science is "supratemporal."[44] A philosophy based on a worldview must, hence, give up the pretense of being science.[45]

"Philosophy as Rigorous Science," like most of Husserl's writings, is a meditation on the problem and the difficulty of finally making a correct, or radical, beginning of philosophy as science once and for all. The view of phenomenology that emerges from his reflection on this problem is centrally concerned with the limitless task of direct intuition of essences. "Thus the greatest step our age has to make," Husserl writes, "is to recognize that with the philosophical intuition in the correct sense [that is, direct intuition], the phenomenological grasp of essences, a limitless field of work opens out. . . ."[46]

In subsequent writings, Husserl further develops, deepens, and alters his position, often in basic ways. *Ideas* I, which appeared in 1913, is intended once again as a general introduction to what Husserl begins to call pure phenomenology. The realism of *Logical Investigations* has in the meantime given way to transcendental idealism. Husserl now recommends what he calls the "phenomenological reduction" as bringing about a readjustment of viewpoint from the natural attitude to the so-called "sphere of transcendental phenomenology."[47] This procedure requires two steps: the reduction to the transcendental plane, and then the eidetic reduction, or further reduction to the eidetic sphere. Through the phenomenological reduction, the phenomenological subject initiates a change of standpoint from the ordinary standpoint, also called the natural standpoint, to the transcendental standpoint, in which original and pure description is carried out. As a consequence, the being of the world, or existence, is bracketed in concentrating only on what is immediately given to the subject in consciousness. In Husserl's opinion, the resultant phenomenological or transcendental phenomenology is not in any sense psychology, but remains strictly parallel to empirical psychology. The phenomenological reduction, Husserl contends, reaches the transcendental-philosophical standpoint or, as he also says, a transcendental-phenomenological Idealism or, again, idealism that has attained the status of science, which Husserl sharply distinguishes from psychological idealism.

In the "Author's Preface to the English Edition of Ideas" (1931), Husserl signals that though he has only treated transcendental solipsism incompletely, objections against it are incorrect.[48] His reference is to his recent *Cartesian Meditations* (1929). Husserl, who earlier stressed the relation of phenomenology to Kant, here underlines its relation to Descartes. As part of his new interest in Descartes, he takes up the problem of transcendental intersubjectivity, which, in his opinion, provides the definitive answer to the problem of solipsism. Solipsism (from L. *solus* + *ipse*), or the possibility that only the subject exists, surfaces as a problem in Descartes's *Meditations on First Philosophy* (1641, 1644). At the end of the Second Meditation, he looks out of a window and sees hats and cloaks passing in the street, which, he says, might be automatons, but which he infers through judgment are in fact men.[49] A similar problem recurs in Husserl after the phenomenological reduction, as a result of which the subject withdraws from the world into itself. In the first of the *Cartesian Mediations*, Husserl characterizes the philosophical standpoint as that of "transcendental solipsism."[50] In the fifth of the *Cartesian Meditations*, he argues that the transcendental ego constitutes other egos in an intersubjective community. Husserl here adapts a conception of empathy (*Einfühlung*) borrowed from Theodor Lipps. He argues that our knowledge of others arises indirectly through what he calls appresentation (*Appräsentation*) on the basis of analogy. Yet though crucial to Husserl's mature position, few of his followers were convinced by this argument.[51]

A final stage in Husserl's heroic effort over many years to work out his conception of phenomenology is provided in still another introduction to phenomenology that he left unfinished at his death, *The Crisis of the European Sciences and Transcendental Phenomenology: An Introduction to Phenomenological Philosophy.* The concept of crisis is already lurking as it were in the conceptual shadows of his thought from the time of his initial phenomenological breakthrough. The term "*Krisis*" in the title can be traced to the Greek "*krisis*," meaning "choice or selection, judgment or trial, crisis or critical moment." This latter pair of meanings is well conserved in the cognate terms in modern European languages, such as in the English "crisis," which translates Husserl's unusual use of the Greek transliteration "*krisis*," as well as in the more usual German synonym, "*Krise*." Speaking broadly, Husserl uses the term to refer to a problem constitutive of rationality.

Husserl, who understands phenomenology as linking objective knowledge and subjective interests, establishes a connection between rigorous philosophy and an implicit ethical goal.[52] In the *Crisis*, where he relates the crisis of science[53] to human being, he contends that in seeking objective knowledge, philosophers are "*functionaries of mankind*."[54] Like Kant, he maintains that human interests are served through philosophical reason as the guide for human life.[55] In the Vienna Lecture (1935), the basis of the book, Husserl naïvely presents his vision of philosophy as the only effective bulwark against Nazism.[56] Several years later in the *Crisis*, he acknowledges that in our time of crisis "science has nothing to say to us."[57] The difficulty does not lie in the intrinsic limits of philosophy, but rather in the failure to defend the correct conception of philosophy as rigorous science that alone can realize the "philosophico-historical idea (or the teleological sense) of European man."[58]

In the *Crisis*, Husserl returns to earlier themes and develops new ones. In "Philosophy as Rigorous Science," he alludes in passing to Galileo's central role in the rise of modern science.[59] Husserl now provides a detailed analysis whose result – Galileo successfully applied mathematics to nature – may seem less than surprising.[60] He also develops the concept of the life-world, which begins to occur earlier in his writings. Husserl here criticizes Kant's unexpressed "presupposition" of taking the surrounding world for granted.[61] He develops an elaborate analysis leading to the idea that all science presupposes phenomenology. Phenomenology studies the pre-given surroundings from which we rise through reduction to the transcendental plane.[62] According to Husserl, a scientist simply presupposes that objective scientific results relate to the pre-given surroundings, or life-world. "The knowledge of the objective-scientific world is 'grounded' in the self-evidence of the life-world."[63]

Like the German idealist Fichte, Husserl was obsessively concerned with finding a way to present his basic insight. His commitment to philosophy, which he identifies with life itself, led him, as he grew older, to despair about ever finally making the true beginning that alone would make of philosophy a rigorous science in the form of phenomenology, or later as transcendental phenomenology. In a passage charged with emotion from *Ideas* I, Husserl writes about his work: "The author sees the infinite open country of the true philosophy, the 'promised land' on which he himself will never set foot."[64] In another passage from the *Crisis*, in surveying his life and work as an old man, Husserl famously writes: "Philosophy as science, as serious, rigorous, indeed apodictically rigorous, science – the *dream is over*."[65]

Heidegger and Post-Husserlian Phenomenology

Husserl was influential in his own time in forming a group of disciples, who rapidly spread his teachings. Later phenomenology develops through interpreting, accepting, and further developing, or criticizing and rejecting, his key insights. His *Logical Investigations* served as the cornerstone of the emerging phenomenological school, though Husserl, who was never satisfied with any of his writings, immediately began to revise it. A second edition appeared in 1913 but without the revised version of the Sixth Meditation, which was only published in 1921. Husserl later claimed that his chief error in the first edition lay in characterizing "phenomenology" as descriptive psychology.[66] Since his view changed, even radically changed as he developed it, different followers were attached to different phases in the evolution of his position. The group of thinkers influenced by Husserl, which is long and distinguished, includes such important philosophers as Max Scheler, Nicolai Hartmann, and Martin Heidegger in Germany, and such French figures as Gabriel Marcel, Jean-Paul Sartre, Maurice Merleau-Ponty, Paul Ricoeur, and even Jacques Derrida. All of these figures differed, often in important ways, from Husserl. It is far from clear that later phenomenology in the twentieth century carries forward even the spirit of Husserlian phenomenology.

Given the enormous wealth of often very important thinkers influenced by Husserl and the limited space at our disposal, it will be necessary to be very selective. Arguably Husserl's single most significant and certainly most controversial follower is the German phenomenologist Martin Heidegger (1889–1976), whom many observers see as equally important as or even more important than Husserl.

Heidegger initially studied Catholic theology with the intention of becoming a Jesuit. He gradually changed his mind after reading Brentano's dissertation "On the Several Senses of Being in Aristotle" (1862). After studies in theology and mathematics, especially mathematical logic, he wrote a doctoral thesis on "The Doctrine of Judgment in Psychologism"

(1913), which was followed by a *Habilitationsschrift* on "The Categories and the Doctrine of Meaning in Duns Scotus" (1915). After completing his studies, as was and still is customary in Germany Heidegger begin to teach as an unsalaried lecturer, in Freiburg im Breisgau. in 1915. When Husserl arrived the following year, Heidegger became his assistant. During the so-called "war emergency" semester Heidegger began to hold lectures criticizing Husserl as well as Jaspers and Dilthey. Heidegger taught at Marburg from 1923 to 1928. In 1928, when Husserl retired, Heidegger succeeded him in the chair of philosophy in Freiburg. He remained in Freiburg from 1928 to 1944, a period interrupted only when he was rusticated at the end of the Second World War. He returned in the winter semester of 1950–1 and remained in Freiburg after his retirement.

Heidegger's relation to Husserl is a key problem in comprehending twentieth-century phenomenology. This problem is clouded by Heidegger's distinct sympathy for National Socialism.[67] Though he was clearly interested in and influenced by Husserl, scholars of Heidegger often study his ideas apart from Husserl's. Yet Husserlian insights as well as reactions to them are woven throughout Heidegger's early position. In a short autobiographical sketch, Heidegger reports his fascination with Husserl's *Logical Investigations*, which he read repeatedly, with special attention to the problem of categorial intuition in the Sixth Investigation. He was convinced that Husserl, who criticized psychologism, later fell back into it. He eventually came to the conclusion that Husserl's effort to apprehend the self-manifestation of phenomena was covered much earlier and in greater depth by Aristotle.[68]

In comparison to Husserl, Heidegger is equally prolific, even more difficult to read, and an at least equally influential thinker. Though Heidegger claims to be a phenomenologist, he understands what he is doing very differently from Husserl. Philosophically, other than the claim to be doing phenomenology, which Heidegger appears later to give up, the two thinkers are opposed on nearly every significant point. Heidegger, for instance, rejects the very idea of phenomenological reduction, hence transcendental phenomenology, that Husserl came to see as the cornerstone of his position. Heidegger also rejects the phenomenological approach to epistemology that Husserl describes as early as the second volume of *Logical Investigations*. Heidegger, on the contrary, understands phenomenology as phenomenological ontology. Husserl relies on conceptions of the analysis of consciousness and intentionality. Heidegger abandons the terms "consciousness" and "intentionality" altogether. Heidegger was and was correctly perceived by Husserl as a strong critic of his own position, which Heidegger does not so much continue as attempt to destroy. Both cannot be right about phenomenology. If Heidegger is right, Husserl is surely wrong; and, conversely, if Husserl is right, then Heidegger must be wrong.

Heidegger's often-stated, single, obsessive, lifelong concern, which begins with his reading of Brentano's dissertation, is the problem of being, as distinguished from beings, or in other terms the being of beings. Heidegger's first and most important discussion of this problem occurs in *Being and Time* (1927), a philosophically very ambitious book. As soon as it appeared, it was hailed as a philosophical classic, at least as important as any other single philosophical treatise in the twentieth century. Though this work is dedicated to Husserl, and though Husserl's influence on Heidegger's thinking is apparent, Heidegger here takes a very different view of phenomenology.

In a short passage prior to the introduction to the book, Heidegger very effectively raises his main theme through the device of citing and commenting on a short passage from Plato's *Sophist*, a dialogue in which Plato works out the outlines of a new theory of being. In the passage Heidegger cites, Theatetus and the Visitor are discussing "being." A standard translation of the passage says: "Then clarify this for us, since we're very confused about it. What do you want to signify when you say *being*? Obviously you've known for a long time. We thought we did, but now we're confused about it."[69] Heidegger, who cites this passage in Greek, and translates it into German, comments that now as before we are not puzzled by "*the question of the meaning of being*."[70] He describes his aim as reawakening an understanding for this question through "the Interpretation of *time* as the possible horizon whatsoever of Being."[71]

This short passage helps us to understand the question motivating Heidegger and his typical procedure. Heidegger typically links the question concerning the meaning of being that concerns him throughout his writings to the history of philosophy. Here as elsewhere, ancient Greek philosophy serves as Heidegger's point of reference. He possesses an unusual grasp of the history of philosophy but is virtually unaware of contemporary debate outside his native Germany. Heidegger's way of stating his thesis suggests the influence of Husserl. "Horizon" (*Horizont*) is an obviously Husserlian term. In *Ideas*, in discussing the natural standpoint, Husserl points, *inter alia*, to the temporal horizon of the world.[72] He indicates that his analysis will be both concrete – the concrete nature of his analyses is one of the most interesting features of his discussion – and, since it is concerned with any possible horizon whatsoever, transcendental.

Being and Time is a fragment of a larger work, which was never finished. The published part is divided into two divisions: the preparatory fundamental analysis of Dasein and temporality, as well as eighty-three numbered sections. In the introduction, Heidegger immediately argues that the question of the meaning of being is *the* central philosophical question. According to Heidegger, this question was already central for Plato and Aristotle, and remains so for Hegel. A second point is that the necessary clue to the question that has never been answered lies in the fact of the vague, unthematized understanding of being that we all possess. According to Heidegger, human being, which he understands under the name of "Dasein" – literally "being there" or "existing" – is basically concerned with the question of the meaning of being: "The very asking of this question is an entity's mode of *Being*; and as such it gets its essential character from what is inquired about – namely, Being. This entity which each of us is himself and which includes inquiring as one of the possibilities of its Being, we shall denote by the term '*Dasein*'."[73] So far, Heidegger has argued that the question that interests him can be raised by human beings, and is central to their being in some way. He goes on to insist that the question about the meaning of being is ontologically prior to all other questions as the ground of all the sciences. This question is further ontically prior since Dasein (or human individuals) always understands itself in relation to its "existence," that is, "in terms of a possibility of itself: to be itself or not itself."[74] Individuals can act or fail to act in ways that realize their potential, pointing in this way to a conception of authenticity. Yet since the question of being belongs to the being of human beings, any answer to the question of the meaning of being requires a preliminary analysis of the being of human beings.

Heidegger needs to choose a *modus operandi* to carry out the proposed analysis of Dasein. He elects to concentrate on the ordinary way in which Dasein shows itself "*proximally and for the most part*, in its average *everydayness*."[75] As for being in general, so for Dasein time functions as the horizon. This task requires what Heidegger calls "destroying the history of ontology," that is, exposing and freeing oneself from the prior tradition that transmits, but in his opinion also conceals ontology in order to arrive at the meaning of being. The function of this proposed destruction is positive. In this connection, Heidegger notes that Kant, the only one who has made any progress on human temporality, was blocked from going further by his dependence on Descartes, who himself depended on medieval ontology. More generally, such interpretation allows us to appropriate the ancient Greek interpretation of the being of beings in nature in terms of time, more specifically with respect to presence (*Anwesenheit*, *parousia*). According to Heidegger, every later discussion of time depends on Aristotle's account.[76] The question of the meaning of being only becomes concrete in "destroying," or revealing the errors of, the history of ontology.

Heidegger, who believes that the appropriate method is phenomenological, now forges a link between phenomenology and ontology. Like Husserl, Heidegger understands this approach as permitting access to what the former already calls the things themselves (*die Sachen selbst*), that is, to what is directly given in experience, as distinguished from Kant's thing in itself (*das Ding an sich*), which is not and cannot be given in experience. Heidegger diverges from Husserl in studying the concepts of phenomenon, *logos*, and phenomenology by examining their Greek etymologies in order to cast essential light on their original meanings. This part of the discussion is at least as closely related to Kant's treatment of the terms "phenomenon" and "appearance" as to his own account of ancient Greek etymologies. According to Heidegger, "phenomenon" means appearing in the sense of "not showing itself." A phenomenon announces something that shows and fails to show itself.[77] "*Logos*" means "discourse which lets something be seen." Phenomenology, which is the science of the being of entities, hence ontology, is descriptive, and description is interpretive, or hermeneutical. This line of argument culminates in a single sentence, which significantly occurs twice in the book, where Heidegger very obviously summarizes his understanding of phenomenology: "Philosophy is universal phenomenological ontology, and takes its departure from the hermeneutic of Dasein, which as an analytic of *existence*, has made fast the guiding-line for all philosophical inquiry at the point where it *arises* and to which it *returns*."[78]

The early Heidegger is a systematic thinker. The remainder of *Being and Time* rigorously develops the argument advanced thus far in original and often incisive ways. Heidegger denies that his position rests on philosophical anthropology. He insists that the analysis of Dasein is deeper than such sciences as anthropology, psychology, or biology. According to Heidegger, who here parts company with any transcendental conception of the subject, Dasein is always in the world, and knowing is only a derivative, not a primary, way of being of human beings.

Heidegger also studies what he calls the worldliness of the world, or the essential property or properties that make it the world. He draws attention to a distinction between things – he uses the term "equipment" (*Zeug*) – that are ready to hand, that is, which can be used or fail to be used, and those that are merely present to hand, or just there. This is roughly the difference between objects as they are meaningful to us in terms of our goals, and objects which just are. In this context, Heidegger gives the famous example of the hammer that supposedly shows itself as it is in terms of the uses to which it can be put, that are intrinsic to it, and that depend on the context, or world in which it is encountered.[79] His point seems to be that human beings structure what is in the world in terms of their goals. He applies this distinction to criticize Descartes, who, because he fails to raise the question of the meaning of being, fails to apprehend the worldliness of the world.

Heidegger devotes a great deal of space to the general idea of authenticity, a theme he simply takes over without attribution from Kierkegaard. In his discussion, Heidegger plays on the distinction between what Dasein is, which is mine, which roughly corresponds to individual human potentials, and Dasein's tendency to exist, or be actual, in ways that, since they reflect the influence of others, differ from what it could be in ignoring others to realize itself. According to Heidegger, one's mood discloses the way the world is. In this connection he distinguishes between fear, which is transitive, that is, fear of someone or something, and anxiety, which is a free-floating way of being. Heidegger suggests that human beings rely in everything they do, including the interpretation of being, on understanding.[80] "*Understanding is the existential being of Dasein's own potentiality-for-Being; and it is so in such a way that this Being discloses in itself what is Being is capable of.*"[81] Unlike Husserl, for whom description is without presuppositions, Heidegger argues that interpretation is never presuppositionless, but always dependent on an interpretive structure.[82] This amounts to the claim that the interpretive capacity characteristic of human beings functions in a circular way. "The 'circle' in understanding belongs to the structure of meaning, and the latter phenomenon is rooted in the existential constitution of Dasein – that is, in the understanding which interprets."[83] Though the individual has capacities that can be realized in simply being who one is, for the most part as inauthentic beings we tend to fall into idle talk (*Gerede*). Heidegger goes on to englobe all the characteristics of the human individual in care (*Sorge*). In reviewing the possibility of inauthenticity, which Heidegger reads as a "*fleeing in the face of itself* and in the face of its authenticity,"[84] he argues that what an individual is, in his language the being of Dasein, is care. We cannot follow this detailed analysis other than to note that for Heidegger individuals are always concerned with various possibilities, in short, with what one could be, or, as he says, with "Being-ahead-of-oneself."[85]

In passing, Heidegger provides an influential, if flawed, account of truth. Earlier in the book he has inconsistently presented views of truth as transcendental (*veritas transcendentalis*)[86] and as hermeneutical.[87] He traces the familiar correspondence view of truth back to Aristotle in arguing that to say of an assertion that it is true means that it uncovers what is as it is. "The *Being-true* (*truth*) of the assertion must be understood as *Being-uncovering*."[88] Through analysis of the Greek term for truth (*aletheia*), Heidegger contends that the first letter (*alpha*) has a privative role which means taking out of hiddenness, or disclosing. Since truth depends on what individuals do, Heidegger goes on to claim that truth is relative to human beings. "*Because the kind of Being that is essential to truth is of the character of Dasein, all truth is relative to Dasein's Being.*"[89]

In *Being and Time*, Heidegger insists on the relation between his own phenomenology and his reading of the history of philosophy. His later writings dealt increasingly with themes in the history of philosophy. Heidegger's next major work is *Kant and the Problem of Metaphysics* (1929). To the best of my knowledge every major commentator takes an epistemological approach to Kant's critical philosophy. Heidegger is an important if controversial exception. In a famous series of lectures and debates with the German neo-Kantian Ernst Cassirer in Davos, Switzerland, he developed the main lines of a rival ontological reading of the critical philosophy.[90] In *Being and Time*, he suggests that Kant begins to analyze but draws back from a full analysis of temporality (time).[91] In his important study of Kant, Heidegger casts himself as Kant's legitimate successor, the only one who resolves Kant's concern.[92] Heidegger implies that the critical philosophy, which was left unfinished in Kant, and which the post-Kantian German idealists and the German neo-Kantians later sought to develop, is only brought to an end in his own position. Since the post-Kantian German idealists also determine to take the critical philosophy beyond Kant in thinking it through to the end, Heidegger is clearly casting himself as a rival to them.

Some time in the next few years, by his own account, Heidegger undertook a still mysterious turning (*Kehre*) in his position. Opinions are divided about whether this turning is traceable only to his philosophical position, to his political engagement with National Socialism, or both. As a result of this change, Heidegger altered the focus of his thought. He now abandons the idea of taking up again and completing the early Greek philosophical concern with ontology, understood as the question of the meaning of being, hence to completing what, at least in his early account, is arguably the main aim of the Western philosophical tradition. Perhaps because in the meantime he came to believe that the original task he set himself simply could not be carried out, hence Western philosophy could not complete its self-assigned task, Heidegger's new interest lies in breaking with or going beyond philosophy. During this period, Heidegger held a series of lecture courses on the German Romantic poet Friedrich Hölderlin.[93] In the *Republic*, Plato famously argues that poets and artists are twice removed from reality, hence from truth.[94] In his discussion of Hölderlin, Heidegger makes the anti-Platonic argument that only the great poet can, as he puts it, tell us who we are. In lectures on Nietzsche, he argues that the Western philosophical tradition comes to an end in Nietzsche's position.[95] In the *Letter on Humanism* (1947), Heidegger clearly states his view that deeper than philosophy lies thinking (*Denken*), which he depicts as "a humanism that thinks the humanity of man from nearness to Being."[96] Heidegger also developed a theory of technology based on the ancient Greek concept of *techne* in arguing that in modern times human beings have come under the sway of an inauthentic technology whose essence is a way of revealing beings as a totality.[97]

Sartre, Merleau-Ponty, and French Phenomenology

Later phenomenology owes at least as much to Heidegger as to Husserl. The influence of their very different positions leads to an unusually wide series of reactions. Though Husserl was vastly influential, Heidegger was arguably even more so, particularly in France, to the point where he can legitimately be regarded as the French master thinker from roughly the end of the Second World War to the end of the century.[98] Throughout this period, phenomenology was the single most important tendency in France.

The peculiar French interest in phenomenology depends on the French reception of Hegel. During the 1930s, Alexandre Kojève gave a famous series of lectures on Hegel in Paris that influenced a number of thinkers who later became prominent throughout French culture, including French philosophy. It has been argued that all of French philosophy from the end of the 1930s, when Kojève's lecture series came to a close, until at least the end of the 1970s can be understood as a series of reactions to Hegel, who functions as the master thinker in twentieth-century French philosophy.[99] Hegel was already studied in France during his lifetime. Victor

Cousin, a prominent French philosopher, was a friend of his. Interest in Hegel, which later waned, was revived at the end of the 1920s in an important study of Hegel and Kierkegaard by Jean Wahl.[100] Husserl studies began early in the 1930s. Emmanuel Levinas, who emigrated to France from Lithuania, studied with (and was attracted to) both Husserl and Heidegger. He played a key role in introducing the former to French students. When Husserl presented lectures on the *Cartesian Meditations* at the Sorbonne in 1929, the text was translated into French by Levinas (and Gabrielle Pfeiffer). He also published an early book in French on Husserl.[101] Heidegger was initially translated into French in the early 1930s. After the war, interest in his thought grew in reaction against Sartre, by that time world-famous, but still flirting with the French Communist Party. In a public lecture delivered after the war, *Existentialism Is a Humanism* (1946), Sartre defended himself against antihumanist criticism of existentialism in claiming that, like Heidegger, he was a humanist.[102] Interest in Heidegger, who claimed in the *Letter on Humanism* (1947) to be misinterpreted by Sartre,[103] and who called attention to a distinction between Sartrean existentialism and his own phenomenological ontology, was also ceaselessly promoted by Jean Beaufret, a French phenomenologist. Heidegger was also a philosopher of choice for French philosophers in revolt against Sartre's enormous hegemony over French culture after the war. By the end of the 1950s or at the latest the early 1960s, Heidegger replaced Sartre as the French master thinker. At the time, it seemed that virtually every young French thinker not only flirted with Marxism but was also a Heideggerian.

Existentialism, a philosophical position centered on the fact of human existence, was arguably invented in reaction to Hegel by the Danish philosopher Søren Kierkegaard (1813–55). Various forms of this general position later flourished in France. Existentialism and phenomenology are related and often difficult to distinguish. If existentialism is included in phenomenology, then French "phenomenology" includes such important figures as Sartre, Merleau-Ponty, Gabriel Marcel – an existentialist who never claimed to be a phenomenologist – Levinas, Michel Henry, Paul Ricoeur, Jacques Derrida, perhaps Albert Camus, perhaps Simone de Beauvoir, and, among the younger generation, Jean-Luc Marion. Of these figures, phenomenologically speaking, the most important are without doubt Sartre and Merleau-Ponty.

Those working in phenomenology are often inspired by Hegel, or Husserl or Heidegger. A peculiarity of the French phenomenological discussion – as noted above, they are understood to employ the same method – is that French phenomenologists tend to draw their inspiration from all three thinkers. Sartre studied Husserl intensively for some four years. Though his command of German was imperfect, he struggled with Heidegger's thought in the original. And he seems to have absorbed Hegelian ideas, which were in the air, without ever studying Hegel directly or attending Kojève's lectures. The resultant synthesis is on display in *Being and Nothingness: A Phenomenological Essay on Ontology* (1943). It is not by chance that when it appeared during the war this work, which insisted on total freedom during the Nazi occupation of France, immediately made Sartre world-famous.

French philosophy and culture has been decisively influenced by Descartes over centuries. Sartre (1905–80) has often been called the last of the Cartesians. Merleau-Ponty (1907–61), who is critical of his French colleague, is often said to be the first post-Cartesian French thinker. Like Heidegger, Sartre and Merleau-Ponty also read intentionality as naming an irreducible ontological relation with the world. In an important early article, Sartre criticizes Husserlian idealism from the vantage point of realism.[104] In *Being and Nothingness*, his most important philosophical work, Sartre works out an impressive dualistic ontological analysis based on the distinction between the in-itself and the for-itself. In Sartre's hands, this Hegelian terminology refers, respectively, to the difference between things, which just are, and human beings, who choose what they wish to be in terms of a project. Sartre typically holds that human beings find themselves in a world they did not make, which is meaningless, but to which they give meaning in choosing their own ways of being. In an early article, Sartre discussed "Cartesian Freedom."[105] He picks up on that theme here in implausibly maintaining that we are always and wholly free.

Sartre is influenced by, but differs from, earlier phenomenologists. In the detailed introduction to *Being and Nothingness*, he develops a realistic approach to phenomenology in which the subject transcends mere appearances of the phenomenon, which also transcends knowledge that we have of it. This leads to an ontology defined as "the description of the phenomenon of being as it manifests itself."[106] Sartre immediately breaks with Heidegger in insisting on consciousness. He also breaks with Husserl, whose idealism he understands on the model of Berkeley, in promoting realism. Sartre understands consciousness as the transphenomenal dimension of the subject. Through consciousness we are directed toward objects that are out there in the world. "The first procedure of a philosophy," he writes, "ought to be to expel things from consciousness and to reestablish its true connection with the world. . . ."[107] Consciousness is always grounded in an immediate, non-reflective self-consciousness. Sartre understands consciousness along the lines of a causal theory of perception in which the object causes the phenomenon which is perceived and to which it cannot be reduced. "[T]he being of the phenomenon, although coextensive with the phenomenon, cannot be subject to the phenomenal condition, which is to exist only in so far as it reveals itself – and that consequently it surpasses the knowledge which we have of it and provides the basis for such knowledge."[108]

Sartre is not only a gifted philosopher, he is also a gifted literary critic and novelist who was awarded the Nobel Prize for literature, which he refused. His literary gifts are on display in a novel, *Nausea* (1938), in which, in a brilliant passage, he famously describes the nausea supposedly secreted by the roots of a chestnut tree.[109] *Being and Nothingness* contains a similarly brilliant passage about what Sartre calls "The look" (*le regard*), in which he analyzes ways in which we objectivate, or objectify, others. For instance, in a passage on shame, Sartre writes: "Pure shame is not a feeling of being this or that guilty object but in general of being *an* object; that is, of *recognizing myself* in this degraded, fixed, and dependent being which I am for the other."[110]

Sartre later went on to many other projects. For a time he turned to Marxism – he did not distinguish Marx and Marxism – in attempting, many observers think unsuccessfully, to synthesize his own brand of existentialism with both. According to Sartre, Marxism, which he calls the ideology of our time, is in danger of collapse without existentialism.[111] He worked out his view of Marxism in a huge, unedited study, *Critique of Dialectical Reason* (1960), in which he moved away from his earlier view of human individuals as always and wholly free in taking a contextual, historicist view of reason.[112] As part of his later concern to grasp individuals in the historical context, he produced an enormously long, but never completed, and unfortunately also unedited study of the French novelist, Gustave Flaubert.[113]

As a philosopher, Sartre, who had many other interests, always gave the impression of being an amateur of genius, but nonetheless still an amateur. As he grew older, he became increasingly self-indulgent, writing as much as fifty pages a day, which he published without editing or even rereading. In comparison with Sartre, Merleau-Ponty is a more orthodox thinker. Like Sartre, Merleau-Ponty also studied at the École normale supérieure, a select institution for the brightest students. Sartre, who taught in the French *lycée* before the war, never returned to teaching.

After the war, Merleau-Ponty taught in Lyons, Paris, and then at the Collège de France, an extremely prestigious institution where chairs are specifically created for and awarded to only one or two outstanding figures in a particular field. For a time Sartre and Merleau-Ponty were closely associated on various projects – for instance, they were co-founders of the important French intellectual journal *Les Temps Modernes* – but they later fell out after Sartre, who quarreled with virtually every intellectual figure of the time, attacked his colleague's views.[114] At odds with the often clannish, hothouse world of French philosophy, Merleau-Ponty, who thought for himself, possessed an original voice, and was critical of his colleagues, though in a very measured, more precise way than the unusually excitable Sartre. Unlike Sartre, who is mainly dependent on the traditional three Hs of French philosophy – Hegel, Husserl, and Heidegger – Merleau-Ponty draws on other sources, such as the French thinker Henri Bergson.

One area where the difference in style between Merleau-Ponty and Sartre is important is the history of philosophy. Though Sartre mentions historical figures, he rarely studied philosophical texts and is at best an uncertain commentator of other figures. Merleau-Ponty was much better at interpreting the history of philosophy, more aware of the significance of philosophical precedent. In an important remark about Hegel, he credits the German philosopher with being the central figure in nineteenth-century philosophy, the person who set the agenda for the twentieth-century discussion, including the French debate: "All the great philosophical ideas of the past century – the philosophies of Marx and Nietzsche, phenomenology, German existentialism, and psychoanalysis – had their beginnings in Hegel."[115] This passage suggests, correctly I think, that Hegel is not only a singularly important thinker, but that his theories largely determine the contemporary French debate, including the reception of Heidegger.

Merleau-Ponty died prematurely, before he had a chance to work out his full range of views. His writings fall very schematically into two main groups, philosophical psychology and phenomenology, which he considers together, and political philosophy. He was especially interested in Gestalt psychology, though critical of Wolfgang Köhler's work on brain states and of behaviorist claims about the supposed causal relation between mental activities and the physical organism. His critical relation to phenomenology, leading to his own position, turns on the Husserlian concept of reduction. For Merleau-Ponty, phenomenology must either be phenomenology without a phenomenological reduction or it is not possible at all. The preface to *Phenomenology of Perception* (1945), his most single most important treatise, comparable in importance to *Being and Nothingness*, contains a detailed critical discussion of Husserlian reduction. Merleau-Ponty here reacts against the later Husserl's conviction that reduction from the natural attitude to the transcendental plane, hence to the transcendental ego, must be the cornerstone of phenomenology. He objects that reduction is a process of infinite length. In a famous passage, he writes: "The most important lesson which the reduction teaches us is the impossibility of a complete reduction."[116]

This view of reduction led Merleau-Ponty to take a critical stance toward both Husserl and Heidegger. Noting that they propose very different conceptions of phenomenology, he writes in an important statement in the initial paragraph of *Phenomenology of Perception*:

> One may try to do away with these contradictions by making a distinction between Husserl's and Heidegger's phenomenologies; yet the whole of *Sein und Zeit* [*Being and Time*] springs from an indication given by Husserl and amounts to no more than an explicit account of the "natürlicher Weltbegriff" or the "Lebenswelt" which Husserl, toward the end of his life, identified as the central theme of phenomenology, with the result that the contradiction reappears in Husserl's own philosophy.[117]

This remark is doubly important. On the one hand, it points to a difficulty in Husserl's effort at pure, unfettered, presuppositionless description in his early breakthrough to phenomenology. If phenomenology depends on the life-world, or the natural attitude, then not only Kant, but also Husserl depends on unacknowledged presuppositions which undermine the very idea of philosophy as presuppositionless science. On the other hand, there is a deep contradiction in Heidegger, who refuses the reduction, hence the Husserlian conception of the subject as a transcendental ego, in favor of Dasein that is always already in the world. According to Merleau-Ponty, "Heidegger's 'being-in-the-world' appears only against the background of the phenomenological reduction."[118] The contradiction lies in the fact that Heidegger refuses but also depends on the phenomenological reduction.

Merleau-Ponty bases his phenomenology on a theory of perception he develops in the *Structure of Behavior* (1942)[119] and the *Phenomenology of Perception*. The former mainly presents his critique of various rival theories, especially behavioristic and causal perceptual models. The latter presents his own theory. Like Sartre, Merleau-Ponty typically insists that perceptual experience carries with it a relation to a world that transcends consciousness. He considers perception to be the privileged mode of access to that world. The problem lies in constructing an acceptable theory of perception. Merleau-Ponty undertakes to do this in the *Phenomenology of Perception*, to begin with through criticizing the familiar sense-datum approach. He rejects this thesis as misrepresenting the basic level of experience as consisting of "pure" sensations. Holding that perception always and necessarily refers to a world that cannot merely be reduced to our perceptions of it, he regards a sense-datum analysis of perception as the product of a mere intellectual analysis. He goes on to describe an original view of the role of the body in perception[120] in arguing that all perception is always from a point of view, or perspective. It is in terms of the body that we approach and perceive anything else. According to Merleau-Ponty, theories of the body and of perception are inseparable since, as he argues, the body is already a theory of perception.[121] He elaborates this theory in later chapters in the book, specifically applying it to the problem of knowledge. Merleau-Ponty's views of the primacy of perception, and consequences for the traditional problem of knowledge, are most concisely stated in a short presentation before the French Philosophical Society (Société française de philosophie). In arguing for the intrinsically historical character of knowledge, Hegel thinks that claims to know are dependent on, or relative to, hence circumscribed by, the historical moment. In a passage that marks his distance from Husserl and Heidegger and brings him close to Hegel, Merleau-Ponty makes a similar point. According to him, all our cognitive claims are imperfect, hence never absolute, always dependent on the historical moment. "But in reality the ideas to which we recur are valid only for a period of our lives or for a period in the history of our culture. Evidence is never apodictic, nor is thought timeless. . . ."[122]

Like Sartre, Merleau-Ponty wrote on political theory and political events. Sartre, who was originally apolitical, later moved closer to theoretical Marxism. Merleau-Ponty, who was originally close to Marxism in practice, especially the French form of Trotskyism, later distanced himself from it. In *Humanism and Terror* (1947), he took a rather indulgent view of Marxism in suggesting that certain difficulties in real human politics cannot be avoided.[123] In the *Adventures of the Dialectic* (1955), he later criticized Marxism for incorrectly attempting to claim total knowledge of history.[124]

Heidegger's Hermeneutical Students: Gadamer and Derrida

The influence of Husserlian phenomenology, both directly and indirectly through later thinkers he influenced, was strong throughout the entire twentieth century and remains strong in the debate. The list of those who belong to the wider phenomenological family is very long. Though many others could be mentioned – Paul Ricoeur and Michel Henry are particularly deserving of separate treatment in view of their importance – arguably the two most influential phenomenologists at the end of the twentieth century were Heidegger's two closest followers, the German thinker Hans-Georg Gadamer and, if he is a phenomenologist, the French thinker Jacques Derrida.

Other than their strong relation to Heidegger, these two thinkers are very different. Gadamer (1900–2002) studied with Heidegger, by whom he was very strongly influenced and to whom he remained loyal both personally and philosophically. Because of his link to National Socialism, after the war Heidegger was forced out of the University of Freiburg. Gadamer later intervened to make it possible for him to return to teaching.

During Gadamer's unusually long career – more than eighty years – he did important work in Greek philosophy and in hermeneutics, for which he is best known. Gadamer's work is generally characterized by an unusually strong grasp of the history of philosophy and culture in general. He began as a specialist in Greek philosophy. His dissertation was on Plato[125] and over the years he published several other books on aspects of Greek philosophy.[126] He also published often very interesting studies of a number of earlier philosophical figures and even poets,[127] as well as on specific themes in emphasizing the relation to the historical moment. For instance, in arguing against the idea of timeless reason, he pointed usefully to the need to understand reason differently after the increasing separation between science and philosophy due to the rise of modern science.[128]

His career did not really begin to take off until the appearance of *Truth and Method* (1960), an important study of hermeneutics he published at age 60.[129] The title, which suggests a method leading to truth, perhaps even a Cartesian method, is misleading. In place of method, Gadamer substitutes a form of hermeneutics, or interpretation. Heidegger raises this theme in *Being and Time* in his accounts of interpretation and understanding. In *Truth and Method*, Gadamer pursues this theme in a different way in resituating it in the lengthy prior debate about hermeneutics, which Heidegger mainly ignores.

Hermeneutics (from Gr. *hermeneuein*, "to interpret") is already discussed by Aristotle.[130] Since the work of Friedrich Schleiermacher, the great German Protestant theologian and Plato scholar, who was a close contemporary of Hegel, in the first quarter of the nineteenth century,[131] hermeneutics has been associated with Protestant interpretation of sacred texts. Gadamer's main aim in his book lies in clarifying the concept of understanding, both in itself and in relation to what he calls "the methodology of the human sciences."[132] According to him, understanding, which is not confined to knowledge, is literally everywhere involved in the way we relate to the world. Gadamer, who points out that even natural science relies on understanding functions within science – this is for him an unclarified term – is mainly interested in claims for truth through understanding outside science, particularly in the appropriation of the central texts of the philosophical tradition and in what he calls "the experience of truth that comes to us through the work of art."[133]

Gadamer's view of hermeneutics is influenced by Husserl's understanding of phenomenological description, Dilthey's attention to the historical horizon as the background for all philosophy, and Heidegger, whose ideas resonate everywhere in his former student's writing. In his theory of hermeneutical understanding Gadamer usefully corrects Heidegger. Heidegger's concern to recover the question of the meaning of being as it was originally raised in early Greek philosophy suggests that one can go back behind the historical tradition. Gadamer, on the contrary, insists on the unavoidable embeddedness of interpretation in an ongoing historical context, which cannot be bracketed, or put out of play. He also resists in this way Husserl's device of phenomenological reduction. On that specific point, he is close to such other phenomenologists as Hegel and Merleau-Ponty, who also stress the importance of history.

According to Gadamer, all interpretation of whatever kind always take place in a cultural context, which changes through history. Any interpreter of any text belongs to a particular culture. The work of interpretation consists in an interplay between past and present, what Gadamer calls a fusion of horizons, between the text to be understood and the present perspective within which the interpreter is situated. We never know what is really in any particular text since there is no way to go beyond our present perspective, which always functions as a horizon, or limit, that structures our understanding.

Derrida (1930–2004) wrote prolifically on an unusually wide number of topics. He was born in Algeria, and only later emigrated to France as a young man to study at the École normale supérieure. Yet he is in a number of ways quintessentially French. Derrida is a cross-over figure whose work combines philosophical and literary themes. His main influences lie in such widely scattered figures as Husserl, Heidegger, Nietzsche, Freud, and Levinas. He has long been vastly more influential in the US, where his work spawned a minor cottage industry, especially in literary studies of various kinds, than in France. In France, he was mainly active outside the usual educational channels, earlier as a teacher at the École normale supérieure and then for many years at the School for Advanced Studies in the Social Sciences (École des hautes études en sciences sociales).

Derrida began as a strong critic of Husserl. As a student, he studied Husserl very closely and criticized him in several early texts.[134] He then turned to Heidegger, whose writings and concepts he commented on in a long series of unusually detailed analyses.[135] During this period, he also produced a lengthy, nearly impenetrable study of Hegel, *Glas*, mentioned above, intended to refute the very idea of total system he attributes to the German thinker, as well as studies of Freud[136] and other figures. He later turned to a series of other themes, whose relation is not always clear, including Marx[137] and religion.[138]

His work combines the typical French literary concern with close textual analysis (*explication de texte*), which he applies to philosophical texts, with an often playful, ambiguous writing style in availing himself of the ambiguities of the French language. He is best known for the term "deconstruction" (*déconstruction*), which he introduced into philosophy in the late 1960s. Derrida never defined this term in any of his writings and in fact strenuously resisted any effort to provide a clear description of his position.[139] This term is arguably best understood in the context of his strenuous effort to subvert the very possibility of knowledge. Heidegger uses the term "deconstruction" (*Abbau*) as part of his effort to return to the question of the meaning of being as it was arguably originally raised by destroying the subsequent history of ontology, hence stripping away the later accretions that have grown up around it. Derrida, who writes in Heidegger's wake, after the ostensible failure of the latter's effort, uses the same term negatively in order, like Rorty, with whom he is sometimes compared, to undercut the very possibility of a positive argument for knowledge

Derrida is an epistemological skeptic of a peculiar kind. He does not, like Rorty, claim that no argument for knowledge works. He, rather, attempts to demonstrate that no argument for knowledge can possibly work. His argument consists in two steps. First, he indexes everything to language through the simple device of claiming, as he puts it, "There is nothing outside the text."[140] If there is nothing outside the text, then any argument for knowledge must be made on a textual basis. The counter-argument that no such argument can be made is borrowed from Hegel. Early in the *Phenomenology of Spirit*, Hegel suggests in effect that since language is general, you cannot say what you mean nor mean what you say.[141] Hegel, who is not a skeptic, is merely pointing to the difficulty in bringing words together with objects as part of his formulation of a theory of knowledge. His point can be formulated as the claim that words are inherently general but things to which they refer are singular. Derrida, who is a skeptic, extends Hegel's argument to any effort to say things with words in undercutting the very possibility of definite reference. If knowledge requires us to pick out objects through words, then Derrida shows that no argument can suffice to do so. It follows that, if this argument goes through, knowledge is impossible.

6

Anglo-American Analytic Philosophy

This chapter will consider Anglo-American analytic philosophy, understood as a specific approach that came into being toward the beginning of the last century at the University of Cambridge in England before later spreading to the US and then rapidly around the world. The difficulty of identifying which thinker belongs to which tradition, which Marxism settled through political criteria, is a philosophical problem in analytic philosophy. Over a long period that now seems to be ending, analytic figures continually featured a political unity in refuting other main positions. It should not be forgotten that this tendency arose in the successful revolt against and clear defeat of British idealism. Yet from the start analytic philosophy was marked by sharp differences in concept and content. The political unity of analytic philosophy was important in the evolution of this tendency in two main ways. As in Marxism, a front united against other, rival philosophical movements worked well to conceal divergences, even sharp oppositions, between the various thinkers. Though they quarreled among themselves, Marxists always, or nearly always, united behind political leaders and political doctrines for the purpose of taking political power in society as a whole. Analytic thinkers, who seek political power within the academy, are content to work within it. The concern with political hegemony among philosophers in the academy later led on to visible, even major, tensions manifest in the unusually sharp struggles between the main analytic thinkers resulting in what currrently looks very much like the growing dissolution of whatever "Anglo-American analytic philosophy" has come to mean in the wider philosophical discussion.

When, where, and with whom analytic philosophy begins depends on the observer. According to Anthony Quinton, analytic philosophy only began in 1912 with the arrival of Wittgenstein at Cambridge.[1] For Morris Weitz, analytic philosophy employs a method, called philosophical analysis, which was invented by Russell and then only later refined by others.[2] In the opinion of Michael Dummett, analytic philosophy is a misnomer for Austro-American philosophy, which includes both phenomenology, originated by Husserl, and what later became Anglo-American analytic philosophy, which begins in Frege.[3]

The difficulty in describing analytic philosophy is a function of the unusual way it came into being. With the exception of analytic philosophy, all the main tendencies of the last century at least initially centered on the ideas of no more than a single important thinker – Marxism on Engels, so-called continental philosophy on Husserl, and pragmatism on Peirce. As a direct consequence, each of these three movements at least began with a central focus that even initially analytic philosophy never possessed. Analytic philosophy differs from the other main philosophical tendencies of the last century in that it was always less the result of the intervention and later influence of a single striking figure than a kind of coalition that came together for a specific purpose, namely opposing British idealism, the reigning position in Britain as analytic philosophy was emerging around 1900. The fact that analytic philosophy never, even as it was beginning, possessed a single central focus akin to those of the other main philosophical approaches gives it not only a comparative richness leading to its extension in many different directions but also an important series of differences, even disparities, in the views of the main early protagonists that makes it very difficult, more so than for the other main tendencies in this period, even to name the main analytic themes.

On the Analytic Revolt Against Idealism

There is a difference between the origins of Anglo-American analytic philosophy and those of analytic philosophy *per se.* Although, in different ways, philosophical analysis and, by extension, analytic philosophy arguably go back to the Greek tradition, analytic philosophy as we know it today is much younger.

Speaking generally, Anglo-American analytic philosophy was founded by three thinkers active in the University of Cambridge early in the twentieth century, two Englishmen, Bertrand Russell and G. E. Moore, and the Austrian Ludwig Wittgenstein, as well as the German Gottlob Frege, who taught in Jena. Through Russell, Frege, who did more than anyone to invent modern logic and modern mathematical logic, has always been very influential on analytic philosophy. Wittgenstein, who came to Cambridge as Russell's student, later eclipsed his teacher. Yet the main figures of early analytic philosophy as it was emerging in England around the turn of the twentieth century, before Wittgenstein's arrival in Cambridge, were unquestionably Moore and Russell.

In order to understand the origins of Anglo-American analytic philosophy, it will be useful to say a word about philosophical idealism. Idealism dominated the philosophical scene in Germany from Kant at least to Hegel and, depending on how he is interpreted, through Marx. As noted above, though idealism was still strongly dominant in German philosophy when Hegel died in 1831, after his death it went into a decline, which was only interrupted when it made a comeback in the 1860s through the return to Kant, leading to different German schools of neo-Kantianism. Starting in 1865 with the publication of Stirling's *The Secret of Hegel*,[4] idealism spread rapidly through British philosophy. British idealism, which began earlier, is often said to include such names as Samuel Taylor Coleridge, J. F. Ferrier, T. H. Green, Edward Caird, F. H. Bradley, J. M. E. McTaggart, and Bernard Bosanquet.[5]

As analytic philosophy began to emerge in England around the turn of the twentieth century, British idealism was still the dominant philosophical tendency. The origins of analytic philosophy in England lie in Moore's and Russell's shared revolt against idealism. The proto-analyst Frege criticized Husserl before he turned to phenomenology and perhaps even to idealism. Yet there is no reason to believe he was ill-disposed toward idealism. Since he published in an idealist journal, it has been suggested he may even have considered himself to be an idealist.[6] Like Frege, Wittgenstein, another of the central early analytic thinkers, was also not much concerned with idealism. His important early work, *Tractatus Logico-Philosophicus*, has only a single reference to this doctrine. In a passage on why the logic of facts cannot be represented, Wittgenstein remarks in passing, in alluding to Kant, that the idealist view of space fails to explain its many forms.[7]

It is unclear precisely how Moore and Russell, the founders of analytic philosophy in England, related to idealism. As undergraduate students of the Cambridge idealist McTaggart, they may have been, or at least may have considered themselves to be, idealists.[8] In the short preface to his dissertation, which became his first book, *An Essay on the Foundations of Geometry* (1897), Russell says that in logic he has learned the most from Bradley, Sigwart, and Bosanquet.[9] Similarly, in Moore's first paper, "In What Sense, If Any, Do Past and Future Time Exist?" (1897), he follows Bradley, and his methods, in arguing that time is unreal.[10] Yet Moore seems to have rapidly changed his mind and, as early as 1898, to have convinced Russell that Bradley and, by extension, idealism were profoundly mistaken.[11] The identification with idealism, if it was one, was superficial and of short duration, since both Moore and Russell quickly became almost viscerally opposed to it.

Moore engineered the analytic turn away from idealism in his famous, but now little-read, article "The Refutation of Idealism" (1903).[12] This influential text was directed against idealism in all its forms, including British idealism, Hegel, Kant, and Berkeley. In the second edition of the *Critique of Pure Reason*, Kant has added his famous "Refutation of Idealism."[13] However, as an empirical realist and a transcendental idealist, his concern was to refute *bad* idealism, and not idealism *per se*. Here and in other passages, he rejects any effort to question the existence of the external world, which is supposedly placed in doubt by bad idealism. Moore generalizes but also transforms Kant's complaint in a direct attack on idealism of all kinds. His article represents an attempt, not to continue Kant, but rather to resolve the problem which, by implication, Kant had not resolved.

Moore's refutation rests on five unidentified, related claims growing out of Kant's earlier effort to refute idealism. First, Kant's attempt points to an important, but still unresolved, problem; second, there is a view, position, or theory that corresponds to the term "idealism"; third, idealism as a whole turns on a single, central, identifiable, mistaken doctrine; fourth, this doctrine consists of wrongfully denying the existence of the external world; and, fifth, this mistaken position can be defeated through a justified, but common-sense claim for direct knowledge.

Each of these claims is either false or at least undemonstrated and indemonstrable. As part of the justification of his own intervention in the debate, Moore apparently assumes – but without demonstration – that Kant's refutation fails. Moore further assumes there is something called idealism, which turns on a central, shared doctrine, though there are only a number of disparate idealisms that have no single identifiable doctrine in common. No main form of idealism, and perhaps none at all (Moore names none), denies the existence of the external world. And for Moore's supposed refutation of idealism to count – his proposed alternative consists in the reassertion of what he took to be common-sense claims, such as "Here is one hand . . . and here is another"[14] – he needs not merely to assert such claims dogmatically but further to show why they should be accepted, say through an epistemological argument.

Though weakly argued, Moore's refutation of idealism was extremely influential in the British discussion. It effectively vanquished British idealism, which quickly disappeared with little trace. Furthermore, it led to an enduring analytic turn against idealism of all kinds, which has never been revoked and about which few analytic thinkers were even tolerably informed,[15] and, by extension, to a certain disdain for the history of philosophy. Thus Rorty reports Quine's quip about the contrast between those interested in the history of philosophy and those interested in philosophy.[16]

The remark attributed to Quine reveals a dismissive attitude about the history of philosophy linked to a certain resistance among analytic thinkers about acknowledging the historical nature of the philosophical discipline. Like a number of earlier thinkers, such as Descartes and Kant, analytic philosophers tend to concentrate on problems not people, arguments and not texts. Analytic thinkers, who often know little about the history of philosophy, were for many years distinguished by the conviction that there is little or nothing to be learned by studying earlier philosophers. The unfortunate result was to make it more difficult for analytic thinkers to learn from a philosophical tradition that they, like Kant, thought was on the wrong track and often neglected to study. For many years, analytic philosophy took an anti-historical view of philosophy, and an ahistorical view of analytic philosophy. Hilary Putnam, for instance, mistakenly attributes to Hegel the view that "mind *makes up* the world,"[17] and describes idealism as the idea that "objects that are not perceived make no sense."[18] This tendency has now begun to change from within, as it were. Hans Sluga claims that analytic philosophy wrongly depicts its own history as non-historical and attacks Dummett, an important Frege scholar, for wrongly attributing an ahistorical approach to Frege.[19] More recently, analytic philosophy has produced a series of often excellent historians. They include such specialists of ancient philosophy as G. E. L. Owen and Myles Burnyeat, and, more generally, Ayer, Dummett, D. F. Pears, John Passmore, Alberto Coffa, Michael Friedman, Peter Hylton and others.

Analysis, Analyticity, and Analytic Philosophy

Analytic philosophy makes a point of practicing analysis, for which there has never been any single or even widely accepted definition, conception, or method. As remarked above, different forms of analysis go all the way back to Greek philosophy. Analytic thinkers see Aristotle and Hume as among their main predecessors. Kant, who insists on the distinction between analytic and synthetic propositions, famously holds that analytic propositions are not ampliative but merely explicative. Yet following Quine's celebrated attack on the analytic–synthetic distinction, analytic thinkers are generally careful about endorsing any version of the Kantian view.[20]

There is no agreement about the nature and limits of philosophical analysis as it is understood in analytic philosophy. Different analytic thinkers disagree among themselves. It is generally thought that all those committed to analysis share the ideal of a careful, detailed, rigorous approach that illuminates our concepts by examining how we utilize them in language. After that minimal claim, opinion differs. Analysis cannot be assimilated to a doctrine, since there is no common doctrine that all analytic thinkers share. Often it is directed against metaphysics, and even more often against idealism, though it is never clear what "metaphysics" or "idealism" means. It is also sometimes suggested that, like chemistry, analysis consists in studying the parts of the things under investigation and their various forms of interrelation.

Analysis reached a new stage in the writings of Moore and Russell. Indeed, it is sometimes said that Russell was the first to articulate the method of analysis as well as its most important practitioner. Yet the two thinkers' approaches to philosophical analysis are very different, even incompatible.

Moore is sometimes held to believe that philosophy consists in analysis. He practiced different forms of analysis but only described what he thought he was doing after many years. For Moore, the philosopher's task lies in formulating definitions as a way of clarifying philosophical claims. He suggested in reply to a critical article[21] that analysis consists in finding in a proposition an equivalent but not mentioned concept, as "male sibling" yields the analysis of "brother." Yet unlike later linguistic analysts, Moore explicitly claims not to analyze verbal expressions.[22] For him, analysis of propositions, which has only an indirect epistemic role, turns attention away from questions about whether a proposition is true or whether it can be known to be true.

In Russell's account, philosophy sounds like conceptual chemistry that decomposes things into their constituent parts, out of which they are then synthesized. He specifically says that philosophy consists in "logical analysis . . . followed by logical synthesis."[23] Russell's view of analysis derives from his work in logic and mathematics. Since, for Russell, logic is central to philosophy,[24] philosophy largely becomes the study of logic understood as philosophical method.[25] In his work in logic, Russell extended the findings of Frege, who showed that arithmetic could be reduced to pure logic,[26] but did not deal with other branches of mathematics. Russell's logicism generalized this approach to mathematics in all its many forms. He went to great lengths to define the basic concepts of mathematics in purely logical terms but, working with Alfred North Whitehead, was less successful in deriving the fundamental principles of mathematics from purely logical laws.[27] The *locus classicus* of his view is contained in his theory of descriptions. Here Russell distinguishes between two main kinds of knowledge, that is, knowledge by acquaintance and by description.[28] J. S. Mill introduced the distinction between denotation, that is, the individual entities to which a term applies, which is also called its extension, and connotation, or the attributes by which it is defined, also called its intension. Following Mill's distinction, Russell worked out a theory of denoting that he presented in a famous article entitled "On Denoting" (1905). According to Russell, the surface forms of language hide a rather different logical form that can only be brought out through analysis. He influentially claims that the statement "the present king of France is bald" can be analyzed as the conjunction of no less than three statements: there is a present king of France, there is one and only one king of France, and he is bald. Since there is no present king of France, the statement is false.[29] Russell's theory of descriptions was later attacked by P. F. Strawson in an influential paper on the grounds that it requires an unwarranted revision of our ordinary conception of speech.[30]

Later analytic thinkers extend the conception of analysis in various ways. Analysis has often been understood as in principle reductive or eliminative, that is, as committed either to reducing one kind of item, either a linguistic statement, or again a thing, to another statement or thing, or to eliminating it entirely. According to the empirical criterion of meaning, statements that cannot be verified empirically are said to be meaningless. Carnap relies on the idea that what cannot be known empirically is obviously not real, and on the further idea that merely cognitive reference cannot be meaningful. He famously attacks Heidegger in "The Elimination of Metaphysics Through Logical Analysis of Language" (1931)[31] in arguing for the meaninglessness of all metaphysics. Following the early Wittgenstein's view[32] that metaphysical sentences are unverifiable, hence meaningless, he argues that statements either asserting or denying the reality of the external world are mere pseudo-statements. At this point, when Carnap understood "metaphysics" as consisting in claims about the essence of things which transcend empirical experience, he was very close to what Kant understood as bad metaphysics. Like Peirce, Carnap's version of the scientific worldview is similar to the concern with good metaphysics which already motivated Hume and Kant.

Physicalism, or the doctrine that everything is physical, is a variant of materialism, which goes back to ancient Greek materialism. Physicalism comes in a profusion of varieties. Some physicalists, such as Carnap, argue that all the sciences can be replaced through physics.[33] Philosophy of mind, which is related to physicalism, goes all the way back to Plato and Aristotle. Analytic philosophers of mind often argue some version of the view that the mind is the brain, as in so-called "mind–brain identity theory" – also called type-identity theory or reductive materialism, illustrated by J. J. C. Smart, U. T. Place and David Armstrong – or defend eliminativism, that is, the view that all mental talk can be replaced by physical talk, or champion functionalism, as Putnam has done. Others adopt an intermediate view. Thus Donald Davidson argues for anomalous monism, according to which mental events just are physical events, but the former cannot be replaced by the latter.[34]

Strawson advances an influential conception of what he calls descriptive metaphysics, understood as an alternative to rational reconstruction in ideal, as contrasted with ordinary, language. Descriptive metaphysics is roughly the effort, as Strawson puts it, "to describe the complex pattern of logical behavior which the concepts of daily life exhibit."[35] He does this most prominently in his book entitled *Individuals* (1959),[36] in which he develops the view that material objects are basic particulars, and a further thesis concerning the traditional mind–body problem. In respect to the latter, he attacks as incoherent two main approaches, including the familiar Cartesian ascription of states of consciousness to mental substance and the so-called "no ownership" theory, for which states of consciousness are not ascribed to anything or anyone. A version of the latter is defended by Gilbert Ryle, who, in his well-known attack on Cartesianism, tries to exorcize what he regards as the ghost in the machine as a mistaken way of speaking about mind as the counterpart of the body as well as in order to support behaviorism.[37]

A rather different conception of analysis is illustrated by Dummett, an original thinker as well as an analytic historian of philosophy. Dummett, who relies on Frege, believes that analytic philosophy exemplifies a linguistic turn. Philosophy can account for thought through a philosophical account of language and only in this way.[38] Dummett points toward the early Wittgenstein's idea that the problem does not lie in investigating phenomena, but rather in "the *kind of statement* that we make about phenomena."[39] Today we are used to the idea that analytic philosophy is centrally dependent on the concern with language. In an anthology of classic papers that appeared around the time the linguistic approach was already waning, Rorty popularized the term "linguistic turn"[40] as referring to "linguistic philosophy," "linguistic philosophers," and "linguistic methods." Yet this influence was not immediately recognized. Thus as late as 1918, Russell felt compelled to write: "The influence of language on philosophy has, I believe, been profound and almost unrecognized."[41] Dummett goes on to argue that in concentrating on the particular linguistic mode of expression, analytic thinkers like Wittgenstein turned away from old philosophical questions in favor of new ones.[42] A similar point is made by Quine, who suggests, in reference to Carnap, the importance of semantic ascent, which he understands as the shift from talking about objects to talking about words.[43] A more radical form of linguistic turn lies in the early Wittgenstein's view that most of the problems and questions that make up the philosophical debate are not false, but nonsensical, due to the failure to understand how language works.[44] This leads to the view that philosophy in all its many forms consists in the critique of language.[45]

Moore, Russell, and Early Analytic Philosophy

Idealism, materialism, and realism are often thought of as incompatible. Both Marxism and analytic philosophy are not only opposed to, but further understand themselves through their rejection of, idealism. The analytic rejection of idealism brings together often very disparate thinkers, beginning with the founders of Anglo-American philosophy, Moore and Russell. These two thinkers, who were undergraduates at the same time at Cambridge and later stayed on to teach there, were very different, in some ways sharply opposed. They share a common role in founding analytic philosophy by refuting British idealism, as well as a general commitment to empiricism – Moore favored an intuitive form of empiricism and Russell favored a logical form of empiricism, and an effort to avoid epistemology through some kind of claim for immediate acquaintance based on either common sense, sense-data, or both. Yet beyond this very circumscribed, minimal agreement, they seem otherwise to have little in common. Two more different thinkers, unlike in nearly every respect, have rarely been associated within a single conceptual tendency.

Moore and Russell, who are both important thinkers, and who are often treated together,[46] are like two enormous horses that, though hitched to the same analytic cart, are pulling in different directions. Their differences begin with their respective backgrounds. Moore, who began in classics, was always concerned with details, whereas Russell, who studied mathematics, painted with a much broader brush. Though they often talked about similar topics, such as sense-data,[47] or analysis, their views were usually different, often incompatible. The contest between them, which was complex, continued over many years, during which each influenced the other. During this period the emergence of Vienna Circle positivism, which was allied to Russell, tipped the balance in his favor. The result was less to resolve the differences between Moore and Russell, for instance by working out a common program, which was never accomplished, than to create a gradual analytic disaffection for Moore, who has been thoroughly superseded and now belongs to the past – oddly enough for a major thinker, his books are now out of print – in favor of Russell, who in many ways remains the key figure of Anglo-American analytic philosophy despite his later eclipse by his student Wittgenstein.

Moore (1873–1958) and Russell (1872–1970) were close contemporaries. Moore did work once regarded as groundbreaking in epistemology and moral philosophy. Somewhat like Berkeley, he typically believed that many of the ordinary philosophical views simply ran against the largely correct views of the ordinary person. Like Thomas Reid, he was a defender of common sense, which he variously equated with views that a great number of people hold at a given time or are disposed to hold. In "A Defense of Common Sense" (1925), he claimed there is a vast body of shared convictions about "the world." For instance, he claimed to know with certainty there are other human beings with whom he can communicate. Indeed, according to Moore, the common-sense view cannot be denied since it is only meaningful if people hold the view, that is, if it is true.[48]

In the context of early analytic philosophy, Moore's appeal to common sense is important for two reasons. First, it provides a way of countering idealism that, at least on Moore's account, advances claims everyone knows to be wrong. The appeal to common sense is designed to restore philosophical sanity by disqualifying much of what passes for philosophy. Second, common sense points to a way around the difficult problem of justifying claims to know in showing how to make epistemological assertions without needing to justify them. According to Kant, the difference between dogmatism, which merely asserts its claims, hence must in all cases be rejected, and philosophy, which is critical, hence possibly acceptable, is that only the latter argues its claims. In Moore, analytic philosophy returns to what for Kant would be a form of dogmatism. Moore believes that the question of whether we know or how we know can be satisfactorily solved merely by asserting, Kant would say dogmatically asserting, what everyone already knows.

When he wrote "The Refutation of Idealism," Moore believed in immediate knowledge of material things. Later he took the position that we are directly cognizant of sense-data that refer to material things. Analysis of ordinary propositions about familiar objects – "This is a hand" – bring in sense-data, and the problem consists in understanding the relation between the sense-data and the object.

Moore's work is mainly piecemeal. Other than many articles, his main work is *Principia Ethica* (1903), in which he argued for the indefinability of "good" and discussed what he called the naturalistic fallacy. According to this fallacy, no definition of good is satisfactory, since it resists definition, analysis, or any attempt to pin it down.[49] In refuting ethical naturalism, Moore argues for an objectivist position as opposed to judgments about the good on the grounds that they refer not to natural but rather to non-natural properties.

Moore was an essentially private and uncontroversial figure, wholly devoted to philosophy. Somewhat like his pragmatist colleague Dewey, Russell was not only an important philosopher, but also a public figure, and in Russell's case a very controversial one. Russell, who was interested in education and social reform, intervened in the public debate on such themes as pacifism, which he recommended, and nuclear arms, which he opposed. Unlike Moore, Russell wrote a great many books on a wide variety of popular or semi-popular topics, such as Bolshevism – Russell thought the price to pay could not be justified and in any case communism was likely to miscarry;[50] *Marriage and Morals*, in which he extolled the importance of the institution of marriage but advocated premarital sex;[51] *The ABC of Relativity*, which he explained in simple terms, accessible to the layman;[52] and his autobiography.[53] He also wrote many books, too numerous even to mention individually here, on a virtually limitless series of more technical "philosophical" topics.

His main "philosophical" contributions are usually regarded as falling under three headings: philosophical logic, which turns on the idea that mathematics just is logic, also known as logicism; the foundations of mathematics; and epistemology and metaphysics. Yet he also wrote at length on individual thinkers, including an important early book on Leibniz,[54] on the history of philosophy,[55] on ethics,[56] and on religion,[57] among other topics.

Russell cites Moore often in his early writings. At the time he wrote the *Principles of Mathematics* (1902) he generously believed that the main features of his position on the basic problems of philosophy all derived from Moore.[58] Yet even here, his position was very different from his Cambridge colleague's. One difference is his distrust of intuition, which Moore favored. Another is his concern with science and mathematics, which never interested Moore. A third is the complex interaction with Frege. In briefest terms, Frege, who was also committed to logicism, attempted to show in a two-volume work that arithmetic can be constructed on the basis of pure logic and set theory. The first volume appeared in 1893. As the second volume was going to press in 1903, Russell pointed out a paradox, which later became known as Russell's Paradox. This paradox, which concerns the self-membership of classes, results from the formation of the class of all classes that is not a member of itself. In a word, if such a class exists, it is a member of itself if and only if it is not a member of itself.[59]

Russell's critique was devastating for Frege's program. Though he destroyed Frege's specific commitment to logicism, Russell, who, as noted above, was much influenced by Frege, remained committed to the general logicist ideal. Frege's influence is visible in Russell's own logicism as well as in his commitment to making set theory work, an interest which continued until he finally dispensed with classes or sets in his so-called "no-class theory" of classes. The latter, which can be understood as intended to solve the problem created by the self-membership of classes, consists in segregating, or dividing, properties, relations and sets, or classes, into types. Russell later claimed that his logical atomism, his most distinctive philosophical contribution, was strengthened by his theory of types.[60]

Under Frege's influence, Russell did important work at the confluence of logic and mathematics. His most influential philosophical contribution is arguably his theory of logical atomism. Since the time of the British empiricists, British philosophy has always favored empiricism of various kinds. Distantly following Reid, Moore developed an intuitive form of empiricism. In combining traditional British empiricism and the latest logical techniques, Russell, who distrusted intuition, worked out a logical form of empiricism under the heading of logical atomism.

Russell's theory of logical atomism – the term occurs in a paper as early as 1911[61] – was most fully described in a series of eight public lectures delivered early in 1918. Wittgenstein, who is sometimes regarded as the leading analytic philosopher of the twentieth century, came to Cambridge to study with Russell, whom he deeply influenced, in 1912. In the published version of his text, Russell prefaced his lectures by saying he will be explaining ideas derived from his friend and pupil Wittgenstein.[62]

In calling attention to his logicist view that mathematics depends on logic, he notes that he eschews a monistic, or holistic, logic, which he describes as generally Hegelian, in favor of an atomistic logic. The world, he comments, consists in "many separate things," hence it does not consist in "a single indivisible Reality."[63] The task of his lectures lies in justifying what he calls "the process of analysis" supporting this approach in terms of "absolutely undeniable data."[64] He calls his doctrine logical atomism. He intends to arrive not at ultimate physical constituents of the universe, the kind of thing one might expect from natural science, but rather at so-called "logical atoms," or particulars as the end point of philosophical analysis. "The reason that I call my doctrine *logical* atomism," he writes, "is because the atoms that I wish to arrive at as the sort of last residue in analysis are logical atoms and not physical atoms."[65] In disregarding traditional views of substance, or matter, Russell construes these logical atoms as "little patches of colour or sounds, momentary things,"[66] what he later in the lectures calls sense-data.

There are in general two ways to justify this claim. One is to argue empirically that experience leads to logical atoms. The other is to argue on a priori grounds that this must be the case. Russell, who is an empiricist, wants to show that the right kind of empiricism will support his claim. His problem in justifying philosophical analysis as leading to logical atoms lies in rebuilding traditional British empiricism on a firm foundation by taking into account the latest logical techniques. His argument is based on facts as the sort of thing that everyone will grant and which are, as says, "the kind of thing that makes a proposition true or false."[67] Facts are not subjective but objective, out there in the world, so to speak.

Russell presupposes that since there is not an infinite regress, words correspond to things at a certain point in philosophical analysis. In order to justify his claim, Russell needs to show that facts can be analyzed. Propositions are composed of and analyzable into their component words. There is a difference between description and acquaintance. The meanings of words depend on description, but description finally depends on acquaintaince, as knowing the meaning of red depends, as Russell observes, on seeing red things.[68]

In an ideal language there would be a one-to-one correspondence of one word for one thing. For Russell, who denies the holistic approach, parenthetically defended by Leibniz, according to which every single .thing is internally related to, hence, implies everything else, in ordinary language we have to do with independent particulars. He also believes the simpler is easier to know than the more complex.[69] According to

Russell, material objects, or particulars, yield to analysis as a series of sense-data. He observes that a given thing, which appears differently at different times, consists in all the ways it appears, which are mere sense-data.[70] In a word, what we see when we see a thing, say a chair, is not the chair, or the particular, but "the same sense-datum of that chair at that moment," that is, how it appears to us.[71]

On Wittgenstein

It is not easy to talk about Ludwig Wittgenstein (1889–1951), who simply defies ordinary forms of classification, other than in superlatives. He is arguably the most influential, still the most important, the most interesting, and finally the most elusive of all the analytic thinkers. Wittgenstein, an Austrian who was born in Vienna, studied mechanical engineering in Linz, Berlin, and Manchester before going to Cambridge to work with Russell, whose *Principles of Mathematics* he happened to have read. He served in the Austrian Army during the First World War, during which time he also completed the *Tractatus Logico-Philosophicus* (1921), his first, highly enigmatic book, and the only book he published during his lifetime. After the war, he worked as a schoolteacher in two villages in Austria – Wittgenstein, who was very rigid, beat the children – and as a self-taught architect in Vienna before returning to Cambridge in 1929, where, except for some interruptions, he remained for the rest of his career. A member of an extremely rich family, he gave away all his money. He suffered as a severely repressed homosexual in England at a time when homosexuality was illegal. It should not be forgotten that about the same time another repressed homosexual, the brilliant English mathematician, Alan Turing, who made important early contributions to the relation between computers and the mind, committed suicide two years after facing trial on account of his sexual identity. It is sometimes said that the obscure last proposition of the *Tractatus* – "what we cannot speak about we must pass over in silence"[72] – was Wittgenstein's way of alluding to what he could not bring himself to mention.

Almost everything Wittgenstein did in philosophy was influential. The transition from a kind of equilibrium between Moore and Russell to a situation in which the latter's influence became dominant was largely brought about by Russell's brilliant student, friend and younger colleague. Already in the *Tractatus*, where Wittgenstein expresses his indebtedness to Frege and Russell, there are some thirty references to Russell – and a dozen and a half to Frege, who was just as important for Wittgenstein – but only a single one to Moore. The neglect later turned to open criticism. *On Certainty* (published posthumously in 1969) is largely devoted to refuting Moore as well as to providing a non-empiricist alternative to his common-sensism. Yet ironically, after Moore retired, Wittgenstein succeeded him in the chair of philosophy at Cambridge in 1939.

Wittgenstein plays different roles as a singularly important thinker and as the link in and major instigator of the transition between early and later Anglo-American analytic philosophy. In philosophy, Wittgenstein's main contributions fall into the areas of language, logic, psychology, and mathematics, and a new conception of philosophy.

The most elaborated form of logical atomism is provided in Wittgenstein's famous, but exceedingly enigmatic, *Tractatus Logico-Philosophicus*, a very short – a mere seventy-five pages – work composed in sybilline sentences, ranging widely over a large number of themes. They include logic, metaphysics, representation, solipsism, ethics, among others.

Generally speaking the *Tractatus* represents the high point of the line of thought Russell derived from Wittgenstein and which Wittgenstein later developed independently. Wittgenstein here goes over the same ground again in a way that deepens the kind of logical empiricism he and Russell were committed to during this period while exposing flaws that Wittgenstein and a host of others later criticized in detail.

Like Russell in *The Philosophy of Logical Atomism*, in the *Tractatus* Wittgenstein develops an atomistic conception of knowledge starting from the idea that the world consists of facts. In his introduction, Russell describes Wittgenstein's theory without comment as if he agreed with it. Yet Wittgenstein thought that Russell misunderstood the doctrine he expressed in the book. Though superficially similar to Russell's position, Wittgenstein's view in this book is finally very different. In the *Tractatus*, he develops a theory based on a truth-functional, propositional approach to knowledge of the "world," understood as "everything that is the case" (1),[73] where "what is the case," or a "fact," refers to the "existence of states of affairs" (2), and where "[a] logical picture of fact is a thought" (3) that is "a sentence with a sense" (4).

Two main differences between Russell and Wittgenstein with respect to logical atomism are the insights that representation is based on formulating a picture of reality and that all forms of philosophy necessarily miscarry. Wittgenstein's central idea is that any form of representation answers to reality, so the structure of a true proposition literally is a picture that mirrors the structure of the world. For instance, in 4.01 – the propositions are numbered – he writes: “A proposition is a picture of reality. A proposition is a model of reality as we examine it.” This claim follows from the idea that there is a way the world is (2.024). The cognitive process is one in which, he says, “[w]e picture facts to ourselves” (2.1), where by “picture” we mean depicting a state of affairs, in short the world. Since in a picture the parts are related to one another in a determinate way (2.14) – as Wittgenstein also says, “[a] picture is a fact” (2.141) – we know that a picture is true or false in comparing it with reality.

Wittgenstein’s picture view of representation, which has many original features, harks back behind Russell to Francis Bacon’s early British empiricist view. According to Bacon, if we keep our eye steadily fixed on the facts of nature in perceiving them as they are, we can keep it from distorting what it sees,[74] or, again, from acting like a false mirror, which distorts what it sees.[75] This view points toward the empirical form of foundationalism already implicit in Bacon and in many intermediate figures before Russell, then again in Wittgenstein, and in later Vienna Circle theorists. It points as well toward Wittgenstein’s form of what later came to be called the linguistic turn, more precisely his view that the problems of philosophy are mere pseudo-problems due to a misuse of language. This misuse is to be exposed and criticized but, since the problems are not real, they cannot be solved. Wittgenstein recommends that when someone tries to say something metaphysical, we point out to him that “he had failed to give a meaning to certain signs in his propositions” (6.53). It is often noted that if every philosophical proposition is only an instance of bad grammar, it would seem that all the sentences in the *Tractatus* are nonsensical.

Like Russell, the early Wittgenstein presupposes a general, but controversial, correspondence between language and reality.[76] For Wittgenstein as for Russell, at some point in the analysis words must actually stand for things. Thus Wittgenstein repeatedly indicates his desire to cut off the possibility of an infinite regress (2.0299–2.022, 3.23–3.24). Unlike Russell, who relies on empirical argument, Wittgenstein deduces the necessary correspondence between words and things as an a priori argument through his analysis of language. His position later undergoes a radical change. In later writings, including the posthumous *Philosophical Investigations* and *On Certainty*, Wittgenstein directly criticizes his own earlier approach in abandoning a priori argumentation in favor of close study of the actual functioning of language. In the preface to the *Tractatus*, he states his belief that he has found the final solution to the problems with which he is concerned. He later changed his mind. In the preface to the *Philosophical*

Investigations,[77] which is widely regarded after the *Tractatus* as his second masterpiece, Wittgenstein reports that in rereading his earlier work he has become aware that it contains grave mistakes.

Both early and late, Wittgenstein adopted a therapeutic approach to the problems of philosophy. As in the *Tractatus*, where Wittgenstein suggests that the problems of philosophy arise from misunderstanding the logic of our language, in the *Philosophical Investigations* he continues to believe that such problems are due to linguistic errors. "Philosophy is a battle," he writes in a typical passage, "against the bewitchment of our intelligence by means of language."[78] In most other respects, the view in the *Investigations* is not only different from, but also contradicts most, perhaps all, of the main doctrines of the earlier Tractarian period. The later position is not aimed at a final determination of the relation of words to things, or language to the world. It is not foundationalist, but anti-foundationalist, no longer anti-contextualist, but contextualist. Absent is the distinctive doctrine from the earlier period in which language is said to picture the world. Instead of holding that one name stands for one thing, and so on, Wittgenstein now holds that meaning is determined by use. In a typical passage, he writes: "Look at the sentence as an instrument, and at its sense in its employment."[79] Wittgenstein now gives up any vestige of logical atomism, hence of the advanced scientific form of empiricism he earlier favored, and, it may be said, empiricism itself.[80] The view that there is a universal form of language gives way to the later conviction that there is nothing common to the various forms of the language, which he now calls language games (*Sprachspiele*). At best there is no more than a family resemblance of relationships that overlap. Finally, in a long passage on what has come to be known as the private language problem, Wittgenstein argues that language is not essentially private but constituted in the public realm.[81] In sum, in place of the earlier effort to grasp the world as it is by matching up words to things, he adopted a very different conception of constative claims as relative to shifting conceptual frameworks determined by the context.

Wittgenstein, the Vienna Circle, and Ordinary Language Philosophy

Though Wittgenstein did not found Anglo-American analytic philosophy, his enormous and continuing influence largely determined its later evolution. In different ways he is located at the confluence of three main later developments in analytic philosophy. One is the Vienna Circle form of philosophy of science that was based on a variation of the logical atomistic theme worked out by Russell and the early Wittgenstein. A second is the form of the linguistic turn that emerged in Oxford ordinary language philosophy. A third is a form of analytic philosophy that flourished in the US after the Second World War and that now, at least in its present instantiation, seems to be coming to an end.

The Vienna Circle and what is known as Oxford ordinary language philosophy emerged as very different reactions to Wittgenstein and others. The term "Vienna Circle" (*Wiener Kreis*) refers to a group of scientists and philosophers with strong scientific and mathematical interests that emerged from discussions beginning in 1907 between Otto Neurath, a philosopher, economist, and sociologist, Hans Hahn, a mathematician, and Philip Frank, a physicist. The main philosophical members were Carnap, Herbert Feigl, Neurath, Moritz Schlick, and Friedrich Waismann. Schlick, who filled Ernst Mach's chair in Vienna in 1922, and became the nominal leader of the Vienna Circle, was later assassinated by a student in 1936. After Hitler came to power, the other members of the Circle, many of whom were Jewish, Marxist, or both, emigrated. Carnap, who came to the US, immediately established a strong beachhead of analytic philosophy in the New World that endures to this day.

The thinkers of the Vienna Circle drew on a variety of eclectic influences, including Mach's anti-metaphysical view of science, the Polish logician Alfred Tarski's work on the semantics of formal languages, the English philosopher Karl Popper's investigation of the difference between science and pseudo-science, and Wittgenstein's early Tractarian views. During the period he spent as an architect in Vienna, Wittgenstein came into contact with Schlick and Waismann and even attended one or two meetings of the group, which studied the *Tractatus* intensively, line by line.

The thinkers of the Vienna Circle worked out a form of logical atomism, or logical empiricism, known as logical positivism, a name initially applied to the philosophical ideas of the group, in a variety of specifically scientific domains as part of the effort to establish rigorously scientific philosophy.[82] Their most distinctive doctrine, which separated them from logical atomism, was the principle of verifiability, or, more formally, the empirical criterion of meaning.[83]

This principle was initially formulated by Waismann in 1930, and then reformulated by others. It can be understood in relation to Kant's triple distinction between analytic a priori, synthetic a priori, and synthetic a posteriori propositions. Kant believed that knowledge of all kinds depended on the possibility of synthetic a priori propositions. The logical positivists denied synthetic a priori propositions in maintaining that meaningful statements are either analytic or empirically verifiable. On this basis, they claimed that many statements of traditional philosophy, which did not respect this distinction, and were unverifiable, were not false but rather meaningless. Yet as it was later seen, since the verifiability principle is neither analytically true nor empirically verifiable, it is itself subject to the same objection.

The closest analogy to the spirit of logical atomism in the Vienna Circle was the early Carnap's effort to weave a seamless, foundationalist web from experience to science in relying on Wittgenstein, who felt he was misunderstood specifically by Carnap and by the members of the Vienna Circle in general. Like Wittgenstein, Carnap understands protocols as propositions not requiring proof, as related to immediate experience, and as serving as the basis for all other propositions of science. He assumes there is only a single correct analysis of the relation between a sign and what it represents.[84]

This project was immediately countered by Neurath, who opposes the foundationalism implicit in the early Wittgenstein and explicit in Carnap and Schlick. Neurath objects to the very idea of a protocol as little more than a fictitious presupposition of an ideal language. According to Neurath, "The fiction of an *ideal language* constructed of clean atomic sentences is just as metaphysical as the fiction of Laplace's spirit."[85] In this context, he makes a famous comment about the similarity between a clean protocol sentence and repairing a ship on the open sea,[86] which Quine cites in the exergue in *Word and Object*.[87] Neurath objects to the idea of an incorrigible relation between concepts and things as an impossible requirement for scientific theory. Long before Quine, he sees that the problem of direct reference has no formal solution; in other words, that the project of semantics as it runs through the entire analytic debate beginning with Frege cannot be carried out. A successful reconstruction of the epistemological ship would presuppose an ideal language allowing no more than a single correct analysis. In place of Carnap's foundationalist approach, Neurath prefers a real language that permits an unlimited number of possible analyses, the same point Quine later works out in his theory of the indeterminacy of translation.[88]

Carnap, who acknowledges the importance of Neurath's critique, immediately abandoned the idea of basing science on incorrigible empirical constatations. In giving up empirical foundationalism as anything more than an unrealizable ideal and in adopting a fallback position based on an ideal language, he continued to defend the idea of a rigorous translation from a real to an ideal language. Following Wittgenstein's view of definitions as rules for translation from one language into another, he contended that in an ideal language, unlike a real language, there are precise rules for the translation from protocol propositions.[89]

Moore and then, to a greater extent, the later Wittgenstein were concerned with ordinary language, which Moore recommended and Wittgenstein analyzed. Moore believed that ordinary language pointed to items of common sense that could not be denied and Wittgenstein was interested in the alleged misuse of ordinary language that led to the pseudo-problems of philosophy. The general interest in ordinary language later developed into the movement known as Oxford ordinary language philosophy.[90]

Philosophy has been taught in Oxford at least since the early thirteenth century. The term "Oxford ordinary language philosophy" is usually taken to mean a particular form of linguistic philosophy that was introduced at the University of Oxford starting in the 1930s through the epistemologist H. H. Price. Price, who was influenced by Cook Wilson, who taught at Cambridge, published a book on *Perception* (1932)[91] in which he contends that sensing is a form of knowing and that we immmediately know sense-data. The claim for knowledge of sense-data is still another form of traditional British empiricism. Thus according to Locke, we do not directly know objects, but we directly know ideas that relate one to one to objects. This type of philosophy based on the analysis of language was developed in different ways by such diverse figures as Gilbert Ryle, J. L. Austin, and, later, A. J. Ayer.

These three thinkers hold distinctly diverse views. Ayer spent time in Vienna absorbing the Vienna Circle theories. As a young man, he was the leading English exponent of logical positivism. His early book, *Language, Truth and Logic* (1936),[92] takes a kind of belligerent approach to theories he did not like that became typical of a certain form of English and later American analytic philosophy. Ayer contributed to bringing about a widespread attitude among many English analytic philosophers that there was one and only one way to do philosophy. In this book, Ayer accepts a form of verificationism sufficient, he believes, to disqualify metaphysical statements of any kind. Elsewhere, he echoed Carnap's complaint in saying that Heidegger's statements contributed to his theories and appeared profound, but could not be evaluated and were therefore meaningless.[93] Ayer typically contends that the real function of philosophy is analysis. Philosophical analysis does not consist in breaking up complexes into their constituent elements, or atoms. It is, rather, analysis of language, of which Russell's theory of descriptions is an illustration. Ayer is also associated with phenomenalism, or the position that physical objects can be reduced to sensory experiences, often identified as sense-data. For Ayer, the choice between sense-datum language and material object language is entirely free. In *The Foundations of Empirical Knowledge* (1940), he later took the view that ordinary sentences about material objects can be wholly translated into sense-datum language.[94] In the preface to the second edition of *Language, Truth and Logic* (1946), Ayer deals again with a series of difficulties engendered by the theories expounded in that book.

Ryle, who is the best known of the Oxford ordinary language philosophers, differs from many analytic colleagues in his interest in continental philosophy. For instance, he wrote an early and partly sympathetic review of Heidegger's *Being and Time.*[95] In an important early article, "Systematically Misleading Expressions" (1932),[96] Ryle takes an early Wittgensteinian line. He holds that philosophy is not composed of a series of doctrines but is rather a therapeutic activity which consists in revealing the real form of facts while detecting misleading constructions and absurd theories. This approach is pursued in *The Concept of Mind* (1949), in which Ryle exhibits the confusions of a Cartesian approach to what he called the ghost in the machine.[97]

In J. L. Austin, the movement in philosophy begun by logical atomism and attention to language comes full circle in the attention to language not to further but rather to destroy logical atomism. Austin, who believes that ordinary language is the final court of appeal, provides the best analytic example of close consideration of language. "Our common stock of words," he writes, "embodies all the distinctions men have found worth drawing, and the connexions they have found worth making, in the lifetimes of many generations."[98] In *Sense and Sensibilia* (1964),[99] which appeared posthumously, Austin denies that what we initially perceive are sense-data, and further denies that propositions concerning sense-data can serve as the incorrigible foundations of knowledge.

Analytic Philosophy in the US

Analytic philosophy was later imported to the United States through Carnap – who emigrated to the US in 1935 – and others who either belonged to or were associated with the Vienna Circle. They include the German physicist and philosopher of science Hans Reichenbach, the Polish logician Alfred Tarski, the Austrian logician and mathematician Kurt Gödel, and the Austrian philosophers Herbert Feigl and Gustav Bergmann. The new import was strengthened by the presence of Russell, who taught in the US in the later 1930s and early 1940s.

American analytic philosophy has for a long time been influenced by the Vienna Circle approach. This is reflected, *inter alia*, in a largely formal, ahistorical conception of philosophy of science largely influenced by Carnap and others which prevails unchanged in the English language debate; in emphasis on technical competence over historical knowledge; in a turn away from traditional British empiricism, which in different forms was typical of both Moore and Russell, through an anti-empiricism including such major figures as the later Wittgenstein, Wilfrid Sellars, and Donald Davidson; and in scientism. According to scientism, which is widely popular in analytic circles, science is the best and perhaps even the only real source of knowledge.

The American analytic hostility to other approaches, as well as the inclination toward scientism, largely derives from the later Carnap, who, after his defeat by Neurath, retreated to an effort to construct a language of science. In imitation of the general logicist program, in *The Logical Syntax of Language* (1934), Carnap, who was still committed to the project of making logic a science, treats philosophy as a branch of logic he calls the logic of science. Once again he argues that metaphysics can be shown to be meaningless in adding that the only meaningful philosophical questions concern the language of science as part of the effort to "*substitute logical syntax for philosophy.*"[100] Scientism, strongly suggested by this form of Carnap's view, and a leading feature of the American debate,[101] was developed by a number of thinkers, including Wilfrid Sellars.

Sellars links scientism with a rejection of the idea of the given and a commitment to what he enigmatically refers to as the logical space of reasons. He distinguishes between the so-called "folk" view, or approach of the ordinary individual, and that of science, and argues that science and only science tells us what is true.[102] He links this view with a frontal attack on classical empiricism, which he calls the myth of the given, in borrowing insights from Hegel. At the beginning of the *Phenomenology of Spirit*, Hegel's target is any claim for immediate knowledge, which presupposes an epistemological given, in English empiricists such as Bacon and Locke, and in different, more sophisticated fashion in Kant's critical philosophy.[103] In restating Hegel's argument in an analytical idiom, Sellars rejects the idea of direct givenness – in Hegelian terms, immediacy – as no more than a myth in favor of the justification of claims to know within the so-called "logical space of reasons."[104]

The four most important figures in American analytic philosophy since the Second World War are Quine, Davidson, Putnam, and Rorty. Quine, who is certainly the single most important American analytic thinker of the second half of the twentieth century, made numerous important contributions, too many even to be enumerated here.[105] He has also played a central role in moderating many of the more excessive views in paring down, as it were, central analytic doctrines to more manageable, more defensible form, hence protecting the unity and even on occasion the continued viability of the analytic debate. Yet in other ways, he is a maverick, out of tune with many of the central analytic ideas and themes. Thus he was always a redoubtable opponent of the very idea of strict reference, more generally the effort to solve the semantic problem along formal lines that in one way or another runs throughout the entire analytic discussion from Frege, through Russell, Strawson, Kripke, and others right up to the present.[106]

One of Quine's most significant contributions lies in his important criticism of Carnap. In the context of his response to Carnap, Neurath makes the famous remark, referenced above, about the similarity between a clean protocol sentence and repairing a ship on the open sea, where, by analogy, the successful reconstruction of the epistemological vessel would presuppose an ideal language allowing no more than a single correct analysis.

Quine begins *Word and Object* (1960) in indicating his agreement with Neurath on a number of points. In "Two Dogmas of Empiricism" (1953),[107] perhaps the single most influential analytic article, even the most influential article in the twentieth century, certainly the conceptual axis of analytic philosophy in the last half of the century, Quine continues Neurath's attack on Carnap. Carnap's aim was always to work out a scientific form of empiricism, which was already on the agenda in Russell and Wittgenstein. To see the point of Quine's attack, it is useful to note the link between Carnap's earlier and later views. It has already been noted that after Neurath's critique, Carnap gives up empirical foundationalism as anything more than an unrealizable ideal and adopts a fallback position based on an ideal language. Yet he continues to defend the idea of a rigorous translation from a real to an ideal language. Following Wittgenstein's view of definitions as rules for translation from one language into another, he contends that in an ideal language, unlike a real language, there are precise rules for the translation from protocol propositions. In attacking the analytic–synthetic distinction, which Carnap presupposes in his later position, Quine "destroys" Carnap's own distinction between a natural and an ideal language, hence, decisively undercuts the revised form of Carnap's project after his early defeat by Neurath. The consequence is to block the translation program for which *Principia Mathematica* once seemed paradigmatic and to undermine the attempt to find a formal solution to the problem of reference that is a main theme in the analytic debate since Frege. In its place, Quine suggests the doctrine of the indeterminacy of translation. According to Quine, it is not possible to match up theories with reality, since reference is not transparent but, rather, opaque.[108] An important consequence that Quine draws is a shift toward pragmatism in which claims are adjudicated not piecemeal but, rather, from a holist perspective.

Davidson, who is often regarded as Quine's faithful lieutenant, something the latter does nothing to discourage, is in fact his strong critic. Davidson, who wrote no books,[109] composed many important articles, many of which were unusually influential. In "On the Very Idea of a Conceptual Scheme" (1974),[110] he exorcizes what he calls the third dogma of empiricism, that is, the distinction between form and content. It may have seemed and no doubt still seems to many analytic thinkers that Davidson was only extending Quine's position. On the contrary, the result of his argument is not further to undermine but rather to re-establish the concept of reference that Quine almost single-handedly did so much to undercut. In criticizing the form–content distinction, Davidson re-establishes a certain form of empiricism in making clear how to understand reference. According to Davidson, since we understand ourselves, we necessarily share a single world that we know as it is through language. In a position that he was later to abandon,[111] he formalizes this view in another extremely influential article, entitled "A Coherence Theory of Truth and Knowledge" (1983), in which he argues that coherence suggests correspondence, that is, the coherence of the parts of a theory suggest that it corresponds to the way the world is.[112]

Putnam studied with Carnap, and is the figure in contemporary analytic philosophy most similar to him. He is distinguished by an unusual combination of great technical competence and a selective interest in the history of philosophy – as part of his turn toward pragmatism he has been concerned over many years with James – as well as an unusually labile position. Putnam, who is a keen critic, has no compunctions in changing his mind. Often the main target of his critical capacity is one of his own earlier views, which he consistently devises, develops, and then abandons. Putnam's entire career turns on the effort to defend different forms of realism, which he has espoused one after the other in serial fashion, most recently in a form of what he calls natural realism.[113]

Putnam was originally committed to logical positivism, especially Carnap. He later formulated an influential theory of internal realism that he elaborated in *Reason, Truth and History* (1981), the most influential of his many books. Externalist theorists hold that there is a neutral, God's-eye point of view in terms of which to answer the question: what objects does the world consist of? Putnam rejects the striking idea of what he calls a brain in a vat.[114] Internalists hold there is no such perspective but that different theories provide different perspectives on the same world. In the internalist view, claims to know do not isolate objects independently of, but rather only within, conceptual frameworks. According to Putnam, " 'Objects' do not exist independently of conceptual schemes. We cut up the world into objects when we introduce one or another scheme of description."[115] For an internalist like Putnam, truth is no more than a limit concept, a *Grenzbegriff*.[116]

We can end this brief account of analytic philosophy with even briefer mention of the *enfant terrible* of American analytic philosophy. Rorty, who is an anomaly within American philosophy *tout court*, can be described as an analytic epistemological skeptic turned pragmatist. Rorty's main attack on epistemology is developed in *Philosophy and the Mirror of Nature* (1979). This book, which appeared in the aftermath of the Vietnamese War, in a time of national self-doubting, and which reflected the widespread disillusionment of the historical moment in what to many seemed like an attack on philosophy itself, was an enormous success. For Rorty, epistemology requires justifying claims to know, hence going beyond what Dewey calls warranted assertibility, though there is no possibility of such a justification.[117] Rorty, who here and later appears to uncritically identify any possible solution of the problem of knowledge with analytic foundationalism, recommends that we give up epistemology as a bad bet. Philosophy cannot solve the problem of knowledge, about which there is nothing useful to say. Rather than continue the conversation, which is simply fruitless, without any possibility of progress, one does better to change the subject.

Rorty's rejection of epistemology illustrates the general Wittgensteinian view that the problems of philosophy are not genuine but rather generated by confusions about knowledge that cannot be solved but can only be dissipated. The difference is that Rorty, who rarely analyzes language, makes an argument leading to a similar conclusion by welding together insights borrowed from Wittgenstein, Heidegger, and Dewey, his three acknowledged philosophical heroes, as well as a number of leading analytic thinkers (Quine, Sellars, Putnam). These three heroes later gave way to Dewey as the single superhero, but a Dewey that few would recognize. Rorty still later turned increasingly to the history of philosophy, about which he often expresses what can only be qualified as deliberately perverse views. An example among many is his view that Hegel's historicism amounts to the idea that the world will not be destroyed by a giant comet.[118] For Rorty, the only legitimate role of philosophy lies in helping us cope, that is, enabling us to get through the day.

7

Kant and Twentieth-Century Philosophy

My very general account of some main aspects of twentieth-century philosophy centers on four main movements or tendencies. The need to adopt something like an average view of each of these movements in limited space clearly does not do full justice either to the wide variety of positions they include or to their nuances. One way to put the point is that few if any positions wholly or even solely exemplify any one tendency. The different positions are invariably more complex, hence often more interesting, than an average depiction suggests.

A further point concerns the very idea of associating particular positions with one or another tendency. Classification of individual thinkers is inevitably arbitrary. Membership in a particular philosophical tendency is often more related to a political decision, to a conscious desire to be associated with one group rather than another, than to genuine philosophical affinities. There is no shortage of figures who overflow easy, average descriptions. Thus the position of Husserl, a pillar of continental philosophy, has strongly analytic aspects that attract someone like Dummett. Analytic figures like Neurath and Carnap, mainstays of the Vienna Circle positivist movement, and Quine, the most significant analytic thinker since the Second World War, reject foundationalism in stressing pragmatism while arguably remaining very far from the central insights of Peirce, its founding father. Davidson, who arguably defers only to Quine as an analytic thinker in the second half of the twentieth century, was for a time interested in the hermeneutical thinker Gadamer. Though Quine has no discernible interest in or knowledge of continental philosophy, his interest in holism has sometimes been held to place him in relation to Hegel. Habermas, who once seemed to be the heir to the Marxist tradition, at least as filtered through Frankfurt School neo-Marxism, has drawn close to Kant as well as increasingly to what sounds like analytic philosophy with a German accent. Rorty was attracted in his early writings to analytic thinkers, then later to Heidegger, and still later to pragmatism, especially to Dewey but emphatically not to Peirce.

The modern tendency toward specialization leads to "self-compartmentalization" of philosophers, who naturally tend to identify with a favored tendency, often in restricting activity within it to a subfield, problem, or concern, such as analytic moral theory, phenomenology, or the early Hegel. It is considered bad form, even suspicious behavior, to be interested in a wide variety of approaches, figures, and problems, an indication of a lack of hard-nosed thinking about the few significant philosophical problems. Jobs are often advertised in the discipline in terms of very narrow specialties in a way that corresponds to a normative view many have of the discipline itself. One tends to look for someone interested in either Ryle or Heidegger, but not both, though Ryle was himself interested in Heidegger. Those specialized in one tendency are all too often ignorant of and more often simply unconcerned about other tendencies, other ways of doing things. In the eyes of many observers everything happens as if there were in fact a royal road and those within a particular tendency were already on it, though there is considerable difference about what the main features of that road happen to be. Among the movements surveyed here, pragmatism is arguably the only one that did not at some point during the twentieth century feature a version of this claim. Someone like Cassirer, an immensely well-read thinker who routinely ranged widely and very knowledgeably across the entire philosophical tradition, including all or nearly all the main problems and figures, would seem oddly out of place today in our increasingly specialized academic environment.

The debate in this period mainly developed within rather than between tendencies in the give and take between representatives of one or another movement. To put the point simply but not inaccurately, for reasons of interest and competence, analytic thinkers debate with analytic thinkers, pragmatists with pragmatists, Marxists with Marxists, and so on. Once upon a time, important philosophers felt competent and even compelled to delve into virtually any topic. It would simply make no sense to ask what Plato's or Kant's area of specialization was. There seems to be no area or question they were unconcerned with. Yet as part of the increasing and increasingly rigid professionalization that has been a main feature in modern times, informed efforts to engage across the board, as it were – to read and think extremely widely, which was earlier typical of many of the best thinkers – have become increasingly few and far between.

The separation of philosophical tendencies in order to think wholly or solely within one or another of them is regrettable, for at least three reasons. First, it turns attention away from the very idea of a single Western philosophical tradition within which various tendencies emerge through the deceptive strategy of simply eliminating it from view. In place of the idea of a single tradition developing over time, in modern times Descartes and Kant each suggest versions of a rival account. According to this view, philosophy worthy of the name owes little or nothing to earlier views, which are probably or at least possibly false, undemonstrated, and not a proven source of claims able to withstand doubt of all kinds; it emerges out of their ruins, as it were. Kant, for instance, very clearly identifies the only philosophy worthy of the name with the critical philosophy. Variations on this theme are especially clear in politically orthodox Marxism as well as in various forms of phenomenology and analytic philosophy. Second, the separation of philosophical tendencies makes it difficult, perhaps impossible to evaluate what might be called philosophical progress. Is philosophy advancing or is it standing still? Does all the activity point to an accomplishment of some sort? It seems that this kind of question is best answered not by pointing to the development of a single tendency, say the progression of continental philosophy since Husserl, but rather through the confrontation of different tendencies with respect to a problem or theme common to them all. Third, the compartmentalized approach obscures the more specific question, germane to the present study, of what in retrospect was accomplished in twentieth-century philosophy.

Questions about how to evaluate philosophy and how to evaluate twentieth-century philosophy are obviously related. Now evaluation is difficult, especially in the cognitive disciplines, where at stake is whether a contribution to knowledge is really being made. There seems to be no way to offer a decision procedure valid for all cognitive disciplines. The appropriate procedure depends on the particular discipline. Many forms of natural science, for example, routinely appeal to prediction in evaluating cognitive claims. Einstein's general theory of relativity points to the deviation of light in the vicinity of a massive body as an appropriate test. If the bending of light had not been detected in the eclipse of the sun in 1919, that would have suggested the need for further measurements. If these still did not produce a measurable result witihin the appropriate range of tolerance, the failure would have cast doubt on the theory. Yet for philosophy, which has no predictive dimension, there is simply no easy way to tell whether progress is being made in general or only within a particular, often fairly narrow perspective.

It is difficult to determine if philosophy is advancing, certainly more difficult than in the natural sciences to know if the abundant activity is moving the debate forward in more than a very restricted sense. Efforts to imitate science, to transform philosophy into a science (Husserl), or to reduce philosophy in some way to commenting on science (Carnap), or again to use words rigorously, do not enable the evaluation of philosophy in a way that is the same as or even similar to that of natural science.

A better approach might be to claim to go further than other rivals in solving scientific problems, for instance through inventing new types of prediction. Thus the general theory of relativity goes beyond Newtonian mechanics through its capacity to account for the precession of the perihelion of Mercury, the technical term for that planet's oddly shaped orbit. Yet it seems that philosophy, which does not make empirical predictions, cannot, like the natural sciences, rely on the relation between philosophical theories and experience to justify its claim to knowledge. A different strategy consists in exploiting a difference between philosophy and natural science. The latter is concerned with particular problems of knowledge, for instance with discovering a new planet or, once it has been discovered, with calculating its orbit. Philosophy is concerned with the problem of knowledge in general. This suggests that we can measure philosophical progress in philosophy in terms of an advance in epistemology.

Various strategies have been suggested to solve the problem of knowledge, some of which we have reviewed above. The most common approach is some variety of metaphysical realism, or the claim to know the mind-independent external world as it is. Though exceedingly common, this claim, which goes all the way back in the tradition to Plato, has never been demonstrated. Since, as repeatedly emphasized, there is no way to know that we do in fact grasp the real as it is, replacement strategies have been suggested. With the model of Euclidean geometry in mind, Descartes insists on epistemological foundationalism, which can be informally described as weaving a seamless web from an initial principle or set of principles known to be true through rigorous deduction of ideas that can be held with certainty to grasp the world. Yet in this case certainty falls short of truth, for there is no way to show that our ideas of the world match up with it either one to one or in general. This same difficulty besets later variants on the foundationalist theme. Kant deduces a set of categories to allow us to infer from representations to noumena, or things in themselves; analytic philosophers beginning in Frege analyze the problem of reference to determine how words relate to things, or again how language hooks onto the world; and Husserl invents reduction in order to intuit essences with the aim of studying the life-world from the transcendental plane. Each of these models is meant to lead to knowledge in a way that, if they functioned, would solve the epistemological problem through a form of foundationalism, thereby exhibiting genuine philosophical progress.

There is surely progress in ruling out older views, in inventing new moves, in proposing variations on old themes and in discovering new ones. Yet if the measure of progress lies in being able to demonstrate knowledge of the metaphysically real, then it is far from clear that there is any such knowledge, hence any philosophical progress. Kant, whose deduction of the categories probably satisfies no one, can no more justify the inference from representations to objects than Descartes can do so from ideas to the world. Though he is on the right track in discarding God as an epistemological principle, Kant fails to solve Descartes's problem concerning the relation of ideas in the mind, which Kant calls appearances (or representations), to the mind-independent external world. Husserl also fails in the same task, but for a different reason. The retreat from the life-world into the transcendental ego provides no way to return to the world, hence no way to justify the claim to explore the life-world on the transcendental plane.

There is no reliable way to claim that one or another theory has in fact finally solved the problem of knowledge. All the "solutions" so far proposed have always led to counterarguments, which only extend the debate with apparently no real prospect of ever bringing it to an end.[1] It seems difficult to measure progress in philosophy by linking it to a proposed "answer" to the problem of knowledge. Another, perhaps more promising approach lies in inspecting the relation of a later state of the discussion to a prior moment in the debate.

This point can be clarified through a remark about the difference between two views of the nature of philosophy. Something important happened in the transition from Socrates as he is depicted in the Platonic dialogues to Platonism as it later arose in Plato's wake. Platonism is a collection of views whose precise relation to Plato cannot be known since his own position also remains unknown and cannot now be recovered. We have already noted that Platonism features the idea, already formulated by Parmenides, that to know requires knowledge of mind-independent reality. For a Platonist, claims to know are true in virtue of the claimed relation of the knower to the cognitive object. Socrates, by contrast, makes a weaker, very different, perhaps more plausible claim. In Socratic practice, claims that arise in debate are tested through further discussion, and then are accepted or more often rejected in terms of their relation not to the mind-independent world, but to the ongoing debate.

The difference between the two approaches is huge and directly relevant to the problem of how to evaluate philosophy. All philosophical theories lay claim to truth, though "truth" is understood in different ways. We can usefully oppose well-known claims about metaphysical truth and a weaker dialectical approach. For a Platonist, and those influenced by this very influential approach, it is meaningful to assert claims to know, which are absolute, not comparative. This approach is reflected in similar claims by Descartes, Kant, Husserl, and others. An observer who has access to reality as it is must be content to present the truth as it has supposedly emerged within the chosen perspective. Yet for someone like Socrates, philosophical claims are never absolute but always relative, always indexed to discussion featuring the dialectical clash of different points of view.

Philosophy has mainly followed Plato and not Socrates in eschewing debate and relative claims in favor of absolute claims to know. Yet, since absolute claims to know conflict, I would like to suggest that a better way to assess philosophical claims is to adopt some version of a dialectical model in which recognizably different perspectives are confronted. Thus it is useful to ask, within the pragmatic approach, whether Peirce or James has a better theory of truth. But it is even better, if we are interested not in a specifically pragmatic theory of truth, but rather in truth without restriction of perspective, to compare the main approaches that emerge in this part of the debate, including the views of, say, not only Peirce and James, but also Heidegger and Tarski, Lukács and Davidson.

Is Kant the Background of Twentieth-Century Philosophy?

In order to know if there is not only smoke but also fire in twentieth-century philosophy, we require a standard of some kind, a way of evaluating what has been and still is taking place in the often arcane reaches of professional philosophy. Different standards recommend themselves. One might, for instance, look at prizes won, lectureships held, who publishes what with which press, whose books are translated and whose work is more frequently or more favorably discussed. A better, more useful standard is provided by Kant. Kant's *Critique of Pure Reason* is certainly one of the most important[2] and perhaps even the most influential single work in the modern tradition. If, as I believe, Kant lies at the basis of much that has taken place since his time, then we can do no better as a way of approaching what went on in philosophy in the last century than to ask how it relates to Kant.

In what follows I will be developing the idea that general claims for philosophy in the twentieth century can be assessed in relation to Kant as a backdrop for much of what went on in that period. This is certainly ironic since Kant believes that real philosophy is essentially unrelated either to the prior or to the later tradition. According to Kant, there was no philosophy before him and, since he brings it to an end in the critical philosophy, there can be none after him. Kant's contemporaries took a different view. Though inspired by him, they believed, with rare exceptions, that his theories were incomplete and needed to be further developed. The post-Kantian tradition is largely composed of a series of direct and indirect reactions to his position. Nineteenth-century German idealism, often known as post-Kantian German idealism, as its name suggests, can usefully be understood as a series of reactions to Kantian idealism. This is true as well for later nineteenth-century philosophy, including the dissolution of the Hegelian school after Hegel's death in 1831 leading to the increasing, but qualified return to Kant in Germany in the second half of the nineteenth century, culminating in a series of neo-Kantian schools. And it is finally true for the complicated development of twentieth-century philosophy, which directly and indirectly can largely be understood as a series of reactions to Kant.

The advantage of considering the twentieth-century debate in relation to Kant is two-fold. First, it provides a way to understand the various positions as knowingly or unknowingly part of a debate larger and deeper than any single position, whose beginnings are ultimately shrouded in Greek antiquity. Though the main tendencies that dominated that period each arose at that time, they did not arise autonomously, out of conceptual thin air, as it were, nor were they without precedent. They arose, rather, on the basis of the entire preceding Western philosophical tradition. The second advantage of this approach is that it suggests that twentieth-century philosophy can be evaluated against a shared, hence common, Kantian background.

This claim is obviously controversial. It will be opposed by those who believe they have successfully broken with past philosophy, as Marxists believe they have broken with Hegel and the German idealist tradition, and analytic thinkers contend they have broken with idealism. It might also be opposed by those who detect the continuing influence of other thinkers. Writing in the middle of the last century, Merleau-Ponty, in a passage cited above, suggests that in different ways everything that has happened in the last hundred years is due to Hegel.[3] Yet the two views are not incompatible, for Hegel, who reacts to Kant on virtually every page of his writings, is in many ways the greatest of all the Kantians. It is entirely consistent to treat philosophy in the twentieth century as a series of reactions to Kant and to Hegel while seeing Kant as a crucial influence on Hegel's position.

In different ways, Kant's influence is deeply embedded in each of the twentieth-century movements considered here. Marx is most deeply influenced by Hegel, but Engels, the founder of Marxism, is more deeply influenced by Kant. Though Marx is inseparable from Hegel, this is not true for Marxism, which is, rather, inseparable from Kant. Engels, who knew Kant poorly, presents a view of German idealism from Kant to Hegel as concerned to solve the problem posed by Kant's concept of the thing in itself. Marxism applies a Kantian argument to Kant in arguing that Kant and post-Kantian German idealism are unable to solve Kant's problem, which is only later solved by Marx. The Kantian dimension in Marxism is later reinforced by Lukács, the single most important Marxist philosopher, and others. Kant's Copernican revolution in philosophy turns on the idea that the form of cognition must be adequate to grasp its object. Following this insight, Lukács argues in detail that in capitalism what Marxists call bourgeois philosophy, and, by extension, bourgeois thought of all kinds, is inadequate to know modern industrial society, which can only be known by Marxism.

Marxism retains Kant's insight that thought must be adequate to its object but revises Kant's anti-contextualism. It claims that in virtue of its relation to the surrounding social context, classical German philosophy, its name for German idealism, is inadequate to grasp its object. In general terms, pragmatism rejects Kant's theoretical apriorism in transforming the problem of knowledge into a practical problem or problems, through what Marxists would call a shift from theory to practice.

Kant's critical philosophy is an enormous step on the way to realizing the impulse behind Cartesian foundationalism. Peirce's criticism of Descartes, his rejection of Cartesian epistemological foundationalism, counts as a rejection of Kant's critical philosophy. His relation to Kant can be expressed as a series of doctrines that he substitutes for corresponding Kantian doctrines that he rejects in the course of elaborating pragmatism. For certainty, he substitutes belief as the result of going beyond doubt. For an a priori, deductive approach, he substitutes a resolutely a posteriori, experimental approach, which can never claim to know mind-independent reality, which Peirce rejects as an absurd goal. For the philosophical effort to ground natural science, which is supposedly not able to guarantee its own truth claims, he offers natural science as emancipated from philosophy and as its own warrant for claims to know. For apodictic, hence incorrigible, assertions that are the hallmark of both Descartes and Kant, he substitutes assertions that are in principle never apodictic and always later corrigible. All of these changes bring Peirce, as he was aware, into Hegel's orbit, with the single, basic exception of his failure to consider the knowing process as intrinsically historical.

Kant's influence on continental philosophy is unusually complex. The epistemological thrust of the critical philosophy lives on in Husserl's effort finally to constitute philosophy as a rigorous science, the main project in his phenomenological period, in terms of his reading of and reaction to Kant. This project is reflected on multiple levels in his writings: in the very Kantian attack on psychologism in the first volume of the *Logical Investigations*, as well as in carrying Kant's distinction between pure and applied logic beyond the point at which he left it in his position[4] with the aim of elaborating the conditions of the possibility of science in general.[5] Kant's influence on continental phenomenology is equally strong in Heidegger's anti-Husserlian reformulation of phenomenology as ontology. Heidegger was a redoubtable Kant scholar. References to and analyses of Kant and Kantian ideas are widely present throughout his writings, including *Being and Time*, which is liberally scattered with them. Heidegger rereads Kant's critical philosophy as an effort at ontology which is prolonged, deepened and perhaps completed in his own position. In *Kant and the Problem of Metaphysics*, Heidegger casts himself as Kant's only authentic successor. According to Heidegger, Kant points to but pulled back from the analysis of the transcendental imagination.[6] This claim points to Heidegger as the one who recognizes and completes Kant's project.

The analytic relation to Kant is deep – Moore and Russell were both concerned with Kant in their dissertations: Moore wrote on Kant's ethics and Russell elaborated a non-Kantian view of geometry – and very complex. Speaking generally, analytic thinkers tend to refuse synthetic a priori judgments, to further turn away from transcendental idealism as part of the turn away from idealism, and to be concerned with the problem of reference that is central to Anglo-American analytic philosophy's attempts to make good on Kant's concern with a representationalist approach to knowledge.

It has been argued that analytic philosophy emerged in reaction against Kant: for instance, through the rejection of his conception of the a priori.[7] It has further been argued that analytic philosophy develops through a series of rejections of key Kantian doctrines.[8] Perhaps the clearest positive link of analytic philosophy to Kant lies in the analytic effort ever since Frege to develop a formal theory of reference.[9] Kant's original view of the problem of knowledge as requiring an analysis of the relation of the representation to the object arguably lives on in the analytic effort to understand how, as it is sometimes informally put, words hook onto things, or language hooks onto the world. The difference is in the refocusing of Kant's epistemological concern with a representational solution to the problem of knowledge as a logical puzzle, or series of puzzles, about the relation of language to referents. Though never a popular theme, this concern runs like a red thread through the entire warp and woof of analytic thinking from Frege's distinction between sense and reference, through Russell's concept of "standing for" as a means of understanding reference, then Strawson's view that Russell conflates reference and assertion, again Kripke's acccount of rigid designators as applying in all possible worlds in what is sometimes called a causal theory of reference, and so on.[10] If a formal solution of the problem of reference could have been devised, at least as concerns language, it would have provided the account of the relation of the representation to the object that Kant calls for but fails to deliver.

What Was Accomplished in Twentieth-Century Philosophy?

The twentieth century was full of important thinkers who were responsible individually and collectively for an impressive body of writings and some very clever, occasionally even brilliant, insights. Yet if we have in mind progress in respect to the main themes that Kant analyzes in the *Critique of Pure Reason*, then we must conclude that the twentieth-century discussion is perhaps most interesting not when it addresses Kantian themes but rather when it diverges from Kant in order to invent new themes and new answers to new questions rather than new solutions to old concerns. To put the same point differently: if Kant is the standard, then it seems there is little progress with respect to his own specific concerns. Later thinkers are arguably most successful, hence contribute most, not in going further down the Kantian path, but rather in changing the subject while providing variations on older, pre-Kantian themes or in inventing and exploring new ones.

Among the twentieth-century movements surveyed here, analytic philosophy arguably comes closest to directly engaging with Kant on an epistemological level. I have been stressing Kant's simultaneous, but inconsistent commitment to different, irreconcilable representationalist and constructivist approaches to knowledge. Before Kant, the main modern approach to knowledge was representationalism associated with Descartes, Locke, and other followers of the so-called "new way of ideas." Analytic philosophy is strongly influenced by this approach. In all its many forms, it remains close to the representationalist way Kant originally poses the epistemological problem of knowledge.

The analytic debate about reference counts as an often very ingenious, ultimately unsuccessful, attempt by many hands to devise a formal solution to the epistemological problem along representationalist lines. The analytic approach is loosely based on Frege's pioneer distinction between sense, or meaning, and reference. Frege intends his distinction to help him deal with puzzles of identity, as in the relation between the morning star and the evening star.[11] His view that reference is determined by sense later led to an ongoing, very complex debate about representational theories of reference and of meaning. Some main entrants in this debate include Russell's theory of denoting, Wittgenstein's early picture theory of language – later abandoned in favor of a theory of meaning in use – Russell's logical atomism, Quine's attack on theory of meaning, and Davidson's fallback appeal to Tarski.

Each of these arguments is ingenious and complex. There is no space here to consider them in the detail they deserve. Suffice it to say there is general agreement that analytic efforts to devise a formal solution to the problem of reference, hence to make good on a representationalist approach to knowledge that Kant earlier sketched, have failed. Indeed, the fact that the formal analytic approach to reference is widely seen to have failed is certainly one of the reasons why Brandom's informal, so-called "inferentialist" approach to reference is currently attracting so much attention.[12]

Analytic philosophy has many other merits. Yet it misfires as an effort to carry forward Kant's specific concern with a representational solution to the problem of knowledge. This failed effort unintentionally confirms Kant's own dissatisfaction with a representational solution to the problem of knowledge.

Like analytic philosophy, both Marxism and pragmatism are concerned with knowledge; pragmatism less so than Marxism. The Marxist analysis relies on reworking basic distinctions which are still central for Kant and

Hegel. For Kant, phenomena are appearances that represent a mind-independent external object. Marxism offers a very different variation on this Kantian theme by invoking a different conception of the subject who knows. Kant is an anti-contextualist, who presupposes that, in making claims to know, the subject is not constrained or limited in any way by its relation to the surrounding world. But Marxism is contextualist, for instance in its reliance on the concept of ideology in claiming that bourgeois thinkers are constrained by their relation to modern industrial society, which they systematically misrepresent. Marxism believes, for reasons that are never adequately articulated, that it alone is able to pierce the veil of ideological illusion contained in false, ideologically distorted appearances.

Marxism shares with representationalism the conviction that under the right conditions we can and in fact do know the world as it is. It differs from standard forms of representationalism in two ways. First, as already mentioned, it invokes contextualism. Second, it relies on the infamous reflection theory of truth and knowledge. The relation of thought to context is both an important insight and a main weakness of the Marxist approach to knowledge. It seems obvious that in some situations cognitive claims are weakened by their relation to the surroundings in which they are formulated. Yet Marxist thinkers seem insensitive to the Hegelian point that thought is inherently and always contextual, that is, that the context not only distorts but also constitutes what we can know.

The new way of ideas depends on making out a claim for the relation of ideas to the mind-independent external world. As concerns the reflection theory of truth, Marxism buys into the new way of ideas, hence falls prey to all its difficulties, including the inability to show that representations represent. The Marxists' claim that what they call "bourgeois philosophy," though not Marxism, is undermined by its relation to its surroundings relies on an implicit appeal to epistemological privilege that is implausible and indemonstrable. It cannot be shown that any given set of cognitive claims, including Marxist claims, are not just another form of distortion, that they in fact correctly depict, or "mirror," the world. Some Marxists distance themselves from the reflection theory, which Lukács regards as an embarrassment. Yet Lukács has no better solution than to maintain that a theory formulated on behalf of working men and women is for that reason and that reason alone able to evade illusion; surely a claim that requires a better justification.

In the form of twentieth-century phenomenology invented by Husserl, the epistemological impulse is strong. It is weakened, though not entirely absent, in such later thinkers as Heidegger, Sartre, Merleau-Ponty, Gadamer, and Sartre.

Husserl aims to realize through phenomenology the ideal of philosophy as rigorous science that he associates primarily with Descartes, Kant, and Fichte. Above I have already pointed to the insuperable difficulty undermining his entire project, namely his inability to show that claims formulated on the transcendental plane apply to or correctly describe what he calls the life-world. This is a direct analogue of Kant's inability to relate what he calls representations (or appearances) to things in themselves. If the problem of knowledge is understood in a Kantian mode, that is, as an explanation about how to know the mind-independent object or, conversely, as knowing the mind-dependent, constructed object, then, since through reduction Husserl brackets existence, hence knowledge of what is, one must say that Husserlian phenomenology is concerned with a different series of issues.

The epistemological theme is not clarified but only further confused by Heidegger. At least officially, Heidegger is not concerned with epistemology at all. Though his insightful reading of Kant is very important, it does not directly contribute to solving the problem of knowledge as Kant sees it. Yet Heidegger's position has many epistemological aspects,[13] not all of which are clearly stated. He is, for instance, committed to different, incompatible views of truth: truth as phenomenological, hence apodictic; and truth as hermeneutical, hence interpretive. Among later phenomenologists influenced by Husserl, Merleau-Ponty is arguably closest to a standard conception of epistemology. Yet since he is closer to Hegel's historical than to Kant's ahistorical conception of knowledge, whatever epistemological progress he makes is arguably due to his interest not in Kant but in Hegel.

I believe that of all the movements important in twentieth-century philosophy, pragmatism goes furthest down the road opened by Kant. Though Peirce is steeped in Kant, his relation to Hegel is arguably more significant for his solution to the problem of knowledge. Peirce's precise relation to Hegel is a mystery. Whatever the truth about it, the theory of inquiry that Peirce sketched in the latter part of the nineteenth century at the same time as he criticized and rejected Cartesian foundationalism is remarkably similar to the theory that Hegel puts forth in the Introduction to the *Phenomenology of Spirit.* Peirce's idea that knowledge is a process of navigating between doubt and belief is similar to, perhaps even modeled on, Hegel's conception of the knowing process as testing a series of theories against further experience. Both are variations on the familiar view of knowledge as the result of a process of trial and error. Peirce's view of reality as the result of the cognitive process is a restatement of Hegel's expectation that at the end of the day what he calls the object for us and the object in itself, roughly the object as it initially appears and finally appears in consciousness, come together when theory about the object fully corresponds to it. Peirce's pragmatic restatement of a Hegelian approach to knowledge is quickly diluted in James and Dewey. James thought little of Kant, and his own efforts at a theory of truth can charitably be described as confused. Dewey's view has epistemological consequences, such as the folly of insisting on certainty, but his effort is not aimed at solving Kant's issues.

Hegel, the Kantian Aftermath, and Twentieth-Century Philosophy

I have been arguing that in different ways the main twentieth-century philosophical tendencies grow out of Kant. Yet in philosophy, later is not better, for lessons are only absorbed after many years and there is resistance to new ideas. We are still in the process of finding out Kant's position. There is continuing controversy about how best to interpret it.[14] Yet if Kant is the standard, it is unclear that the twentieth century carries forward his main lessons.

It has already been noted that in Kant's wake most able thinkers believed his position was incomplete and needed to be carried beyond Kant in order to complete the Copernican revolution in philosophy. If this is the standard, then arguably the most important later innovation, the biggest step in developing and completing Kant's contribution, lies in the post-Kantian transformation of the Kantian approach to knowledge from an ahistorical to a historical conception. The introduction of a historical dimension into the problem of knowledge totally transforms it. At least normatively, Kant's transcendental study of the general conditions of knowledge points to an a priori conception of knowledge unrelated to time and place, hence ahistorical. This changes immediately in Kant's wake. The post-Kantian idealist line of development up to Hegel leads to a thoroughly historical conception of knowledge claims indexed to time and place, hence to the historical moment. One way to put the point is that in building on Fichte and Schelling, Hegel rejects Kantian representationalism in favor of Kantian constructivism, which he understands not as an a priori but as an a posteriori construction by finite human beings in historical space.

Since Hegel is not often linked to epistemology and less often to philosophy of science, it may be useful to provide an illustration. An important statement of this approach occurs in the Introduction to the *Phenomenology of Spirit.* In departing from Kant, Hegel, who depicts knowing as a process, suggests that the conditions of knowing cannot be separated from the process of knowing. According to Hegel, both our cognitive theories and the cognitive object evolve in the process of knowledge. The cognitive process would come to an end if in experience our view of the object agreed with the object of the view. Claims to know are always dependent on theories which are relative to the historical moment in which they are formulated and hold sway, but which may later change.

Hegel's position points toward the historical nature of the process of knowledge, which is understood through thinking through the problem of knowledge in Kant's wake. He develops Kant's insight that we construct the objects we know not a priori, nor ahistorically, but a posteriori, in practice, through a historical process, for instance in the formulation of scientific theories in the course of studying nature. Hegel's insight into the historicity of the knowing process is largely lacking in twentieth-century discussions of knowledge. Peirce, who was arguably closest to Hegel, understands that knowledge arises in a process that he never identifies as historical. The later Wittgenstein sees that claims to know depend on context but never grasps their historical development. I would like to suggest that if Kant's epistemology is our standard, then the most important step toward a solution of the problem of knowledge as he understands it lies in recapturing the historical dimension of epistemology that was the outcome of the nineteenth-century post-Kantian German idealist debate on how to carry forward and to complete the critical philosophy.

Notes

Introduction

1 Peter Strawson, *The Bounds of Sense: An Essay on Kant's "Critique of Pure Reason,"* London: Methuen, 1966, p. 29.
2 William James, "Philosophical Conceptions and Practical Results," in William James, *Writings 1878–1881*, New York: Viking, 1992, p. 1096.
3 For instance, Passmore's very interesting discussion is mainly focused on British philosophy. See John Passmore, *A Hundred Years of Philosophy*, Harmondsworth: Penguin, 1968.
4 See Karl Marx and Friedrich Engels, *The German Ideology*, part one: with selections from parts two and three, together with Marx's "Introduction to a Critique of Political Economy," edited and with an introduction by C. J. Arthur, New York: International Publishers, 1970.

Chapter 1 Toward Interpreting Twentieth-Century Philosophy

1 See "Philosophy as Rigorous Science," in Edmund Husserl, *Phenomenology and the Crisis of Philosophy*, translated and with an introduction by Quentin Lauer, New York: Harper and Row, 1965, p. 115.
2 This joke is reported by Rorty. See Richard Rorty, *Consequences of Pragmatism*, Minneapolis: University of Minnesota Press, 1982, p. 211.
3 For an early instance of the effect of 9/11 on philosophy, see Joseph Margolis, *Moral Philosophy after 9/11*, University Park: Pennsylvania State University Press, 2003.
4 See Michael Friedman, *A Parting of the Ways: Carnap, Cassirer and Heidegger*, Chicago: Open Court, 2000. Friedman seems to be overly generous in his depiction of the extent of Carnap's effort to engage with Heidegger.
5 See Rudolf Carnap, "The Elimination of Metaphysics through the Logical Analysis of Language," in *Logical Positivism*, edited by A. J. Ayer, New York: Free Press, 1959, pp. 60–81.
6 See intro., n. 3 above.

7 See Richard J. Bernstein, *Praxis and Action: Contemporary Philosophies of Human Activity*, Philadelphia: University of Pennsylvania Press, 1971.
8 See Herbert Spiegelberg, *The Phenomenological Movement: A Historical Introduction*, The Hague: Martinus Nijhoff, 1982.
9 See Jürgen Habermas, *The Philosophical Discourse of Modernity: Twelve Lectures*, translated by Frederick Lawrence, Cambridge, Mass.: MIT Press, 1987.
10 "The safest general characterization of the European philosophical tradition is that it consists of a series of footnotes to Plato." Alfred North Whitehead, *Process and Reality*, New York: Free Press, p. 39.
11 See Étienne Gilson, *La Liberté chez Descartes et la théologie*, Paris: Alcan, 1913.
12 See Daniel Garber, *Descartes' Metaphysical Physics*, Chicago: University of Chicago Press, 1992.
13 See Immanuel Kant, *Critique of Pure Reason*, translated and edited by Paul Guyer and Allen W. Wood, New York: Cambridge University Press, 1998, B xliv, p. 123.
14 For an argument that Marx is a full-fledged member of German idealism, see Tom Rockmore, *Marx After Marxism*, Oxford: Blackwell, 2002.
15 See Otto Liebmann, *Kant und die Epigonen* (1865), edited by Bruno Bauch, Berlin: Reuther and Reichard, 1912.
16 See ibid., p. 206.
17 This term occurs frequently under Hegel's pen. See, e.g., G. W. F. Hegel, *The Encyclopedia Logic*, translated by T. F. Geraets, W. A. Suchting, and H. S. Harris, Indianapolis: Hackett, 1991, pp. 87, 175, 177.

Chapter 2 Kant and the Post-Kantian Debate

1 See Martin Heidegger, *Kant and the Problem of Metaphysics*, translated by Richard Taft, Bloomington: Indiana University Press, 1997.
2 See Immanuel Kant, *Prolegomena to Any Future Metaphysics*, translated, with an introduction and notes, by James W. Ellington, Indianapolis: Hackett, 2001.
3 For recent discussion of epistemological foundationalism, see Tom Rockmore, *On Foundationalism: A Strategy for Metaphysical Realism*, Lanham, Md.: Rowman and Littlefield, 2004.
4 See G. W. F. Hegel, *Lectures on the History of Philosophy*, translated by R. F. Brown and J. M. Stewart with the assistance of H. S. Harris, Berkeley: University of California Press, 1990, p. 137.
5 See, for discussion, Richard Popkin, *The History of Scepticism from Erasmus to Descartes*, New York: Humanities Press, 1964.
6 See Third Meditation in *Meditations on First Philosophy*, in *The Philosophical Works of Descartes*, translated by Elizabeth S. Haldane and G. R. T. Ross, New York: Cambridge University Press, 1970, I, p. 159.
7 See ibid., I, p. 160.
8 See Reply to Objections V, in ibid., II, pp. 227–8.

9 Locke uses the term "white paper" in claiming that all ideas are derived from experience. See John Locke, *An Essay Concerning Human Understanding*, collated and annotated, with prolegomena, biographical, critical, and historical, by Alexander Campbell Fraser, New York: Dover, 1959, I, 2, pp. 121–2.

10 "It is an established opinion amongst some men, that there are in the understanding certain *innate principles*; some primary notions, *koinai ennoiai*, characters, as it were stamped upon the mind of man; which the soul receives in its very first being, and brings into the world with it. It would be sufficient to convince unprejudiced readers of the falseness of this supposition, if I should only show (as I hope I shall in the following parts of this Discourse) how men, barely by the use of their natural faculties, may attain to all the knowledge they have, without the help of any innate impressions; and may arrive at certainty, without any such original notions or principles." Ibid., I, pp. 37–8.

11 He enjoins the observer to prevent the mind from distorting what it sees, or acting "like a false mirror, which, receiving rays irregularly, distorts and discolors the nature of the thing by mingling its own nature with it." Francis Bacon, *The New Organon*, edited with an introduction by Fulton H. Anderson, Indianapolis: LLA, 1960, aphorism no. xli, p. 48.

12 See Richard Rorty, *Philosophy and the Mirror of Nature*, Princeton: Princeton University Press, 1979.

13 See Locke, *An Essay Concerning Human Understanding*, II, 25, p. 525.

14 Ibid., introduction 8, p. 32.

15 Ibid., II, 2, 2, p. 145.

16 See ibid., II, 32, 19, p. 523 and II, 32, 25, p. 525.

17 This term seems to have been coined by Bishop Stillingfleet, an early critic of Locke. Locke talks about his way of ideas, which Stillingfleet calls the new way of ideas. See John Locke, *Mr.* ***Locke's*** *reply to the Right Reverend the Lord Bishop of Worcester's answer to his letter: concerning some passages relating to Mr.* ***Locke's*** *Essay of humane understanding, in a late discourse of His Lordships, in vindication of the Trinity*, London: H. Clark, for A. and J. Churchill . . . and E. Castle . . . , 1697, p. 72.

18 See Immanuel Kant, *The Metaphysical Principles of Virtue*, translated by James W. Ellington, with an introduction by Warner Wick, Indianapolis: LLA, 1964, pp. 5–6.

19 See Kant, *Critique of Pure Reason*, B 370, p. 395 (see ch. 1, n. 13 above).

20 See ibid., B xxxvi, p. 120.

21 See the account of the "Second Analogy," in ibid., B 232–57, pp. 304–16.

22 See Kant, *Prolegomena*, p. 5.

23 See Immanuel Kant, "A New Elucidation of the First Principles of Metaphysical Cognition" (1755), in *Cambridge Edition I, Theoretical Philosophy 1755–1770*, translated and edited by David Walford in collaboration with Ralf Meerbote, Cambridge: Cambridge University Press, 1992, pp. 1–45.

24 "Dreams of a Spirit-Seer Elucidated by Dreams of Metaphysics" (1766), in ibid., p. 370: "It is impossible for reason ever to understand how something can be a cause, or have a force; such relations can only be derived from experience."
25 See "Monadology," in G. W. F. Leibniz, *The Monadology*, translation with introduction and notes by Robert Latta, Oxford: Oxford University Press, 1965, §§ 30–1, pp. 234–5.
26 See Kant, *Critique of Pure Reason*, B 246, p. 311, B 365, p. 321, and B 811, pp. 665–6.
27 See ibid., B xxii n., p. 113.
28 See Kant, *Prolegomena*, pp. 2–6.
29 See Kant, *Critique of Pure Reason*, B 274, p. 326.
30 Kant explicitly says that the concept of the subject, in his language the synthetic unity of apperception, "is the highest point" of transcendental philosophy. See ibid., B 314 n., p. 247.
31 See Immanuel Kant, "On the Form and Principles of the Intelligible and Sensible World," in *Cambridge Edition I*, pp. 375–416.
32 Kant's Letter to Marcus Herz, February 21, 1772, in Kant, *Prolegomena*, p. 117.
33 Ibid., p. 118: "The pure concepts of the understanding must, therefore, not be abstracted from the sensation of the senses, nor must those concepts express the receptivity of representations through sense; but they must, to be sure, have their sources in the nature of the soul, though not insofar as they are produced by the object nor insofar as they bring forth the object itself."
34 Ibid., p. 118: "However, I had passed over in silence the question as to how else, then, a representation referring to an object is possible without being affected by the object in some way."
35 Ibid., p. 119: "In mathematics, this agreement is possible because there the objects are quantities and can be represented as such only inasmuch as we can produce their representations by taking a unit a number of times. Hence the concepts of quantities are spontaneous, and their principles can be established a priori."
36 Ibid., p. 119: "But in the relation of qualities, questions arise as to how my understanding is itself to frame entirely a priori concepts of things with which the things are necessarily to agree, and furthermore how the understanding is to lay out real principles regarding the possibility of things, and experience must faithfully agree with these principles even though they are nonetheless independent of experience."
37 Ibid., p. 119.
38 "Idea" signifies a pure concept of reason for which no object of experience can be given. See *Prolegomena*, p. 327.
39 See Kant, *Critique of Pure Reason*, B 833, p. 677.

40 See Ibid., B xxx, p. 117.
41 See *Discourse on Method*, IV, in *The Philosophical Works of Descartes*, I, p. 105.
42 Descartes, who was aware of this objection, denies it. See ibid., p. 129.
43 See Locke, *An Essay Concerning Human Understanding*, introduction 5, p. 29.
44 For a recent discussion, see Stathis Psillos, "The Present State of the Scientific Realism Debate," in *British Journal of the Philosophy of Science* 51 (2000), pp. 705–28.
45 A recent exception is Putnam. See Hilary Putnam, *The Threefold Cord: Mind, Body and World*, New York: Columbia University Press, 1999.
46 See Bertrand Russell, *A Critical Exposition of the Philosophy of Leibniz* (1900), London: George Allen and Unwin, 1967, p. 14.
47 See Hans Blumenberg, "What Is Copernican in Kant's Turning?," ch. 5 in *The Genesis of the Copernican Revolution*, translated by Robert M. Wallace, Cambridge, Mass.: MIT Press, 1987, pp. 595–614.
48 In the first letter of his *Briefe über die Kantische Philosophie*, which appeared in August 1786, hence before the second edition of the *Kritik der reinen Vernunft*, Reinhold refers to the relation between Kant and revolution (see K. L. Reinhold, "Briefe über die Kantische Philosophie," in *Teutscher Zeitschrift*, August 1786, 27, pp. 124–5) and then to Kant and Copernicus (ibid., p. 126).
49 In a *Nachruf* on the occasion of Kant's death, Schelling suggests that Kant intends to make a Copernican turn. "Like Copernicus, his countryman, who transferred motion from the center to the periphery, he initially inverted representation, according to which the inactive and passively receptive subject is impacted by the object, and inversion which, in all branches of knowledge, was transmitted like an electric shock." "Immanuel Kant" (1804), in *Schellings Werke*, Munich: Beck, 1958, Bd. III, p. 599.
50 See Kant, *Critique of Pure Reason*, B 14, p. 143.
51 See Gottlob Frege, *The Foundations of Arithmetic*, translated by J. L. Austin, New York: Harper and Row, 1960.
52 See "Two Dogmas of Empiricism," in W. V. Quine, *From a Logical Point of View*, New York: Harper and Row, 1963, pp. 20–46.
53 See Hans Reichenbach, *The Philosophy of Space and Time*, translated by Maria Reichenbach, New York: Dover, 1958.
54 See Kant, *Critique of Pure Reason*, B x, p. 107.
55 See ibid., B 741, p. 630.
56 See ibid., B 752, p. 636.
57 Ibid., B xi–xii, pp. 107–8.
58 See Kant, *Prolegomena*, § 14, p. 35.
59 See ibid., § 15, p. 36.
60 See ibid., § 17, pp. 36–8.

61 See, e.g., § 9: "Galileo's Mathematization of Nature," in Edmund Husserl, *The Crisis of the European Sciences and Transcendental Phenomenology*, translated, with an introduction, by David Carr, Evanston, Ill.: Northwestern University Press, 1970, pp. 23–59.

62 Kant, *Critique of Pure Reason*, B xxiii, p. 113.

63 "But hitherto I have not been able to deduce from the phenomena the reason for these properties of gravity, and I do not contrive hypotheses. For whatever is not deduced from the phenomena is to be called an *hypothesis*. . . ." Isaac Newton, *Newton's Principia*, translated by I. Bernard Cohen and Anne Whitman, with the assistance of Julia Budenz, Berkeley: University of California Press, 1960, p. 546.

64 "If we proceed still further to the fundamental doctrines of physical astronomy, we find a physical law of reciprocal attraction extending over the whole of material nature, the rule of which is that it decreases inversely as the square of the distance from each attracting point, just as the spherical surfaces through which this force diffuses itself increase; and this law seems to be necessarily inherent in the very nature of things, so that it is usually propounded as cognizable *a priori*." Kant, *Prolegomena*, § 38, pp. 58–9.

65 Kant, *Critique of Pure Reason*, B xvi, p. 110.

66 Ibid., B xiii., p. 109.

67 See, e.g., "Galileo's Mathematization of Nature," in Husserl, *The Crisis.*

68 "All apprehended change of place is due to movement either of the observed object or of the observer, or to differences in movements that are occurring simultaneously in both. . . . Now it is from the earth that we visually apprehend the revolution of the heavens. If, then, any movement is ascribed to the earth, that motion will generate the appearance of itself in all things which are external to it, though as occurring in the opposite direction, as if everything were passing across the earth, though not the earth itself. . . ." Nicolaus Copernicus, *On the Revolution of the Heavenly Spheres*, in *Great Books of the Western World*, edited by Mortimer Adler, Chicago: University of Chicago Press, 1990, Vol. 15, p. 505.

69 Kant, *Critique of Pure Reason*, B xvi–xvii, p. 110.

70 See ibid., B 130–9, pp. 246–50.

71 See ibid., B 134 n., p. 247.

72 Ibid., A ix, p. 100.

73 See ibid., B 132, p. 247.

74 Ibid., B 132, p. 246.

75 See Kant, *Prolegomena*, § 39, pp. 60–2.

76 See Kant, *Critique of Pure Reason*, B 127, p. 225.

77 See ibid., B 116, pp. 219–20.

78 See ibid., A 110, pp. 233–4.

79 See ibid., A 125, p. 241.

80 See *Opus posthumum*, in *Kants-Werke*, Berlin: Akademie-Ausgabe, XXI, p. 115.

81 See "Fragment of a System," in G. W. F. Hegel, *Early Theological Writings*, translated by T. M. Knox, with an introduction and fragments translated by Richard Kroner, Philadelphia: University of Pennsylvania Press, 1971, pp. 309–20.

82 See G. W. F. Hegel, *Philosophy of Right*, translated with notes by T. M. Knox, Oxford: Clarendon Press, 1965, p. 11.

Chapter 3 On Marxism in the Twentieth Century

1 See T. I. Oizerman, *Nauchno-filosofskoe Mirovozrenie Marksizma* [Scientific-Philosophical Worldview], Moscow: Nauka, 1989.

2 See T. I. Oizerman, *Marksizm i utopizm* [Marxism and Utopia], Moscow: Progress, 2003.

3 See Nicholas Lobkowicz, *Theory and Practice: History of a Concept from Aristotle to Marx*, Notre Dame, Ind.: University of Notre Dame Press, 1967.

4 See "Theses on Feuerbach," in Marx and Engels, *The German Ideology*, part one, p. 123 (see intro., n. 4 above).

5 See Adam Schaff, *Marxism and the Human Individual*, introduction by Erich Fromm, edited by Robert S. Cohen, based on a translation by Olgierd Wojtasiewicz, New York: McGraw-Hill, 1970.

6 See especially "Karl Marx and the Classical Definition of Truth," in Leszek Kolakowski, *Toward a Marxist Humanism*, translated by Olga Zielenko Peel, New York: Grove Press, 1968, pp. 38–66.

7 See Leszek Kolakowski, *Main Currents of Marxism*, translated by P. S. Falla, Oxford: Clarendon Press, 1978, 3 vols.

8 "It is no accident that Marx should have begun with an analysis of commodities when, in the two great works of his mature period, he set out to portray capitalist society in its totality and to lay bare its fundamental nature. For at this stage in the history of mankind there is no problem that does not ultimately lead back to that question and there is no solution that could not be found in the solution to the riddle of commodity-*structure*." Georg Lukács, *History and Class Consciousness*, translated by Rodney Livingstone, Cambridge, Mass.: MIT Press, 1971, p. 83.

9 Rockmore, *Marx After Marxism* (see ch. 1, n. 14 above).

10 V. I. Lenin, *The Teachings of Karl Marx*, New York: International Publishers, 1930, p. 10.

11 For discussion of the differences, see Kolakowski, *Main Currents of Marxism*, I, pp. 399–408.

12 See Marx's "Letter to His Father: On A Turning-Point in Life" (1837), in *Writings of the Young Marx on Philosophy and Society*, edited by L. D. Easton and K. H. Guddat, Garden City, N.Y.: Doubleday, 1967, p. 48.

13 See Emil Fackenheim, *The Religious Dimension of Hegel's Thought*,

Bloomington: Indiana University Press, 1968.

14 See Jindrich Zeleny, *The Logic of Marx*, translated by Terrell Carver, Totowa, N.J.: Rowman and Littlefield, 1980.

15 See, e.g., "On the Status of Science and Metaphysics," in Karl Popper, *Conjectures and Refutations: The Growth of Scientific Knowledge*, New York: Harper and Row, 1965, pp. 184–200.

16 See Frederick Engels, "Speech at the Graveside of Karl Marx," in *The Marx–Engels Reader*, edited by Robert C. Tucker, New York: Norton, 1972, p. 681.

17 See Friedrich Engels, *Anti-Dühring*, New York: International Publishers, 1970.

18 See Lukács, *History and Class Consciousness*, p. 83.

19 Ludwig Feuerbach, *Principles of the Philosophy of the Future*, translated by Manfred Vogel, Indianapolis: Bobbs-Merrill, 1966.

20 See Ludwig Feuerbach, *The Essence of Christianity*, translated by George Eliot, New York: Harper and Row, 1957.

21 See Sigmund Freud, "The Future of An Illusion," in *The Freud Reader*, edited by Peter Gay, New York: Norton, 1989, pp. 685–721.

22 See G. W. F. Hegel, *Phenomenology of Spirit*, translated by A. V. Miller, with analysis of the text and foreword by J. N. Findlay, New York: Oxford University Press, 1977, § 209, p. 127.

23 See D. F. Strauss, *The Life of Jesus Critically Examined*, translated by George Eliot, Philadelphia: Fortress Press, 1973.

24 See Feuerbach, *The Essence of Christianity.*

25 See Karl Marx, *Early Writings*, translated by T. B. Bottomore, New York: McGraw-Hill, 1964, p. 52.

26 See "Economic and Philosophical Manuscripts," in *Early Writings*, p. 197.

27 See Marx, *Early Writings*, pp. 126–8.

28 See "Theses on Feuerbach," in Marx and Engels, *The German Ideology*, pp. 121–3.

29 See Friedrich Engels, *Ludwig Feuerbach* in *Marx/Engels Collected Works*, Vol. 26, London: Lawrence & Wishart, 1991, p. 355.

30 See ibid., p. 357; see also Hegel, *Philosophy of Right*, p. 10 (see ch. 2, n. 82 above).

31 See Engels, *Ludwig Feuerbach*, in *Marx/Engels*, p. 358.

32 See ibid., p. 358.

33 See ibid., p. 360.

34 See Francis Fukuyama, *The End of History and the Last Man*, New York: Free Press, 1992.

35 See Engels, *Feuerbach*, in *Marx/Engels*, p. 363.

36 Ibid., pp. 374–80.

37 Ibid., pp. 357–64.

38 Ibid., p. 366.

39 See ibid., p. 366.
40 Karl Marx, *Capital: A Critique of Critical Economy*, translated by Samuel Moore and Edward Aveling, edited by Frederick Engels, New York: International Publishers, 1967, p. 20.
41 See Engels, *Ludwig Feuerbach*, in *Marx/Engels*, p. 374.
42 See ibid., p. 368.
43 Ibid., p. 380.
44 See ibid., p. 381.
45 Ibid., p. 381.
46 Ibid., p. 383.
47 Ibid., p. 383.
48 Ibid., p. 384.
49 See ibid., p. 388.
50 For an important non-Marxist reading of the relation, see Klaus Hartmann, *Die Marx'sche Theorie. Eine philosophische Untersuchung zu den Hauptschriften*, Berlin: De Gruyter, 1970.
51 The most important non-Western Marxist interpreter of Hegel and Hegelian Marxism is the Russian philosopher T. I. Oizerman. All of his many books in one way or another concern a Hegelian approach to Marx and Marxism.
52 See, e.g., Louis Althusser, *For Marx*, translated by Ben Brewster, New York: Pantheon, 1969.
53 See Karl Kosch, *Marxism and Philosophy*, translated, with an introduction, by Fred Halliday, New York: Monthly Review Press, 1971, p. 68.
54 See "On Materialistic Dialectic," in ibid.
55 See Lukács, *History and Class Consciousness*, p. xxix.
56 See Hegel, *Philosophy of Right*, § 67, p. 54: "By alienating the whole of my time, as crystallized in my work, and everything produced, I would be making into another's property the substance of my being, my universal activity and actuality, my personality."
57 See the fourth part of the first of the *Paris Manuscripts*, in Marx, *Early Writings*, pp. 120–34.
58 See Lukács, *History and Class Consciousness*, pp. 131–3.
59 See ibid., pp. 140–8.
60 Ibid., p. 149.
61 See Georg Lukács, *The Young Hegel: Studies in the Relations between Dialectics and Economics*, translated by Rodney Livingstone, Cambridge, Mass.: MIT Press, 1976.
62 See, e.g., Georg Lukács, *The Historical Novel*, translated by Hannah and Stanley Mitchell, introduction by Frederic Jameson, Lincoln: University of Nebraska Press, 1983.
63 See, e.g., Georg Lukács, *Die Eigenart des Ästhetischen*, in *Georg Lukács-Werke*, edited by Frank Benseler, Neuwied: Luchterhand, 1963, Vol. 11, 12.
64 Kolakowski, *Main Currents of Marxism* (see n. 7 above).

65 See Vincent Descombes, *Modern French Philosophy*, translated by L. Scott-Fox and J. M. Harding, New York: Cambridge University Press, 1986.

66 See Alexandre Kojève, *Introduction à la lecture de Hegel: leçons sur La phénoménologie de l'esprit, professées de 1933 à 1939 à l'École des hautes-études*, edited by Raymond Queneau, Paris: Gallimard, 1947, p. 470.

67 See Alexandre Kojève, *Introduction to the Reading of Hegel: Lectures on the Phenomenology of Spirit Assembled by Raymond Queneau*, edited by Allan Bloom, translated by James H. Nichols, Jr, New York: Basic Books, 1969.

68 For a contribution to the history of the Frankfurt School, see Martin Jay, *The Dialectical Imagination: A History of the Frankfurt School and the Institute of Social Research, 1923–1950*, Boston: Little, Brown and Co., 1973.

69 See Kolakowski, *Main Currents of Marxism*, III, p. 342.

70 For an older study encompassing the thinkers of both the first and the second generations, see David Held, *Introduction to Critical Theory*, Berkeley: University of California Press, 1980.

71 See "Traditional and Critical Theory," in Max Horkheimer, *Critical Theory*, translated by Matthew J. O'Connell and others, New York: Herder and Herder, 1972, pp. 188–243.

72 Ibid., p. 194.

73 Ibid., p. 203.

74 Kant, *Critique of Pure Reason*, B 181, p. 273 (see ch. 1, n. 13 above).

75 See Horkheimer, *Critical Theory*, p. 203.

76 Ibid., p. 221.

77 See ibid., p. 233.

78 Ibid., p. 242.

79 See Max Horkheimer, *The Eclipse of Reason*, New York: Seabury, 1947, p. 134.

80 See Herbert Marcuse, *One Dimensional Man: Studies in the Ideology of Advanced Industrial Society*, Boston: Beacon Press, 1964.

81 See "The Question Concerning Technology," in Martin Heidegger, *The Question Concerning Technology and Other Essays*, translated, with an introduction, by William Lovitt, New York: Harper and Row, 1977, pp. 3–35.

82 Max Horkheimer and Theodor Adorno, *Dialectic of Enlightenment*, translated by John Cumming, New York: Herder and Herder, 1973, p. 3.

83 Ibid., p. 24.

84 See André Glucksmann, *Les maîtres Penseurs*, Paris: Gallimard, 1977.

85 See Horkheimer and Adorno, *Dialectic of Enlightenment*, pp. 24–5.

86 See Theodor Adorno, Else Frenkel-Brunswik, Daniel J. Levinson, and R. Nevitt Sanford, *The Authoritarian Personality*, New York: Harper and Row, 1950.

87 See Theodor Adorno, *Minima Moralia*, translated by E. F. N. Jephcott, London: New Left Books, 1974.

88 See Theodor Adorno, *Negative Dialectics*, translated by E. B. Ashton, New York: Seabury, 1973.

89 See Jacques Derrida, *Glas*, Paris: Éditions Galilée, 1974, 2 vols.

90 See Theodor Adorno, *Against Epistemology: Studies in Husserl and the Phenomenological Antinomies*, translated by Willis Domingo, Oxford: Basil Blackwell, 1982.

91 See Theodor Adorno, *The Jargon of Authenticity*, translated by Knut Tarnowski and Frederic Will, Evanston, Ill.: Northwestern University Press, 1973, p. 95.

92 See Martin Heidegger, *Being and Time*, translated by John Macquarrie and Edward Robinson, New York: Harper and Row, 1962, § 35: "Idle Talk," pp. 211–14.

93 See Adorno, *The Jargon of Authenticity*, pp. 92–3.

94 See Herbert Marcuse, *Hegel's Ontology and the Theory of Historicity*, translated by Seyla Benhabib, Cambridge, Mass.: MIT Press, 1987.

95 See Herbert Marcuse, *Soviet Marxism*, Boston: Beacon, 1958.

96 See Herbert Marcuse, *Eros and Civilization*, Boston: Beacon, 1955.

97 See Marcuse, *One Dimensional Man*.

98 See Herbert Marcuse, *The Aesthetic Dimension*, Boston: Beacon, 1978.

99 See Marcuse, *Hegel's Ontology and the Theory of Historicity*.

100 See Herbert Marcuse, *Reason and Revolution: Hegel and the Rise of Social Theory*, Boston: Beacon, 1960.

101 See note 80 above.

102 Alfred Schmidt, *The Concept of Nature in Marx*, translated by Ben Fowkes, London: New Left Books, 1971.

103 See Iring Fetscher, *Hegels Lehre vom Menschen. Kommentar zu den SS. 387–482 der Enzyklopädie der philosophischen Wissenschaften*, Stuttgart: Frommann-Holzboog, 1970.

104 Jürgen Habermas, *The Structural Transformation of the Public Sphere: An Inquiry into a Category of Bourgeois Society*, translated by Thomas Burger with the assistance of Frederick Lawrence, Cambridge, Mass.: MIT Press, 1989.

105 See Jürgen Habermas, *Zur Rekonstruktion des historischen Materialismus*, Frankfurt a. M.: Suhrkamp, 1976.

106 See Jürgen Habermas, *Theory of Communicative Action*, translated by Thomas McCarthy, Boston: Beacon Press, 1984, 1987, 2 vols.

107 See Jürgen Habermas, *The Philosophical Discourse of Modernity: Twelve Lectures*, translated by Frederick Lawrence, Cambridge, Mass.: MIT Press, 1987.

108 See Jürgen Habermas, *Justification and Application: Remarks on Discourse Ethics*, translated by Ciaran Cronin, Cambridge: Polity Press, 1993.

109 See Jürgen Habermas, *Between Facts and Norms: Contributions to a Discourse Theory of Law and Democracy*, translated by William Rehg, Cambridge, Mass.: MIT Press, 1996.

110 See Kant, *Critique of Pure Reason*, B 867, pp. 694–5.

111 See Friedrich Engels, *Introduction to Socialism: Utopian and Scientific*, cited in *A Dictionary of Marxist Thought*, edited by Tom Bottomore, Cambridge, Mass.: Harvard University Press, 1983, p. 206.

112 See Jürgen Habermas, *Truth and Justification*, edited and translations by Barbara Fultner, Cambridge, Mass.: MIT Press, 2003.

113 See "Literaturbericht zur philosophischen Diskussion um Marx und den Marxismus," in *Philosophische Rundschau* 5, 3/4 (1957), pp. 165–235, republished as "Anhang," in Jürgen Habermas, *Theorie und Praxis*, Neuwied: Luchterhand, 1972, pp. 387–464; "Between Philosophy and Science: Marxism as Critique," in Jürgen Habermas, *Theory and Practice*, translated by John Viertel, Boston: Beacon Press, 1973, pp. 195–252; "Knowledge and Human Interests: A General Perspective," in Jürgen Habermas, *Knowledge and Human Interests*, translated by J. J. Shapiro, Boston: Beacon Press, 1971, pp. 301–17; "Toward a Reconstruction of Historical Materialism," in Jürgen Habermas, *Communication and the Evolution of Society*, translated by Thomas McCarthy, Boston: Beacon Press, 1979, pp. 130–77; *Theory of Communicative Action* (see n. 106 above).

114 Habermas, "Literaturbericht zur philosophischen Diskussion um Marx und den Marxismus" (see previous note).

115 "Between Philosophy and Science," in Habermas, *Theory and Practice* (see n. 113 above).

116 "Knowledge and Human Interests," in Habermas, *Knowledge and Human Interests* (see n. 113 above).

117 See "Work and Interaction: Remarks on Hegel's Jena Philosophy of Mind," in Habermas, *Theory and Practice*, pp. 142–69.

118 See n. 113 above.

119 See n. 105 above.

120 See n. 113 above.

121 See n. 106 above.

Chapter 4 Pragmatism as Epistemology

1 See Josiah Royce, *Lectures on Modern Idealism*, New Haven: Yale University Press, 1964, p. 85.

2 See, e.g., Richard Rorty, "Nietzsche, Socrates and Pragmatism," in *South African Journal of Philosophy* 10: 3 (August 1991), pp. 61–3; "Nietzsche: un philosophe pragmatique," in *Magazine Littéraire* (April 1992), pp. 28–32.

3 See Robert Brandom, *Articulating Reasons: An Introduction to Inferentialism*, Cambridge, Mass.: Harvard University Press, 2000, p. 11.

4 See Mark Okrent, *Heidegger's Pragmatism: Understanding, Being, and the Critique of Metaphysics*, Ithaca, NY: Cornell University Press, 1988.

5 See Hubert Dreyfus, *Being-in-the-World: A Commentary on Heidegger's Being and Time, Division I*, Cambridge, Mass.: MIT Press, 1991.

6 See "Thirteen Pragmatisms," in A. O. Lovejoy, *Thirteen Pragmatisms and Other Essays*, Baltimore: Johns Hopkins University Press, 1963, pp. 1–29.
7 See Bertrand Russell, *A History of Western Philosophy*, New York: Simon and Schuster, 1945, p. 151.
8 See A. J. Ayer, *The Origins of Pragmatism: Studies in the Philosophy of Charles Sanders Peirce and William James*, San Francisco: Freeman, Cooper, 1968, p. 3.
9 See Nicholas Rescher, *Realistic Pragmatism: An Introduction to Pragmatic Philosophy*, Albany, NY: SUNY Press, 2000.
10 See John E. Smith, *Themes in American Philosophy: Purpose, Experience and Community*, New York: Harper and Row, 1970.
11 See John E. Smith, *Purpose and Thought: The Meaning of Pragmatism*, Chicago: University of Chicago Press, 1978, p. 8.
12 Kant, *Critique of Pure Reason*, B 852, p. 687 (see ch. 1, n. 13 above).
13 This distinction runs throughout the whole tradition. See Lobkowicz, *Theory and Practice* (see ch. 3, n. 3 above).
14 See Kant's two introductions, in Immanuel Kant, *Critique of the Power of Judgment*, translated by Paul Guyer and Eric Matthews, Cambridge: Cambridge University Press, 2000.
15 See Russell, *A History of Western Philosophy*, pp. 816, 824.
16 Cornel West, *The American Evasion of Philosophy: A Genealogy of Pragmatism*, Madison: University of Wisconsin Press, 1989.
17 Rescher, *Realistic Pragmatism.*
18 See Peirce's review of *Studies in Logical Theory*, in *Collected Papers of Charles Sanders Peirce*, edited by Charles Harteshorne and Paul Weiss, Cambridge, Mass.: Belknap Press, 1960–6, 8.188–90.
19 See, e.g., John Dewey, "The Pragmatism of Peirce," in *Journal of Philosophy* 21 (1916); "Peirce's Theory of Quality," in *Journal of Philosophy* 32 (1935); and "Peirce's Theory of Linguistic Signs, Thought and Meaning," in *Journal of Philosophy* 43 (1946).
20 These include his seminal articles on "The Fixation of Belief," in *The Essential Peirce: Selected Philosophical Writings*, edited by Nathan Houser and Christian Kloesel, Bloomington: Indiana University Press, 1992, 2 vols, I, pp. 109–23; "How To Make Our Ideas Clear," in ibid., I, pp. 124–41; "The Doctrine of Chances," in ibid., I, pp. 142–54; "The Probability of Induction," in ibid., I, pp. 155–69; "The Order of Nature," in ibid., I, pp. 170–85; and "Deduction, Induction and Hypothesis," in ibid., I, pp. 186–99.
21 See "Fraser's *The Works of George Berkeley*," in *The Essential Peirce*, I, pp. 83–105.
22 See C. J. Hookway, *Peirce*, London: Routledge, 1999.
23 See H. S. Thayer, *Meaning and Action: A Critical History of Pragmatism*, Indianapolis: Bobbs-Merrill, 1973.

24 See Murray Murphey, *The Development of Peirce's Philosophy*, Cambridge, Mass.: Harvard University Press, 1961.
25 See "The Fixation of Belief," in *The Essential Peirce*, I, p. 111.
26 See ibid., p. 111.
27 See ibid., p. 120.
28 See "How To Make Our Ideas Clear," in *The Essential Peirce*, I, p. 126.
29 See ibid., p. 128.
30 Ibid., p. 132.
31 See ibid., pp. 138, 139.
32 Ibid., p. 139. This view influenced Dewey, who says: "The best definition of *truth* from the logical standpoint which is known to me is that of Peirce: 'The opinion which is fated to be ultimately agreed by all those who investigate what it is we mean by the truth'." John Dewey, *Logic: The Theory of Inquiry*, New York: Henry Holt, 1938, p. 58.
33 See "The Probability of Induction," in *The Essential Peirce*, I, pp. 167–9.
34 See "Deduction, Induction and Hypothesis," in *The Essential Peirce*, I, p. 197.
35 Ibid., p. 198.
36 See William James, *Pragmatism*, New York: Meridian, 1960, p. 43.
37 See his letter of 1903 to James, cited in Thayer, *Meaning and Action*, pp. 499ff.
38 "The Maxim of Pragmatism," in *The Essential Peirce*, II, 135.
39 See ibid., pp. 143–4.
40 See "The Seven Systems of Metaphysics," in *The Essential Peirce*, II, p. 180.
41 See "What Pragmatism Is," in *The Essential Peirce*, II, p. 333.
42 Ibid., p. 338.
43 See "The Fixation of Belief," in *The Essential Peirce*, I, p. 120.
44 He refers to Peirce as the inventor of pragmatism in a lecture in 1898. See "Philosophical Conceptions and Practical Results," in James, *Writings 1878–1881*, pp. 1078–9 (see intro., n. 2 above).
45 See James, *Pragmatism*, p. 18.
46 See n. 30 above.
47 This characterization and the conclusions James draws from it were stated earlier in almost exactly the same way in his book on religion. See William James, *The Varieties of Religious Experience*, New York: New American Library, 1961, p. 339.
48 James, *Pragmatism*, p. 43.
49 See William James, *The Principles of Psychology*, Frederick H. Burkhardt, general editor; Fredson Bowers, textual editor; Ignas K. Skrupskelis, associate editor, Cambridge, Mass.: Harvard University Press, 1981.
50 See William James, *Psychology: The Briefer Course*, edited by Gordon Allport, Notre Dame, Ind.: University of Notre Dame Press, 1985.

51 Ibid., pp. 18–42.
52 Ibid., p. 26.
53 See ibid., p. 147.
54 See Lecture XVIII, in James, *The Varieties of Religious Experience*, pp. 329–46.
55 Ibid., p. 377.
56 Ibid., p. 388.
57 William James, *The Will To Believe and Other Essays on Popular Philosophy*, New York: Dover, 1956, p. xiii.
58 Ibid., p. 263.
59 Ibid., p. 275.
60 See William James, *Essays in Radical Empiricism*, New York: Longmans, Green, and Co., 1912.
61 See "The Will To Believe," in *The Will To Believe*, § 6, pp. 14–17.
62 See "What Pragmatism Means," in *Pragmatism*, p. 59.
63 See "Pragmatism's Conception of Truth," in *Pragmatism*, p. 135.
64 Russell, *A History of Western Philosophy*, p. 818.
65 Writing in 1945, that is Russell's judgment. See ibid., p. 819.
66 See *Collected Papers of Charles Sanders Peirce*, edited by Charles Hartshorne and Paul Weiss, Cambridge, Mass.: Harvard University Press, 1931–58, 8 vols.
67 There are no references to Peirce in many of Dewey's main writings, including *Reconstruction in Philosophy* and *Experience and Nature*. There is only a single article by Dewey on Peirce in his immense bibliography: "The Pragmatism of Peirce," in *Journal of Philosophy, Psychology and Scientific Methods* 13 (1916), pp. 709–15.
68 "The Development of American Pragmatism," in *John Dewey: The Later Works, 1925–1953*, edited by Jo Ann Boydston, Carbondale: University of Southern Illinois Press, 1981–90, 17 vols, Vol. 2, p. 16.
69 See John Dewey, *Liberalism and Social Action*, New York: Putnam, 1963.
70 See M. H. Thomas, *John Dewey: A Centennial Bibliography*, Chicago: University of Chicago Press, 1962.
71 See John Dewey, *Psychology*, New York: Harper and Bros., 1891.
72 See John Dewey, *Lectures in the Philosophy of Education*, edited, with an introduction, by Reginald D. Archambault. New York: Random House, 1966.
73 See John Dewey, *Reconstruction in Philosophy*, Boston: Beacon Press, 1964.
74 See John Dewey, *Experience and Nature*, La Salle, Ill.: Open Court, 1925.
75 See John Dewey, *Individualism, Old and New*, New York: Minton, Balch & Company, 1930.
76 See John Dewey, *Art as Experience*, New York: Capricorn, 1958.
77 See John Dewey, *The Quest for Certainty: A Study of the Relation of Knowledge and Action*, New York: Putnam, 1960.

78 "Philosophy and the American Way of Life," in *John Dewey: The Middle Works, 1899–1924*, Carbondale: Southern Illinois University Press, 1976–83, 15 vols, Vol. 3, pp. 73–4.
79 See "Kant and Philosophic Method," in *John Dewey: Philosophy, Psychology and Social Practice*, edited by Joseph Ratner, New York: Capricorn, 1963, pp. 35–48.
80 See "Intelligence and Morals," in *The Influence of Darwinism on Philosophy and Other Essays*, Amherst, NY: Prometheus Books, 1997, p. 66.
81 "The Influence of Darwinism on Philosophy," in *The Influence of Darwinism on Philosophy and Other Essays*, pp. 8–9.
82 "The Pattern of Inquiry," in *Logic: The Theory of Inquiry*, *John Dewey: The Later Works, 1925–1953*, Vol. 12, p. 122.
83 Dewey, *The Quest for Certainty*, p. 8.
84 Ibid., p. 17.
85 Dewey, "Darwinism and Philosophy," in *The Influence of Darwinism on Philosophy and Other Essays*, p. 17.
86 Dewey, *Reconstruction in Philosophy*, p. v.
87 The first chapter of his book is devoted to making this point. See "Experience and Philosophic Method," in Dewey, *Experience and Nature*, pp. 1–36.
88 Ibid., p. 59.
89 Ibid., p. 4.
90 Ibid., p. xvi.
91 In a famous paper, he decisively criticizes the very idea of protocol sentences. See Otto Neurath, "Protocol Sentences," in *Logical Positivism*, edited by Ayer, pp. 199–208.
92 See Rudolf Carnap, *The Logical Syntax of Language*, translated by Amethe Smeaton, La Salle, Ill.: Open Court, 2002.
93 See C. I. Lewis, "A Pragmatic Conception of the A Priori," in *The Journal of Philosophy* 20 (1923), pp. 169–77. For his later development of this approach, see C. I. Lewis, *Mind and the World Order* (1929), New York: Dover, 1956, chs. 7–9, pp. 195–308.
94 Quine, "Two Dogmas of Empiricism," in Quine, *From a Logical Point of View* (see ch. 2, n. 52 above).
95 See Hilary Putnam, *Pragmatism: An Open Question*, Oxford: Blackwell, 1995, esp. ch. 3: "The Permanence of William James," pp. 5–26.
96 See Brandom, *Articulating Reasons.*
97 For remarks on Goodman and Davidson as pragmatists, but not Frege, see Rescher, *Realistic Pragmatism.*
98 Rorty, *Philosophy and the Mirror of Nature*, p. 11 (see ch. 1, n. 12 above).
99 Rorty, *Consequences of Pragmatism*, p. 161 (see ch. 1, n. 2 above).
100 See "Introduction: Pragmatism and Post-Nietzschean Philosophy," in Richard Rorty, *Essays on Heidegger and Others, Philosophical Papers, Volume 2*, Cambridge: Cambridge University Press, 1991, pp. 1–6.

101 See Friedrich Nietzsche, *The Gay Science*, translated by Walter Kaufmann, New York: Vintage, 1974, § 374, p. 336.

102 See "On the Very Idea of a Conceptual Scheme," in Donald Davidson, *Inquiries into Truth and Interpretation*, Oxford: Clarendon Press, 1991, pp. 183–98.

103 See Davidson, *Inquiries into Truth and Interpretation*, p. xviii.

104 See "Pragmatism, Davidson and Truth," in Richard Rorty, *Objectivity, Relativism, and Truth, Philosophical Papers, Volume 1*, Cambridge: Cambridge University Press, 1991, pp. 126–50.

105 See "A Coherence Theory of Truth and Knowledge," in Donald Davidson, *Subjective, Intersubjective, Objective*, Oxford: Clarendon Press, 2001, pp. 137–53.

106 In *Philosophy and Social Hope* (London: Penguin, 1999), Rorty perhaps inconsistently describes Putnam as "the leading contemporary pragmatist" (p. xxvii) and Dewey and Davidson as the "paradigmatic pragmatists" (p. 24).

107 See "Hilary Putnam and the Relativist Menace," in Richard Rorty, *Truth and Progress, Philosophical Papers, Volume 3*, Cambridge: Cambridge University Press, 1998, pp. 43–62.

108 See ibid., p. 62.

Chapter 5 Continental Philosophy as Phenomenology

1 This term seems to have been invented by the historian of phenomenology, Spiegelberg. See Herbert Spiegelberg, *The Phenomenological Movement: A Historical Introduction*, The Hague: Martinus Nijhoff, 1982. This book provides a pioneer and still reliable survey of phenomenology in Husserl and his followers. For a more recent survey of roughly the same terrain from a more analytic angle of vision, see Dermot Moran, *Introduction to Phenomenology*, London: Routledge, 2000.

2 See Plato, *Republic*, translated by C. D. C. Reeve, Indianapolis: Hackett, 2004, 511C–514A, pp. 205–7.

3 Kant refers often to this seminal distinction. The most important passage is Kant, *Critique of Pure Reason*, B 566, p. 535 (see ch. 1, n. 13 above).

4 J. H. Lambert, *Neues Organon oder Gedanken über die Erforschung und Bezeichnung des Wahren und der Unterschiedung von Irrtum und Schein*, Leipzig: J. Wendler, 1764.

5 See "To J. H. Lambert, September 2, 1770," in Immanuel Kant, *Philosophical Correspondence, 1759–99*, edited and translated by Arnulf Zweig, Chicago: University of Chicago Press, 1967, p. 59.

6 See "To Marcus Herz, February 21, 1772," in Kant, *Philosophical Correspondence, 1759–99*, p. 71.

7 See Plato, *Phaedo*, translated by G. M. A. Grube, in *Plato: Complete Works*, edited by John M. Cooper, Cambridge, Mass.: Hackett, 1997, 101E, p. 87.

8 See Hegel, *The Encyclopedia Logic*, 25, p. 64 (see ch. 1, n. 17 above).

9 For references, see Spiegelberg, *The Phenomenological Movement*, pp. 14–18.

10 Spiegelberg refers to Brentano's view of Hegel as exhibiting "extreme degeneration of human thought." See ibid., p. 13.

11 See "Philosophie als strenge Wissenschaft," in Edmund Husserl, *Aufsätze und Vorträge (1911–1921)*, edited by Thomas Nenon and H. R. Sepp, Dordrecht: Martinus Nijhoff, 1987, p. 6.

12 In a detailed, recent study, Welton, who is typical, makes no direct reference to Hegel, and only a single reference in the context of Adorno's view of Husserl. See Donn Welton, *The Other Husserl: The Horizons of Transcendental Phenomenology*, Bloomington: Indiana University Press, 2000.

13 This idea seems to have been initially formulated by Kojève in his well-known study of Hegel. According to Kojève, Husserl and Hegel share the same phenomenological method. See Kojève, *Introduction à la lecture de Hegel*, p. 470 (see ch. 3, n. 66). This idea reappears in Derrida. In a reference to a book by Hyppolite (Jean Hyppolite, *Logique et existence*, Paris: Presses Universitaires de France, 1953, p. 39), he notes "the profound convergence between Hegel's and Husserl's positions." Edmund Husserl, *L'origine de la géométrie*, translated, with an introduction, by Jacques Derrida, Paris: Presses Universitaires de France, 1974, p. 58, n. 1.

14 See Gottlob Frege, "Review of Dr. E. Husserl's *Philosophy of Arithmetic*," in *Husserl: Expositions and Appraisals*, edited by Frederick Elliston and Peter McCormick, Notre Dame, Ind.: Notre Dame University Press, 1981, pp. 314–24.

15 For the view that Husserl was reacting to Frege, see Dagfinn Føllesdall, *Husserl und Frege. Ein Beitrag zur Beleuchtung der Entstehung der phänomenologischen Philosophie*, Oslo: Aschehoug, 1958. For the view that Husserl changed his view before Frege's criticism, see J. N. Mohanty, *Husserl and Frege*, Bloomington: Indiana University Press, 1982.

16 See Michael Dummett, "Preface," to Edmund Husserl, *Logical Investigations*, translated by J. N. Findlay, London: Routledge, 2001, I, p. xvii.

17 It is a common objection that Husserl rejects psychologism in the first volume of the *Logical Investigations* only to fall back into it. For Husserl's later refutation of this charge as based on superficial interpretation, see Husserl, *Logical Investigations*, II, p. 178.

18 See Husserl's letter of August 27, 1900 to Meinong, cited in Edmund Husserl, *Gesammelte Werke*, The Hague: Martinus Nijhoff, 1950–, Vol. XVIII, p. xvii.

19 See Husserl, *Logical Investigations*, I, p. 318 n. 6.

20 Ibid., II, § 1, p. 166.

21 Ibid., I, p. 5.

22 See ibid., I, § 65, pp. 149–50.

23 Husserl claims to have only understood this distinction four years later. See Edmund Husserl, *The Crisis of European Sciences and Transcendental Phenomenology: An Introduction to Phenomenological Philosophy*, translated, with an introduction, by David Carr, Evanston, Ill.: Northwestern University Press, 1970, § 70, p. 243.
24 Franz Brentano, *Psychology from an Empirical Standpoint* (1874), translated by A. C. Rancurello, D. B. Terrell, and L. L. McAlister, London: Routledge, 1995, p. 88.
25 Husserl's position in part depends on his understanding of intentionality. Though critical of Brentano's concept, it is sometimes held that he did not have a positive concept of his own. See Moran, *Introduction to Phenomenology*, p. 189.
26 The relation of Husserl's and Heidegger's concepts of truth has attracted attention. See Ernst Tugendhat, *Der Wahrheitsbegriff bei Husserl und Heidegger*, Berlin: de Gruyter, 1967.
27 "Philosophy as Rigorous Science," in Husserl, *Phenomenology and the Crisis of Philosophy* (see ch. 1, n. 1 above).
28 See Wilhelm Dilthey, "Die Typen der Weltanschauung und ihre Ausbildung in den metaphysischen Systemen," in Wilhelm Dilthey, *Gesammelte Schriften*, VII, *Der Aufbau der geschichtlichen Welt in den Geisteswissenschaften*, edited by Bernhard Groethuysen, Göttingen: Vanderhoeck und Ruprecht, 1927, pp. 75–117.
29 Husserl, *Phenomenology and the Crisis of Philosophy*, p. 73.
30 Ibid., p. 73.
31 On Husserl's relation to Kant, see Iso Kern, *Husserl und Kant: Eine Untersuchung über Husserls Verhältnis zu Kant und zum Neukantianismus*, The Hague: Martinus Nijhoff, 1964.
32 See Husserl, *Phenomenology and the Crisis of Philosophy*, p. 76.
33 See ibid., pp. 79–122.
34 Ibid., pp. 122–47.
35 Ibid., p. 80.
36 Ibid., p. 93.
37 Ibid., p. 106.
38 Ibid., p. 110.
39 See Edmund Husserl, *Ideas: General Introduction to Pure Phenomenology*, translated by W. R. Boyce Gibson, New York: Collier Books, 1962, § 61, p. 166.
40 See Husserl, *Phenomenology and the Crisis of Philosophy*, pp. 113–16.
41 Ibid., p. 118.
42 Ibid., p. 120.
43 Ibid., p. 125.
44 Ibid., p. 136.
45 Ibid., p. 143.

46 Ibid., p. 147.

47 See, for discussion of the phenomenological reduction, Husserl, *Ideas*, §§ 31–2, pp. 96–100.

48 See ibid., pp. 11–12.

49 See *Meditations on First Philosophy*, in *The Philosophical Works of Descartes*, I, pp. 155–6 (see ch. 2, n. 6 above).

50 Edmund Husserl, *Cartesian Meditations: An Introduction to Phenomenology*, translated by Dorion Cairns, Dordrecht and Boston: Kluwer Academic Publishers, 1993, § 13, p. 30.

51 For criticism, see Paul Ricoeur, *Husserl: An Analysis of His Phenomenology*, translated by Edward G. Ballard and Lester E. Embree, Evanston, Ill.: Northwestern University Press, 1967.

52 In the first sentence of his programmatic article, he describes it as "the science that satisfies the loftiest theoretical needs and renders possible from an ethico-religious point of view a life regulated by pure rational norms." Husserl, *Phenomenology and the Crisis of Philosophy*, p. 71.

53 See Husserl, *Crisis of the European Sciences*, p. 3.

54 Ibid., p. 17.

55 "Skepticism about the possibility of metaphysics," Husserl writes, "the collapse of the belief in a universal philosophy as the guide for the new man, actually represents a collapse of the belief in 'reason', understood as the ancients opposed episteme to doxa." Ibid., p. 12.

56 "The crisis of European existence," he writes, "can end in only one of two ways: in the ruin of a Europe alienated from its rational sense of life, fallen into a barbarian hatred of spirit; or in the rebirth of Europe from the spirit of philosophy, through a heroism of reason that will definitely overcome naturalism." Husserl, *Phenomenology and the Crisis of Philosophy*, p. 192.

57 Husserl, *Crisis of the European Sciences*, p. 6.

58 Husserl, *Phenomenology and the Crisis of Philosophy*, p. 149.

59 See ibid., p. 100.

60 See Husserl, *Crisis of the European Sciences*, § 9: "Galileo's Mathematization of Nature," pp. 23–60.

61 See ibid., § 28, pp. 103–11.

62 See ibid., part IIIA, §§ 28–53, pp. 103–89.

63 Ibid., § 34e, p. 130.

64 Husserl, *Ideas*, p. 21.

65 Husserl, *Crisis of the European Sciences*, appendix IX, p. 389.

66 See Edmund Husserl, "A Report on German Writings in Logic (1895–1899)," in *Early Writings in the Philosophy of Logic and Mathematics*, *Collected Works*, Dordrecht: Kluwer, 1994, Vol. V, p. 251.

67 Heidegger was Rector of the University of Freiburg im Breisgau for a period before the war, an enthusiastic and early academic member of the German Nazi party (NSDAP), and a supporter of Nazism, from which he

never clearly distanced himself. It is at least arguable that his position and his politics are inseparably intertwined. See Tom Rockmore, *On Heidegger's Nazism and Philosophy*, Berkeley: University of California Press, 1997. Heidegger's treatment of Husserl, after he became Rector, is also controversial.

68 See "My Way Into Phenomenology," in Martin Heidegger, *On Time and Being*, translated, with an introduction, by Joan Stambaugh, Chicago: University of Chicago Press, 2002, pp. 74–82.

69 *Sophist*, translated by N. P. White, in *Plato: Complete Works*, 244A, p. 265.

70 Martin Heidegger, *Being and Time*, translated by John Macquarrie and Edward Robinson, New York: Harper and Row, 1962, p. 1.

71 Ibid., p. 1.

72 In a typical passage, he writes: "This world now present to me, and in every waking 'now' obviously so, has its temporal horizon infinite in both directions, its known and unknown, its intimately alive and its unalive past and future." Husserl, *Ideas*, § 27, p. 92.

73 Heidegger, *Being and Time*, p. 27.

74 Ibid., p. 33.

75 Ibid., pp. 37–8.

76 See Aristotle, *Physics*, in *The Complete Works of Aristotle*, edited by Jonathan Barnes, Princeton: Princeton University Press, 1984, I, delta 10–14.

77 See Heidegger, *Being and Time*, p. 53.

78 Ibid., p. 62. See also ibid., p. 487.

79 See ibid., § 15, pp. 95–102.

80 Ibid., § 31, pp. 182–8.

81 Ibid., p. 184.

82 See ibid., § 32, pp. 188–95.

83 Ibid., p. 195.

84 Ibid., p. 229.

85 Ibid., p. 236.

86 See ibid., p. 62.

87 See ibid., § 32.

88 Ibid., § 44, p. 261.

89 Ibid., § 44, p. 270.

90 See, for the protocol of the lectures by Cassirer and Heidegger, Heidegger, *Kant and the Problem of Metaphysics*, pp. 193–208 (see ch. 2, n. 1 above).

91 See Heidegger, *Being and Time*, § 6, p. 45.

92 See Heidegger, *Kant and the Problem of Metaphysics*, § 31, pp. 112–20.

93 See Martin Heidegger, *Hölderlin's Hymn "The Ister"*, translated by William McNeill and Julia Davis, Bloomington: Indiana University Press, 1996; Martin Heidegger, *Hölderlins Hymne "Andenken"*, Frankfurt am Main: Klostermann, 1982.

94 See Plato, *Republic*, bk 10. 595A–608a, pp. 297–312.

95 See Martin Heidegger, *Nietzsche*, translated with notes and an analysis by David Farrell Krell, San Francisco: Harper and Row, 1979–, 3 vols.

96 "Letter on Humanism," in Martin Heidegger, *Basic Writings*, edited, with general introduction and introductions to each selection, by D. F. Krell, New York: Harper and Row, 1977, p. 222.

97 "The Question Concerning Technology," in Heidegger, *The Question Concerning Technology and Other Essays* (see ch. 3, n. 81 above).

98 See Tom Rockmore, *Heidegger and French Philosophy: Humanism, Anti-Humanism and Being*, London: Routledge, 1995.

99 For this argument, see Descombes, *Modern French Philosophy* (see ch. 3, n. 65 above).

100 See Jean Wahl, *Le malheur de la conscience dans la philosophie de Hegel*, Paris: Rieder, 1929.

101 See Emmanuel Levinas, *The Theory of Intuition in Husserl's Phenomenology*, translated by André Orianne, Evanston, Ill.: Northwestern University Press, 1995.

102 See Jean-Paul Sartre, *Existentialism Is a Humanism*, translated by Bernard Frechtman, New York: Philosophical Library, 1947.

103 See "Letter on Humanism," in Heidegger, *Basic Writings*, p. 208.

104 See Jean-Paul Sartre, *The Transcendence of the Ego: An Existentialist Theory of Consciousness* (1937), translated and annotated, with an introduction, by Forrest Williams and Robert Kirkpatrick, New York: Octagon Books, 1972.

105 "La Liberté cartésiennne," in Jean-Paul Sartre, *Situations I*, Paris: Gallimard, 1947, pp. 314–35.

106 Jean-Paul Sartre, *Being and Nothingness*, translated by Hazel Barnes, New York: Washington Square Press, 1973, p. 7.

107 Ibid., p. 11.

108 Ibid., p. 9.

109 See Jean-Paul Sartre, *Nausea*, translated by Lloyd Alexander, Norfolk, Conn.: New Directions, 1964.

110 Sartre, *Being and Nothingness*, p. 384.

111 See Jean-Paul Sartre, *Search for a Method*, translated by Hazel Barnes, New York: Vintage, 1963.

112 See Jean-Paul Sartre, *Critique of Dialectical Reason*, translated by Quintin Hoare, London: Verso, 1991.

113 See Jean-Paul Sartre, *Family Idiot*, translated by Carol Cosman, Chicago: University of Chicago Press, 1981–93, 5 vols.

114 For Sartre's moving obituary of Merleau-Ponty, see Jean-Paul Sartre, *Situations IV: Portraits*, Paris: Gallimard, 1947, pp. 189–287.

115 "Hegel's Existentialism," in Maurice Merleau-Ponty, *Sense and Non-Sense*, translated by Hubert L. Dreyfus and Patricia Allen Dreyfus, Evanston, Ill.: Northwestern University Press, 1964, p. 63. This idea is later echoed by others. According to Philippe Sollers, Nietzsche, Bataille, Lacan, and

Marxism-Leninism result from "l'explosion du système hégélien." *Bataille*, Paris: 10/18, 1973, p. 36, cited in Descombes, *Le Même et l'autre*, Paris: Éditions de Minuit, 1979, p. 23 n. 5.

116 Maurice Merleau-Ponty, *Phenomenology of Perception*, translated by Colin Smith, London: Routledge, 2003, p. xv.

117 Ibid., p. viii.

118 Ibid., p. xvi.

119 Maurice Merleau-Ponty, *The Structure of Behavior*, translated by Alden Smith, Boston: Beacon Press, 1967.

120 See Part I: "The Body," in Merleau-Ponty, *Phenomenology of Perception*, pp. 77–232.

121 See Merleau-Ponty, *Phenomenology of Perception*, pp. 235–9.

122 "The Primacy of Perception and Its Philosophical Consequences," in Maurice Merleau-Ponty, *The Primacy of Perception and Other Essays on Phenomenological Psychology, the Philosophy of Art, History and Politics*, edited, with an introduction, by James M. Edie, Evanston, Ill.: Northwestern University Press, 1964, p. 13.

123 Maurice Merleau-Ponty, *Humanism and Terror: The Communist Problem*, translated with a new introduction by John O'Neill, New Brunswick, NJ: Transaction Publishers, 2000.

124 Maurice Merleau-Ponty, *Adventures of the Dialectic*, translated by Joseph Bien, Evanston, Ill.: Northwestern University Press, 1973.

125 See Hans-Georg Gadamer, *The Idea of the Good in Platonic-Aristotelian Philosophy*, translated, with an introduction and annotation, by P. Christopher Smith, New Haven: Yale University Press, 1986.

126 See, e.g., Hans-Georg Gadamer, *Idee und Wirklichkeit in Platos Timaios: vorgelegt am 10. Nov. 1973*, Heidelberg: Winter, 1974.

127 Among his studies of particular philosophers, see Hans-Georg Gadamer, *Heidegger's Ways*, translated by J. W. Stanley, with an introduction by D. J. Schmidt, Albany, NY: SUNY Press, 1994; and Hans-Georg Gadamer, *Hegel's Dialectic: Five Hermeneutical Studies*, translated, with an introduction, by P. Christopher Smith, New Haven: Yale University Press, 1976. For an illustration of his study of a poet, see Hans-Georg Gadamer, *Gadamer on Celan: "Who Am I and Who Are You?" and Other Essays*, translated and edited by Richard Heinemann and Bruce Krajewski, Albany, NY: SUNY Press.

128 See Hans-Georg Gadamer, *Reason in the Age of Science*, translated by F. G. Lawrence, Cambridge, Mass.: MIT Press, 1996.

129 See Hans-Georg Gadamer, *Truth and Method*, translated by Garrett Barden and John Cumming, New York: Crossroad, 1988.

130 See Aristotle, "De Interpretatione" ("On Interpretation"), in *The Complete Works of Aristotle*, I, pp. 25–39.

131 See Friedrich Schleiermacher, *Hermeneutics and Criticism*, edited by Andrew Bowie, Cambridge: Cambridge University Press, 1998.

132 See Gadamer, *Truth and Method*, p. xi.

133 Ibid., p. xiii.

134 See Jacques Derrida, *La Voix et le phénomène: introduction au problème du signe dans la phénoménologie de Husserl*, Paris: Quadridge/Presses Universitaires de France, 1993. See also *Le problème de la genèse dans la philosophie de Husserl*, Paris: Presses Universitaires de France, 1990.

135 See Jacques Derrida, *Politiques de l'amitié; suivi de L'oreille de Heidegger*, Paris: Galilée, 1994.

136 See Jacques Derrida, *The Post Card: From Socrates to Freud and Beyond*, translated, with an introduction and additional notes, by Alan Bass. Chicago: University of Chicago Press, 1987.

137 See Jacques Derrida, *Specters of Marx: The State of the Debt, the Work of Mourning, and the New International*, translated by Peggy Kamuf; with an introduction by Bernd Magnus and Stephen Cullenberg. New York: Routledge, 1994.

138 See *Religion*, edited by Jacques Derrida and Gianni Vattimo, Stanford, Calif.: Stanford University Press, 1998.

139 An example is his contribution of a text to a book on his thought, a text whose central aim seems to lie in showing that his thought surpasses anything said about it. See Geoffrey Bennington and Jacques Derrida, *Jacques Derrida*, Chicago: University of Chicago Press, 1993.

140 Jacques Derrida, *Of Grammatology*, translated by Gayatri Spivak, Baltimore: Johns Hopkins University Press, 1997, p. 158.

141 See the account of "Sense Certainty," in G. W. F. Hegel, *Phenomenology of Spirit*, pp. 58–67 (see ch. 3, n. 22 above).

Chapter 6 Anglo-American Analytic Philosophy

1 See Anthony Quinton, "Analytic Philosophy," in *The Oxford Companion to Philosophy*, edited by Ted Honderich, New York: Oxford, 1995, p. 28.

2 See Morris Weitz, "Philosophical Analysis," in *The Encyclopedia of Philosophy*, edited by Paul Edwards, New York and London: Free Press and Macmillan, 1967, Vol. 1, pp. 97–105.

3 See Michael Dummett, *Origins of Analytical Philosophy*, Cambridge, Mass.: Harvard University Press, 1994.

4 See J. H. Stirling, *The Secret of Hegel: Being the Hegelian System in Origin, Principle, Form, and Matter*, London: Longman, Green, Longman, Roberts, & Green, 1865.

5 For discussion, see Jean Pucelle, *L'idéalisme en Angleterre de Coleridge à Bradley*, Neuchâtel: La Baconnière, 1955.

6 According to Hans Sluga, Frege, who published in a leading idealist journal, almost certainly shared a series of contemporary idealist ideas, such as anti-naturalism, anti-psychologism, objectivist epistemology, apriorism, and

rationalism. See Hans Sluga, *Gottlob Frege*, London: Routledge and Kegan Paul, 1980, pp. 59–60. For Gabriel, Frege is a kind of neo-Kantian. See Gottfried Gabriel, "Frege als Neukantianer," in *Kant-Studien* LXVII (1986), pp. 84–101.

7 See Ludwig Wittgenstein, *Tractatus Logico-Philosophicus*, with a new translation by D. F. Pears and B. F. McGuinness, and with the introduction by Bertrand Russell, London: Routledge and Kegan Paul, 1961, 4.0412.

8 For this claim, see Peter Hylton, *Russell, Idealism, and the Emergence of Analytic Philosophy*, Oxford: Clarendon Press, 1990. It is unclear that either Russell or Moore ever had more than the most hazy grip of the idealist theories they later strongly opposed.

9 See "Preface" in Bertrand Russell, *An Essay on the Foundations of Geometry* (1897), New York: Dover, 1956.

10 See "In What Sense, If Any, Do Past and Future Time Exist?," in G. E. Moore, *The Early Essays*, edited by Tom Regan, Philadelphia: Temple University Press, 1986, pp. 17–24.

11 See Bertrand Russell, *The Philosophy of Logical Atomism*, edited and with an introduction by David Pears, Chicago: Open Court, 1998, p. 158.

12 See G. E. Moore (1903), "The Refutation of Idealism," in *Mind*, New Series, 12, 48 (October 1903), pp. 433–53.

13 See Kant, *Critique of Pure Reason*, B 274–7, pp. 326–33 (see ch. 1, n. 13 above).

14 See G. E. Moore, *Philosophical Papers*, London: George Allen and Unwin, 1959, p. 144.

15 Warnock, for instance, seems to know almost nothing about British idealism, which he regards as difficult to describe. See G. J. Warnock, *English Philosophy Since 1900*, London: Oxford University Press, 1958, pp. 2–10.

16 See ch. 1, n. 2 above.

17 Hilary Putnam, *Reason, Truth and History*, New York: Cambridge University Press, 1981, p. xi.

18 Putnam, *The Threefold Cord*, p. 44 (see ch. 2, n. 45 above).

19 See Sluga, *Gottlob Frege*, pp. 2–7.

20 See H. P. Grice and P. F. Strawson, "In Defense of a Dogma," in *Philosophical Review* 65 (1956), pp. 141–58.

21 See C. H. Langford, "Moore's Notion of Analysis," in *The Philosophy of G. E. Moore*, edited by Paul Schilpp, Evanston, Ill.: Northwestern University Press, 1942, pp. 319–42.

22 See "Responses," in *The Philosophy of G. E. Moore*, edited by Schilpp, pp. 660–7.

23 Russell, *The Philosophy of Logical Atomism*, p. 178.

24 See ibid., p. 157.

25 "It is in this way that the study of logic becomes the central study of philosophy: it gives the method of research in philosophy, just as mathematics

gives the method in physics." Bertrand Russell, *Our Knowledge of the External World* (1929), New York: Mentor, 1956, p. 185.

26 See Frege, *The Foundations of Arithmetic* (see ch. 2, n. 51 above).

27 See Alfred North Whitehead and Bertrand Russell, *Principia Mathematica*, Cambridge: Cambridge University Press, 1925.

28 See "Knowledge by Acquaintance and Knowledge by Description," in Bertrand Russell, *Mysticism and Logic*, Garden City, NY: Doubleday, 1957, pp. 202–24.

29 See Bertrand Russell, "On Denoting," in *Readings in Philosophical Analysis*, edited by Herbert Feigl and Wilfrid Sellars, New York: Appleton-Century-Crofts, 1949, pp. 103–15.

30 See P. F. Strawson, "On Referring," in *Mind* 59 (1950), pp. 320–44.

31 Carnap, "The Elimination of Metaphysics through Logical Analysis of Language," in *Logical Positivism*, edited by Ayer (see ch. 1, n. 5 above).

32 See Wittgenstein, *Tractatus Logico-Philosophicus*, proposition 6.53.

33 This is the basis of physicalism. See Carnap, *The Logical Syntax of Language* (see ch. 4, n. 92 above).

34 See "Mental Events," in Donald Davidson, *Essays on Actions and Events*, Oxford: Clarendon Press, 2001, pp. 207–25.

35 See P. F. Strawson, "Analysis, Science, and Metaphysics," in Richard Rorty, *The Linguistic Turn: Essays in Philosophical Method, with Two Retrospective Essays* (1967), Chicago: University of Chicago Press, 1992, p. 313.

36 See P. F. Strawson, *Individuals: An Essay in Descriptive Metaphysics*, London: Methuen, 1959.

37 See Gilbert Ryle, *The Concept of Mind*, Chicago: University of Chicago Press, 1984.

38 See ch. 2: "The Linguistic Turn," in Dummett, *The Origins of Analytic Philosophy*, pp. 4–14.

39 Ludwig Wittgenstein, *Philosophical Investigations*, translated by G. E. M. Anscombe, 2nd edn, Oxford: Blackwell, 1997, § 90, p. 42e.

40 See Rorty, *The Linguistic Turn.*

41 Russell, *The Philosophy of Logical Atomism*, p. 166.

42 See ch. 14: "Conclusion: A Methodology or a Subject-Matter," in Dummett, *The Origins of Analytic Philosophy*, pp. 162–6.

43 See § 56: "Semantic Ascent," in W. V. O. Quine, *Word and Object*, Cambridge, Mass.: MIT Press, 1960, pp. 270–6.

44 See Wittgenstein, *Tractatus Logico-Philosophicus*, 4.003.

45 See ibid., 4.0031.

46 See, e.g., ch. 9: "Moore and Russell," in Passmore, *A Hundred Years of Philosophy*, pp. 201–39 (see intro., n. 3 above).

47 Russell and Moore were among a number of thinkers committed at various times to theories of sense-data. The very idea of sense-data is controversial.

For critical discussion, see J. L. Austin, *Sense and Sensibilia*, edited by G. J. Warnock, Oxford: Clarendon Press, 1962.

48 G. E. Moore, *Selected Writings*, edited by Thomas Baldwin, London: Routledge, 1993, pp. 106–33.

49 G. E. Moore, *Principia Ethica*, Cambridge: Cambridge University Press, 1903.

50 See Bertrand Russell, *The Practice and Theory of Bolshevism* (1920), New York: Simon and Schuster, 1964, p. 101.

51 See Bertrand Russell, *Marriage and Morals*, New York: H. Liveright, 1957.

52 See Bertrand Russell, *The ABC of Relativity*, London: G. Allen and Unwin, 1959.

53 See Bertrand Russell, *The Autobiography of Bertrand Russell*, Boston: Little, Brown, 1967–9, 3 vols.

54 See Bertrand Russell, *A Critical Exposition of the Philosophy of Leibniz* (1900), London: George Allen and Unwin, 1967.

55 Russell, *A History of Western Philosophy* (see ch. 4, n. 7 above).

56 See, e.g., Bertrand Russell, *Human Society in Ethics and Politics* (1952), New York: Mentor, 1955.

57 See, e.g., Bertrand Russell, *Religion and Science*, London: T. Butterworth, 1935.

58 See Bertrand Russell, *Principles of Mathematics*, New York: Norton, 1964.

59 Ibid., ch. X, pp. 101–7.

60 See Russell, *The Philosophy of Logical Atomism*, p. 169.

61 See "Analytic Realism," in *The Collected Papers of Bertrand Russell*, edited by Kenneth Blackwell, London: G. Allen and Unwin, 1992, Vol. VI, p. 135.

62 See Russell, *The Philosophy of Logical Atomism*, p. 35. At this point, during the First World War, Russell did not even know whether Wittgenstein, who was then serving in the Austrian Army, was still alive.

63 Ibid., p. 36.

64 Ibid., p. 36.

65 Ibid., p. 37.

66 Ibid., p. 37.

67 Ibid., p. 40.

68 Ibid., pp. 53–6.

69 Ibid., pp. 65–6.

70 Ibid., p. 147.

71 Ibid., p. 154.

72 See Wittgenstein, *Tractatus Logico-Philosophicus*, 6.54.

73 The sentences of the *Tractatus* are numbered in decimal fashion. The numbers in parentheses in the text refer to the corresponding numbered passages in the *Tractatus*.

74 Bacon, *The New Organon*, p. 29 (see ch. 2, n. 11 above).

75 See ibid., p. 48.

76 This idea has been repeatedly criticized. For a very sharp attack on analytic philosophy focused on this theme, see Ernest Gellner, *Words and Things: An Examination of, and an Attack on, Linguistic Philosophy*, with a foreword by Bertrand Russell, London and Boston: Routledge & Kegan Paul, 1979.
77 See Ludwig Wittgenstein, *Philosophical Investigations*, translated by G. E. M. Anscombe, New York: Macmillan, 1966, p. xe.
78 Ibid., § 109, p. 47e.
79 Ibid., § 421, p. 1263.
80 The central aim of *On Certainty* lies in cutting off the alternative to logical atomism, or logical empiricism, presented in Moore's intuitive empiricism, or common-sensism. Wittgenstein characteristically argues that Moore misuses language.
81 See Wittgenstein, *Philosophical Investigations*, §§ 243–315.
82 The main statement of purpose occurs in a manifesto entitled "The Scientific World View: The Vienna Circle" (1929). See Hans Hahn, Otto Neurath, and Rudolf Carnap, *Wissenschaftliche Weltauffassung: Der Wiener Kreis*, Vienna: Artur Wolf Verlag, 1929, Heft I.
83 For discussion, see Carl G. Hempel, "Problems and Changes in the Empiricist Criterion of Meaning," in *Revue Internationale de Philosophie* 41 (1950), pp. 41–63.
84 See Rudolf Carnap, *The Logical Structure of the World, and Pseudoproblems in Philosophy*, translated by Rolf A. George, Chicago: Open Court, 2003, §§ 67–8, pp. 107–10.
85 Otto Neurath, "Protokollsätze," in *Erkenntnis* 3 (1932/1933), p. 204.
86 Ibid., p. 206.
87 See Quine, *Word and Object*, p. vii.
88 See ibid., pp. 73–9.
89 Carnap proposes this idea in his reply to Neurath. See Rudolf Carnap, "Über Protokollsätze," in *Erkenntnis* 3 (1932/1933), pp. 215–16.
90 See ch. 18: "Wittgenstein and Ordinary Language Philosophy," in Passmore, *A Hundred Years of Philosophy*, pp. 424–65.
91 See H. H. Price, *Perception*, New York: McBride, 1933.
92 A. J. Ayer, *Language, Truth, and Logic*, New York: Dover, 1952.
93 See Editor's Introduction in *Logical Positivism*, p. 16.
94 See A. J. Ayer, *The Foundations of Empirical Knowledge*, New York: St Martin's Press, 1958.
95 See Gilbert Ryle, "Review of Martin Heidegger's *Sein und Zeit*," in *Mind* 38 (1929), pp. 355–70.
96 Gilbert Ryle, "Sytematically Misleading Expressions," in *Logic and Language*, I, edited by A. G. N. Flew, Oxford: Blackwell, 1951, pp. 11–36.
97 See n. 37 above.
98 J. L. Austin, "A Plea for Excuses," in *Philosophical Papers*, Oxford: Clarendon Press, 1961, pp. 175–204.

99 See n. 46 above.
100 Carnap, *The Logical Syntax of Language*, p. 8.
101 For discussion, see Joseph Margolis, *The Unraveling of Scientism: American Philosophy at the End of the Twentieth Century*, Ithaca, NY: Cornell University Press, 2003.
102 See "Philosophy and the Scientific Image of Man," in Wilfrid Sellars, *Science, Perception and Reality*, Atascadero, Calif.: Ridgeview, 1991, pp. 1–40.
103 For his later critique of empiricism, see Hegel, *The Encyclopedia Logic*, §§ 37–60, pp. 76–107 (see ch. 1, n. 17 above).
104 See Wilfrid Sellars, *Empiricism and the Philosophy of Mind*, Cambridge, Mass.: Harvard University Press, 1997, § 36, p. 76.
105 For an accessible general discussion, see Alex Orenstein, *W. V. O. Quine*, Princeton: Princeton University Press, 2002.
106 See, e.g., W. V. O. Quine, *The Roots of Reference*, La Salle, Ill.: Open Court, 1973.
107 "Two Dogmas of Empiricism," in Quine, *From a Logical Point of View* (see ch. 2, n. 52 above).
108 See Quine, *Word and Object*, pp. 144–51.
109 His only "monograph" is in fact a collection of lectures. See Donald Davidson, *Truth and Predication*, Cambridge, Mass.: Belknap Press, 2005.
110 See ch. 4, n. 102 above.
111 See "Afterthoughts," in Davidson, *Subjective, Intersubjective, Objective*, pp. 154–8 (see ch. 4, n. 105 above).
112 See "A Coherence Theory of Truth and Knowledge," in Davidson, *Subjective, Intersubjective, Objective*, pp. 137–53.
113 See Putnam, *The Threefold Cord: Mind, Body, World.*
114 See Putnam, *Reason, Truth and History*, pp. 1–21.
115 Ibid., p. 52.
116 Ibid., p. 216.
117 Rorty, *Philosophy and the Mirror of Nature*, p. 178 (see ch. 1, n. 12 above).
118 Rorty, *Truth and Progress, Philosophical Papers, Volume 3*, p. 305 (see ch. 4, n. 107 above).

Chapter 7 Kant and Twentieth-Century Philosophy

1 See Nicholas Rescher, *The Strife of Systems: An Essay on the Grounds and Implications of Philosophical Diversity*, Pittsburgh: University of Pittsburgh Press, 1985.
2 For a claim that it is by far the single most important work in the modern tradition, see Otfried Höffe, *Kants Kritik der reinen Vernunft. Die Grundlegung der modernen Philosophie*, Munich: C. H. Beck, 2003.
3. See ch. 5, p. 122 and n. 115 above.

4 See Husserl, *Logical Investigations*, I, § 58, p. 214 (see ch. 5, n. 16 above).

5 Husserl's letter to G. Albrecht, dated August 22, 1901, in Iso Kern, *Husserl and Kant*, p. 15 (see ch. 5, n. 31 above).

6 See Heidegger, *Kant and the Problem of Metaphysics*, § 31, pp. 166–76 (see ch. 2, n. 1 above).

7 According to Coffa, analytic philosophy "was born in the effort to avoid Kant's theory of the a priori." Alberto Coffa, *The Semantic Tradition from Kant to Carnap*, Cambridge: Cambridge University Press, 1991, p. 21.

8 This is Hanna's overall thesis. See Robert Hanna, *Kant and the Foundations of Analytic Philosophy*, Oxford: Clarendon Press, 2001, p. 11.

9 According to Hanna, the link is very tight: "I will dub the problem that Kant's transcendental idealism is ultimately designed to solve 'the Semantic Problem'." Ibid., p. 3. Hanna argues this point in ibid., ch. 1: "Kant and the Semantic Problem," pp. 14–66.

10 Ryle says "preoccupation with the theory of meaning could be described as the occupational disease of twentieth-century Anglo-Saxon and Austrian philosophy." Gilbert Ryle, "The Theory of Meaning," in Ryle, *Collected Papers*, New York: Barnes and Noble, 1971, II, p. 350.

11 See "On Sense and Reference," in *Translations from the Writings of Gottlob Frege*, edited P. T. Geach and Max Black, Oxford: Blackwell, 1980.

12 See Brandom, *Articulating Reasons* (see ch. 4, n. 3 above).

13 The epistemological consequences of his position are not well known. See Charles Guignon, *Heidegger and the Problem of Knowledge*, Indianapolis: Hackett, 1983.

14 For a recent study, which argues that Kant features a non-causal variety of representationalism, see A. B. Dickerson, *Kant on Representation and Objectivity*, Cambridge: Cambridge University Press, 2004.

Index

18075753R00127

Made in the USA
San Bernardino, CA
27 December 2014